Software Product Lines in Action

Frank J. van der Linden · Klaus Schmid
Eelco Rommes

Software Product Lines in Action

The Best Industrial Practice
in Product Line Engineering

With 90 Figures and 9 Tables

 Springer

Frank J. van der Linden
Philips Medical Systems
Veenpluis 4-6
5684 PC Best, The Netherlands
frank.van.der.linden@philips.com

Eelco Rommes
Philips Research
Prof. Holstlaan 4
5656 AA Eindhoven, The Netherlands
eelco.rommes@xs4all.nl

Klaus Schmid
Universität Hildesheim
Institut für Informatik
Samelsonplatz 1
31141 Hildesheim, Germany
schmid@sse.uni-hildesheim.de

Library of Congress Control Number: 2007923180

ACM Computing Classification (2007): D.2, K.6.3, H.4

ISBN 978-3-540-71436-1 Springer Berlin Heidelberg New York

Springer is a part of Springer Science+Business Media
springer.com
© Springer-Verlag Berlin Heidelberg 2007

Typesetting: by the authors
Production: Integra Software Services Pvt. Ltd., Puducherry, India
Cover design: KünkelLopka, Heidelberg

Printed on acid-free paper   45/3100/Integra   5 4 3 2 1 0

Foreword

Software product lines represent perhaps the most exciting paradigm shift in software development since the advent of high-level programming languages. Nowhere else in software engineering have we seen such breathtaking improvements in cost, quality, time to market, and developer productivity, often registering in the order-of-magnitude range. Let me say that again: *often registering in the order-of-magnitude range.* Just to be clear, we are talking about software systems built for around one-tenth the cost. With around one-tenth the faults. Delivered in around one-tenth the time. If you know of another way to achieve such a staggering combination of better-faster-and-cheaper, please let me know.

Equally exciting to me are the strategic benefits that accrue to a product line organization, in the form of market agility. At the Software Engineering Institute, we have recorded case study after case study of companies succeeding in one market area with a product line approach, and then taking their production capability to a nearby, under-exploited area of the market, and quickly rising to market dominance in that area as well. And why not? If you can outperform your competitors by order-of-magnitude levels, it's hard to imagine what could keep you from becoming a market leader.

It seems very clear that software product line practice, as a viable and attractive option for software development, is without doubt here to stay. While the underlying concepts are straightforward enough – building a family of related products or systems by planned and careful reuse of a base of generalized software development assets – the devil can be in the details. Successful product line practice can involve organizational change, business process change, and technology change. Bringing comprehensive change to a software development organization isn't easy, and false starts are expensive – or fatal. Better to learn from the experts than strike out through the wilderness on your own.

Which brings us to this book: I fully expect that *Software Product Lines in Action* will become one of the foundational references of this quickly evolving field. It's the most comprehensive treatment of product line practice in existence today. It's all here, the concepts, a full approach, a holistic treatment of product line practice from the standpoint of business, process, and technology, an analysis method, and a rich collection of case studies. In fact, a big reason to be a fan of this book is its wonderful collection of case studies. Nothing teaches like experience, and the unprecedented ten case studies represent (to my knowledge) the largest collection of experiential software product line reports ever gathered in one reference. More than just third-hand reporting, however, the authors themselves have been integral leaders on many of the case studies on which they report. They have been important contributors to this field almost since it was a field, and can rightly take credit for helping to make software product line practice a known, repeatable, software development approach. In fact, they helped make this field a field. I'm proud to call them colleagues. After you read this book and launch a successful software product line of your own, you'll be proud to call them colleagues too.

Austin, Texas,
January 2007   *Paul Clements*

Preface

The software industry is challenged with a continuous drive to improve its engineering practice. Software has to be produced ever faster and more reliable. Increasingly, complex systems are produced with constant, or even diminishing, numbers of people.

Software product line engineering is a strategic approach to developing software. It impacts business, organisation and technology alike and is a proven way to develop a large range of software products and software-intensive systems fast and at low costs, while at the same time delivering high-quality software.

This book captures the wealth of knowledge that eight companies have gathered during the introduction of the software product line engineering approach in their daily practice.

Who This Book Is For

This book is meant for anyone who is interested in the practical side of product line engineering. Those who consider to use a product line approach in their organisations, those who are about to start one and those who want to improve their current practices will find useful information. This book presents a broad view on product line engineering so that both managers and technical specialists will benefit from reading it. Specific emphasis is given to providing real-world data to support managers in deciding on the potential adoption of product line engineering in their organisations. We believe that best practices are best communicated along with what goes wrong if one fails to adhere to them. This book is also a tool on how to do it right (or wrong), and to learn from the experiences of others.

Background knowledge of product line engineering is not required, but the reader is expected to be familiar with current software engineering practices, or to have some experience in software development.

Readers who want a detailed introduction to the subject are referred to the textbook *Software Product Line Engineering* [106], which describes the foundations, principles and techniques of software product line engineering.

What You Will Learn from Reading This Book

This book gives a practical overview to software product line engineering, driven from industrial experiences that were collected from organisations of varying sizes and domains. Practitioners themselves report on practical implementation: *from practitioners to practitioners.*

This book is complemented with business-related information regarding the benefits and drawbacks of the approach. It not only shows how software product lines can improve the software creation process, but also describes problems that may occur and how companies have solved them in their respective contexts.

The core of this book contains ten case studies, covering small and large organisations, acting in all kinds of domains, with different degrees of domain and process maturity. These companies work on a large variety of software intensive systems including medical imaging, mobile phones, software for televisions, utility control, supervision and management, financial services and car electronics.

The reader will

- understand the relevant aspects, regarding business, architecture, process and organisational issues, of applying software product line engineering.
- learn about the current practice of product line engineering in leading companies of different sizes, operating in several countries and working in various domains.
- have the information for performing an informed analysis on the applicability, or improvement, of the product line approach to his or her own organisation.
- have information about the first steps in transitioning, or improving, the product line approach in his or her organisation.

The Case Studies

Starting in the 1990s, massive investments were made in Europe in the area of product line engineering. This was done both inside companies and as a part of large projects in which companies, research institutes and academia from many different countries co-operated, for example the ESAPS, CAFÉ and FAMILIES projects. One of the results was a flourishing community of product line engineering research and practice in Europe.

The case studies in this book reflect the experiences of companies that were involved in these projects. Each case study was written with experts from the case in question.

The majority of these studies deals with software intensive systems, mainly because the software intensive systems industry in general is more advanced when it comes to software product line engineering. There are several reasons for that.

- Experience with platforms and customisation in other engineering disciplines is often already present in these companies.
- Their customers are used to choosing from a range of systems, each with different properties.
- Pure software customers are often acquainted to and mostly accept the one-size-fits-all system, where they can adapt the system to their specific needs.

However, as more and more information systems — especially business-oriented systems — must be adapted to business-oriented workflows, product line engineering becomes increasingly important. Also for these systems, the adaptation and customisation costs for the client may become prohibitive if systems are delivered with too much diverse and undocumented variability.

The Structure of This Book

This book consist of three parts: a high-level introduction to software product line engineering, ten industrial case studies and their analysis.

Part I — Aspects of Software Product Line Engineering

This part sets a common framework for the description of our industrial case studies. It covers the four major concerns of software product line engineering: Business, Architecture, Process and Organisation. These *BAPO* concerns are a main organising principle of this part. Each of them is explained in detail in a separate chapter. In addition, the Family Evaluation Framework is based on these concerns.

Chapter 1 Product Line Engineering Approach provides the basics you need to understand the book. It explains what product line engineering is, provides an overview of the major aspects (BAPO) and introduces the main topics of software product line engineering: variability and the use of a platform.

Chapter 2 Business explains the business aspects of software product line engineering. It deals with the motivation to initiate or continue with this approach and it explains the economical aspects of software product line engineering.

Chapter 3 Architecture deals with the technical aspects of product lines, most importantly how to deal with variability.

Chapter 4 Process describes the processes for software product line engineering. It describes the separation between domain and application engineering, and the relation between these two life-cycles.

Chapter 5 Organisation deals with roles and responsibilities, structures and distribution of the work.

Chapter 6 The Family Evaluation Framework introduces a BAPO-based framework that can be used to evaluate software product line engineering in larger or smaller parts of companies.

Part II — Experience Reports

This part is the body of the book. It consists of eight experience reports from ten different companies of various sizes and working on various domains.

Chapter 7 Experiences in Product Line Engineering describes the origins of the experiences, the part of software product line engineering that is covered and the formats used within each experiment. The following chapters each describe the company's (or division's) experiences.

Chapter 8 AKVAsmart shows a small company introducing a product-line approach for its range of fish-farming products.

Chapter 9 Bosch Gasoline Systems describes how a product line organisation was set up and executed for a large supplier of automotive products.

Chapter 10 DNV Software deals with the introduction of a product line in ship classification software.

Chapter 11 market maker Software AG shows the business impact of the introduction of a product line on a small company producing financial software.

Chapter 12 Nokia Mobile Phones gives information on the way a product line improves the way to deal with quality requirements, in a large telecom product company.

Chapter 13 Nokia Networks shows another part of this big company, describing the impact of the complex organisation to the product line development.

Chapter 14 Philips Consumer Electronics Software for Televisions shows how all BAPO concerns are affected by the introduction of a product line within this large company

Chapter 15 Philips Medical Systems describes another part of this large company, and how they took a different approach in the introduction of product lines.

Chapter 16 Siemens Medical Solutions shows the difficulties a big company may have to introduce only partially a product line.

Chapter 17 Telvent gives details of the application of an architecture pattern for product lines in the network management domain.

Part III — Conclusions

In this part, conclusions are drawn from an analysis of the set of experiences described. It summarises the lessons learned and provides general guidelines on how to get started with software product line engineering.

Chapter 18 Analysis reflects on the experiences and looks at them from a BAPO and FEF perspective.

Chapter 19 Starting with Software Product Line Engineering presents the steps that need to be taken to successfully make the transition towards software product line engineering, using examples from Part II.

Chapter 20 Outlook looks at trends and expectations for the future. It also describes the challenges that still need to be solved.

Acknowledgements

We thank Eureka/ITEA, BMBF (Germany), SenterNovem (Netherlands) and all other public authorities for funding the projects ESAPS (1999–2001), CAFÉ (2001–2003) and FAMILIES (2003–2005). This book is based on the experience obtained in these projects. However, a lot of additional work was done by a lot of people from the various organisations in order to achieve a quality of the case studies that we can now present here. This goes well beyond project-based work. Each of them is named for the respective case studies, as they were strongly involved and contributed to writing the final case studies.

The BAPO model of product line engineering concerns was a result of the Composable Architectures project conducted at Philips Research between 1998 and 2002. The authors thank their organisations for giving them time to finish the book. These are Philips Medical Systems, Philips Research, Fraunhofer IESE and the University of Hildesheim.

Timo Käkölä provided valuable comments on an earlier version of the book. Monika Lamping did a great job at proof-reading and performing corrections on it and Dennis Stender provided assistance with some pictures. Several figures, viz. 1.1, 1.2, 1.4, 1.5, 2.3, 4.1, 4.2 and 5.1 are copies from the book Software Product Line Engineering [106].

And finally, we would like to thank Ralf Gerstner for accompanying this project for such a long time.

Contents

Part II Experience Reports

Part III Conclusions

Aspects of Software Product Line Engineering

1

The Product Line Engineering Approach

Software increasingly becomes the key asset for modern, competitive products. No matter how simple or complex, no matter how large or small, there is hardly any modern product without software. Thus, competitiveness in software development has increasingly become a concern for companies of all sizes and in all markets. As a result, product line engineering has gained increasing attention over recent years. While many introductions of a software product line engineering approach are driven by cost and time to market concerns, it supports other business goals as well. We will discuss the consequences of such an approach on business performance in detail in Sect. 1.1. In Sect. 1.2 we will discuss the historical basis of software product line engineering and compare it with other efforts for software reuse. Section 1.3 gives an overview of the most fundamental concepts of product line engineering. These are variability management, business-centric development, architecture-centric development, and the two-life-cycle approach. We will discuss each of these concepts below in detail in a separate section.

1.1 Motivation

Many different reasons lead companies to embark on a software product line engineering approach. These range from more process-oriented aspects like cost and time over product qualities like reliability to end-user aspects like user interface consistency.

The move towards software product line engineering is usually strongly based on economic considerations. Due to its support of large-scale reuse, such an approach improves mostly the process side of software development, i.e. it reduces costs, time to market and improves qualities of the resulting products like their reliability.

The improvement of costs and time to market are strongly correlated in software product line engineering: the approach supports large-scale reuse during software development. As opposed to traditional reuse approaches [108],

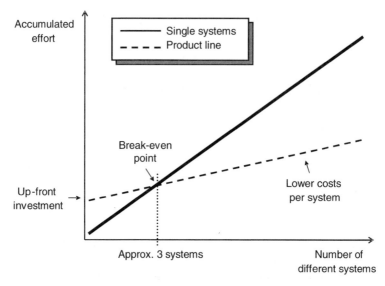

Fig. 1.1. Economics of software product line engineering

this can be as much as 90% of the overall software. Reuse is more cost-effective than development by orders of magnitude. Thus, both *development costs* and *time to market* can be dramatically reduced by product line engineering.

Unfortunately, this improvement does not come for free, but requires some extra up-front investment. This is required for building reusable assets, transforming the organisation, etc. Different strategies exist to make this investment. They range from the so-called *big-bang* approach to an incremental strategy [131], but the underlying need for a set-up investment remains. The positive message is, however, that usually a break-even is reached after about three products, sometimes earlier (cf. Fig. 1.1).

Usually, along with the reduction of development costs a reduction of *maintenance costs* is also achieved. Several aspects contribute to this reduction; most notably the fact that the overall amount of code and documentation that must be maintained is dramatically reduced. As the overall size of the application development projects is strongly reduced, the accompanying *project risk* is reduced as well.[1]

Software product line engineering also has a strong impact on the quality of the resulting software. A new application consists, to a large extent, of matured and proven components. This implies that the defect density of such products can be expected to be drastically lower than products that are

---

[1] Note that this holds only for individual system development. The overall setup of the product line is actually larger than a single system development and, as a consequence, it is usually more risky. This is often compensated by an incremental build-up strategy for the product line [131]

developed all anew. This leads to more *reliable* and *secure* systems. As a result, *safety* is positively impacted as well. Software product line engineering can also support *quality assurance*, e.g. by regarding a product and its simulation as two variants. Especially for embedded systems, simulation enables extensive testing that would be impossible otherwise. If both variants are derived from the same code, simulations can actually be used as a basis for analysing the quality of the final product. While arguments of costs typically dominate the product line engineering debate, the ability to produce higher quality is for some organisations the major argument, especially in safety-critical domains, where major efforts go in the quality assurance and certification efforts.

Beyond process qualities, software product line engineering positively impacts product aspects like the usability of the final product, e.g. by improving the consistency of the user interface. This is achieved by using the same building blocks for implementing the same kind of user interaction, e.g. by having a single component for installation or user registration for a whole set of products instead of having a specific one for each product. In some cases, demand for this kind of unification has been the basis for the introduction of a product line engineering approach in the first case [20].

1.2 A Brief History of Software Product Line Engineering

The dream of massive software reuse is about as old as software engineering itself. Numerous attempts or initiatives to reuse software were made, but usually with little success. These reuse initiatives were usually based on an approach focusing on small-scale, ad hoc reuse (i.e. typically on the code-level – or at least within a development phase; in addition the development of new assets was rarely based on the systematic analysis of future variability).

The concept of focusing on a specific domain as a basis for developing reusable assets was only introduced somewhat later [97]. However, work in this context focused almost exclusively on the fully automatic development of software in a single domain based on generation tools. This lead to domain-specific languages, but so far never scaled to large-scale system development.[2]

Back in the 1970s Parnas [101] already proposed the concept of *product families*. While it was initially aimed at variability in non-functional characteristics, the product line concept can be traced back to this work.

The concept of product lines was fully introduced in the early 1990s. One of the first contributions was the description of the Feature-Oriented Domain Analysis (FODA) method [80]. Around the same time several companies started to address the issue more systematically. For example, Philips introduced the Building-Block method in the early 1990s [146]. These first

---

[2] Current developments in domain-specific languages are revisited in Chap. 20, p. 309

approaches were leveraged by massive investments in Europe in the area of software product line engineering, both inside companies and part of several scientific projects. The following are among them:

- ARES (1995–1998) – Architectural Reasoning for Embedded Systems.
- Praise (1998–2000) – Product-line Realisation and Assessment in Industrial Settings.
- ESAPS (1999–2001) – Engineering Software Architectures, Processes and Platforms [49].
- CAFÉ (2001–2003) – from Concepts to Application in system-Family Engineering [35].
- FAMILIES (2003–2005) – FAct-based Maturity through Institutionalisation, Lessons-learned and Involved Exploration of System-family engineering [51].

These projects supported the systematic building of a community of software product line engineering research and practice in Europe. During the same time, especially, the SEI (Software Engineering Institute) supported the development of software product line engineering in the USA, most notably in the context of governmental organisations.

1.3 Fundamentals of the Software Product Line Engineering Approach

The key difference between traditional single system development and software product line engineering is a fundamental shift of focus: from the individual system and project to the product line. This shift especially implies a shift in strategy: from the ad hoc next-contract vision to a strategic view of a field of business.

Software product line engineering relies on a fundamental distinction of development *for reuse* and development *with reuse* as shown in Fig. 1.2. In *domain engineering* (development for reuse) a basis is provided for the actual development of the individual products. As opposed to many traditional reuse approaches that focus on code assets, the product line infrastructure encompasses all assets that are relevant throughout the software development life-cycle. The various assets cover the whole range from the requirements stage over architecture and implementation to testing. This range of assets together defines the product line infrastructure. A key distinction of software product line engineering from other reuse approaches is that the various assets themselves contain explicit variability. For example, a representation of the requirements may contain an explicit description of specific requirements that apply only for a certain subset of the products.

The individual assets in the product line infrastructure are linked together just like assets in software development. For example, traceability is defined

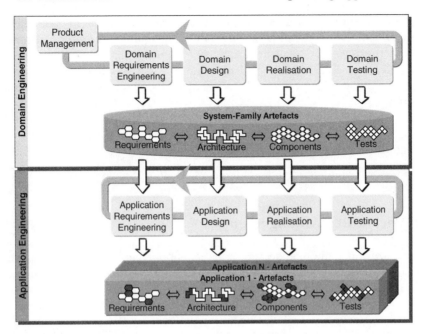

Fig. 1.2. The two-life-cycle model of software product line engineering

among the individual assets, ideally enabling one to take a requirement and identify all related implementation code and test cases.

Application engineering (development with reuse) builds the final products on top of the product line infrastructure. Application engineering is strongly driven by the product line infrastructure, which usually contains most of the functionality required for a new product. The variability explicitly modelled in it provides the basis for deriving the individual products. Basically, when a new product is developed, an accompanying project is set up. Then requirements are gathered and directly categorised as being part of the product line (i.e. a commonality or variability) or product-specific. Then the various assets (e.g. architecture, implementation, etc.) may be instantiated right away, leading to an initial product version. At this stage in the development, up to 90% of the product may be available from reuse; only the remaining 10% must be developed in further steps.

Several principles are fundamental to successful software product line engineering. They can be described as follows:

- *Variability management*: individual systems are considered as variations of a common theme. This variability is made explicit and must be systematically managed.

- *Business-centric*: software product line engineering aims at thoroughly connecting the engineering of the product line with the long-term strategy of the business.
- *Architecture-centric*: the technical side of the software must be developed in a way that allows taking advantage of similarities among the individual systems.
- *Two-life-cycle approach*: the individual systems are developed based on a software platform. These products – as well as the platform – must be engineered and have their individual life-cycles.

In the following sections, we will discuss each of these principles in detail.

1.4 Variability Management

Software product line engineering aims at supporting a range of products. These products may support different, individual customers or may address entirely different market segments. As a result, variability is a key concept in any such approach. Instead of understanding each individual system all by itself, software product line engineering looks at the product line as a whole and the variation among the individual systems. This variability must be defined, represented, exploited, implemented, evolved, etc. – in one word *managed* – throughout software product line engineering. This is what we mean, when we discuss *variability management*.

1.4.1 Types of Variability

When managing variability in a product line, we need to distinguish three main types:

1. *Commonality*: a characteristic (functionality or non-functional) can be common to all products in the product line. We call this a commonality. This is then implemented as part of the platform.
2. *Variability*: a characteristic may be common to some products, but not to all. It must then be explicitly modelled as a possible variability and must be implemented in a way that allows having it in selected products only.
3. *Product-specific*: a characteristic may be part of only one product – at least for the foreseeable future. Such specialties are often not required by the market per se, but are due to the concerns of individual customers. While these variabilities will not be integrated into the platform, the platform must be able to support them.

During the life-cycle of the product line, a specific variability may change in type. For example, a product-specific characteristic may become a variability. On the other hand, a commonality may become a variability as well – for example, if over time the decision is made to support alternatives to the

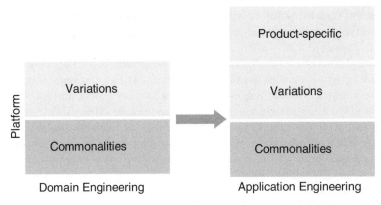

Fig. 1.3. The relation of different types of variability

characteristic (e.g. extending the platform beyond the initial operating system which provided the starting basis).

While commonalities and variabilities are handled mostly in domain engineering, product-specific parts are handled exclusively in application engineering. This is shown in Fig. 1.3.

Variability management is a concern in any software product line engineering approach. It covers the whole life-cycle. It starts with the early steps of scoping, covering all the way to implementation and testing and finally going into evolution. As such, variability is relevant to all assets throughout software development. It is thus a very generic question: How to represent variability?

1.4.2 Variability Representation

Many different approaches to variability representation have been discussed over the years. They differ in several dimensions. The following are among them:

- Which concepts are used to characterise variability?
- Is variability representation integrated with the final assets?

For representing variability several different approaches have been devised. While most modern approaches use features as basic concepts for variability representation, other approaches exist as well. For example, some approaches make the underlying decision that differentiates among various products the basic concept of variability representation. Also, various different interpretations of the term *feature* exist. This opens a very wide spectrum. The major point is that characteristics of the products that differentiate them from other products are core to the representation. Most modern approaches support the characterisation of variability by means of characteristics that cut across different views. This brings us to the second dimension. This dimension describes whether the variability information is fully integrated in other models or not. While initially variability modelling was often integrated in the underlying notation, meanwhile it is generally recognised that approaches to variability modelling that rely on the distinction of a variability model and a main system model are much easier to apply in complex settings and scale much better [10]. The notion of distinguishing between variability model and basic system model is also called orthogonal variability modelling [106]. There are different approaches to describe the variability model: the decision-based modelling approach relies on describing those decisions that must be made in order to derive a specific product line instance. It was initially described in [135], more recent approaches include [96, 128].

Alternatively, the variability can be described based on a graphical notation. For the sake of simplicity, we will use the same graphical notation here that was used in [106], which goes back to [10]. The notational elements of these variability diagrams are described in Fig. 1.4.

These elements have the following meaning:

- *Variation point*: the variation point describes where differences exist in the final systems (e.g. systems may differ with respect to the operating systems they rely on, with respect to whether they support e-mail or not, etc.).

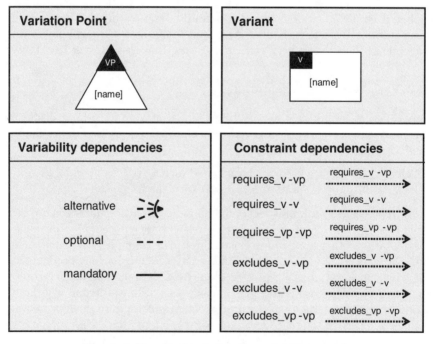

Fig. 1.4. Graphical notation for variability models

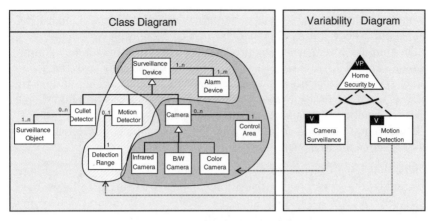

Fig. 1.5. Relation between variability model and class model

- *Variant*: the different possibilities that exist to satisfy a variation point are called variants.
- *Variability dependencies*: this is used as a basis to denote the different choices (variants) that are possible to fill a variation point. The notation includes a cardinality which determines how many variants can be selected simultaneously (e.g. a program may support e-mail, fax, phone, etc. as communication modes even in a single system).
- *Constraint dependencies*: they describe dependencies among certain variant selections. There are two forms:
  1. *Requires*: the selection of a specific variant may require the selection of another variant (perhaps for a different variation point).
  2. *Excludes*: the selection of a specific variant may prohibit the selection of another variant (perhaps for a different variation point).

The variability model on its own is not able to represent the full meaning of variability in software product line engineering. In addition, we need the traditional views on requirements, design, etc. and the relation between these views and the variability, so that we know how variability will have an impact on these individual views. An example of this relationship is given for the case of a UML class model in Fig. 1.5.

1.4.3 Application Engineering and Variability

Setting up the product line infrastructure is not a goal in itself. The ultimate aim is its exploitation during application engineering. This is also called the *instantiation* of the variability.

As new requirements are captured during application engineering, each requirement must be considered and a decision must be made about its future treatment in the life-cycle: shall it be part of the platform and shall it be a variable part there – or shall it be delegated to product development?

The simplest case is when the product line infrastructure already supports the requirement. In this case, it only needs to be checked that the *binding time* of the infrastructure also supports the requirements. The binding time describes when the decision upon selection of a variant must be made. Typical values are compile-time, link time, start-up time, etc.

If the requirement is not supported by the product line infrastructure, there are three different possibilities:

1. One can try to negotiate to drop or replace it. While this may sound strange from a customer-satisfaction perspective, it needs to be evaluated nevertheless. In a product line context, the more variabilities we must support, the more difficult the evolution of the infrastructure gets.
2. The new requirement shall be integrated with the product line infrastructure. There exist systematic approaches to make such a decision: the so-called *scoping* approaches [119] (see Sects. 1.5 and 2.4).
3. The new requirement shall be integrated in an application-specific manner.

The second case leads to a hand-over with domain engineering, while the third case leads to stand-alone software development in application engineering. Typically, all three cases occur for different requirements in the same system development.

1.5 Business-Centric

While traditional software development focuses on the individual system, product line engineering must always address the market as a whole. Product line engineering can only be successful if the product line infrastructure is in the long term an adequate instrument to field new products onto the market very efficiently. As a consequence, development decisions for the individual product are always linked to the product line at large. This relationship must be managed from an economic point of view.

Because of this strong linkage, it is of key importance that the major business goals for the product line initiative are well understood. Typical business goals are effort- (and thus cost-) reduction, as well as time-to-market reduction. Another major set of goals are quality-related. Typical examples are reliability improvement or usability improvement. The goal of usability improvement is supported as product line engineering inherently supports user interface consistency.

The specific set of goals that provides the basis of a product line engineering effort influences decisions about when a requirement should be implemented and whether it should be implemented for the product line as a whole or only for a specific product. As a rule of thumb, the break-even from a cost-point of view is typically about three implementations.[3] When three or more product realisations of a requirement are required, it is usually more cost-effective to implement it once as part of domain engineering. This break-even point shifts as soon as additional goals come in like consistency of user interfaces – in this case a single product-specific implementation may already violate this goal.

A business-centric approach to product line engineering entails that key decisions about which functionality to include in the product line and how this support shall be realised (as part of domain or application engineering) is based on a systematic economic decision. This analysis is also called *scoping*. We can differentiate three major categories [119]:

1. *Product portfolio planning*: this aims at determining the specific products and their functionalities that shall be supported by the product line infrastructure.
2. *Domain potential analysis*: this aims at analysing the potential of the product line domain or specific sub-domains in order to identify whether a promising case for product line engineering exists.
3. *Asset scoping*: this determines which specific components shall be built in domain engineering and which requirements they shall support.

Product portfolio planning aims at capturing the products that shall be part of the product line and identifying their main requirements. At this stage, a first overview of commonalities and variabilities of the products is gained. Product portfolio planning is the first step at which an optimisation can (and should) occur. This activity is mostly performed from a marketing point of view [82], but in the context of product line engineering, technical aspects must be taken into account as they strongly impact the production cost [23].

Domain potential analysis focuses on the systematic analysis of an area of functionality in order to determine whether an investment in software product line engineering shall be made. This is sometimes done on the level of the product line as a whole [12], while other approaches focus on individual areas within the product line [122]. The key issue of this step is always to get a systematic answer to the question where reuse investments should be focused. The overall result of this activity corresponds basically to an assessment.

Finally, asset scoping aims at defining the individual components that shall be built for reuse. In order to adequately define these components, two viewpoints must be brought together. These are the viewpoints of business and of architecture. Thus, this activity can be considered as being on the borderline between business-centric and architecture-centric. The business-centric viewpoint can be addressed by an economic analysis [122], while the architectural viewpoint is usually taken into account by an architectural review.

---

[3] More detailed analysis [123] shows that the break-even point strongly depends on the specific situation. It may range from just above 1 to almost a factor of 10. The underlying driver to this variation is mostly the overhead complexity incurred by the developed genericity

These decisions must be made not only during initial set-up of the product line (where they are the most pronounced), but also during product line evolution. Thus, usually some kind of review board is set up in the organisation which is responsible for the decisions described above throughout the lifetime of the product line.

We will further discuss the business aspects of software product line engineering in Chap. 2.

1.6 Architecture-Centric

Software product line engineering relies on a common product line architecture (also called *reference architecture*). It is thus often termed *architecture-centric*. The central role of a common architecture is a major ingredient of the success of product line engineering compared to other reuse approaches. The reference architecture is designed in domain engineering, in order to provide a coherent picture of the different components that must be developed and to equip them with generic interfaces that can be used throughout the different products. A common architecture defines a single environment for all components that are used in the individual products[4]. This ensures that there is no need to develop multiple components that address similar functionality, and differ only with respect to the environment they work in.

In each application engineering cycle, the reference architecture provides the basis for the derivation of the specific product architecture. As discussed in Sect. 1.4, this product architecture is mainly derived by instantiation of the generic asset. The architectural decomposition provides the basis for work assignment in the development process and for determining how to modify assets to support product-specific requirements. The role of architectures in a product line context is further discussed in Chap. 3.

Most practitioners to date assume a strong role of product line architecture as key for the overall success of a product line engineering initiative. Indeed, most experience reports in software product line engineering report on a strong role of the architecture [38, 25]. There are but few exceptional cases, where it seems that successful product line programs have been set up without major investments in software architecture [34].

1.7 Two-Life-Cycle Approach

Software product line engineering consists of domain engineering and application engineering. These two types of engineering are – in the ideal case – only loosely coupled and synchronised by platform releases. As a consequence, they can be conducted based on completely different life-cycle models. This

---

[4] In terms of the framework for comprehensive reuse, see [15]

distinction of domain engineering and application engineering is a key characteristic of software product line engineering (cf. Fig. 1.2, p. 7).

Domain engineering focuses on the development of reusable assets that provide the necessary range of variability. As domain engineering continues as long as the product line exists, the underlying software development approach must be able to cope with long-term, highly complex system development.

The activities within domain engineering are as follows:

- *Product management*: this activity aims to define the products that will constitute the product line as a whole. In particular, it aims at identifying the major commonalities and variabilities among the products. This realises product portfolio planning as discussed in Sect. 1.5. It also encompasses major economic analysis of the products in the product line. The major output of this activity is the product roadmap.
- *Domain requirements engineering*: this activity starts with the product roadmap and aims at a comprehensive analysis of the requirements for the various products in the product line. It captures these requirements, identifies commonalities and variabilities and constructs an initial variability model, which supports the further development steps.
- *Domain design*: starting from the requirements model, this activity aims at developing the product line architecture (or reference architecture). It thus provides the basis for all future realisation work within the product line.
- *Domain realisation*: this activity encompasses detailed design and implementation of the reusable software components. At this stage the planned variability which has been expressed as a requirement must be realised with adequate implementation mechanisms.
- *Domain testing*: this aims at validating the generic, reusable components that were implemented as a result of the previous activity. Domain testing is much more difficult than testing in a single system context, mainly for two reasons: the implemented variability must be taken into account and there is no specific product which provides an integration context. In addition, domain testing also generates reusable test assets that can be reused in application testing.

As a result domain engineering sets up the common product line infrastructure, including all required variability.

Application engineering focuses on the development of the individual systems on top of the platform. As a large part of development effort and complexity is moved to domain engineering, this activity – and thus the underlying life-cycle model – will usually be profoundly different as it will not need to cope with so much complexity and the development will not span so much time. On the other hand, application engineering is directly involved with the customer and thus will often need to deal with much more rapid changes. As a consequence, a life-cycle model that is able to cope rapidly with changes is required.

Application engineering consists of the following activities:

- *Application Requirements Engineering*: This aims at identifying the specific requirements for an individual product. As opposed to single system requirements engineering, this starts from the existing commonalities and variabilities. It is thus the goal of this activity to stay as close as possible to the existing product line infrastructure.
- *Application Design*: This activity derives an instance of the reference architecture, which conforms to the requirements identified in the previous step. On top of this product-specific adaptations are built. Thus, as far as reusable components are concerned, the architecture is consistent with the reference architecture, enabling plug-and-play reuse.
- *Application Realisation*: Based on the available requirements and architecture, the final implementation of the product is developed. This includes reuse and configuration of existing components as well as building new components corresponding to product-specific functionality.
- *Application Testing*: In this step, the final product is validated against the application requirements. Similar to the previous steps, this builds on reusable assets from the corresponding domain activity.

While the details of the integration of domain engineering and application engineering will strongly depend on the situation, it is important to keep the two apart in terms of different types of activities that are typically performed with different quality criteria and objectives in mind. This is in particular true, if both life-cycles are enacted by the same people, as is often the case, especially in small organisations.

1.8 The BAPO Model

In the description of software product line engineering in this book, we use the BAPO model as a major structuring model. This model is based on the assumption that in the context of software engineering, four concerns need to be addressed: Business, Architecture, Process and Organisation (BAPO). This model has been successfully used in the context of product line engineering [3, 99, 154], Chap. 14.

- *Business*: the costs and profits of the software, the strategy of applying it and the planning of producing it.
- *Architecture*: the technical means to build the software.
- *Process*: the roles, responsibilities and relationships within software development.
- *Organisation*: the people and organisational structures that execute the software development.

As Fig. 1.6 shows, the four BAPO concerns are all interrelated. Applying changes in one concern induces changes in the others.

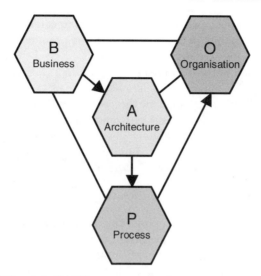

Fig. 1.6. BAPO concerns of software engineering

The BAPO acronym denotes a natural order to traverse these concerns. Business is the most influential factor. This has to be set up right in the first place. Architecture reflects these business concerns in software structure and rules. Processes enable the development of the software, based on the architecture. Organisation hosts this process, assigning units and people who are responsible for business, architecture and process responsibilities.

Throughout this book, we will use the BAPO model as a major structuring principle. The next four chapters will each address a specific aspect of BAPO. Moreover, the relation to BAPO will become explicit in each case-study chapter handled in Part II. We will now briefly discuss each of these concerns in a software product line context.

First, consider business concerns. We emphasised the importance of business aspects in a software product line engineering context in Sect. 1.5. Case studies have shown that the following business advantages can be obtained from product line engineering:

- Reduction to less than 50% time to market (Chap. 15).
- Reduction of code size by more than 70% (Chap. 8).
- Significantly reduced cost of quality (Chap. 11).
- Product defect density reduced to 50% of original rate (Chap. 15).
- Reduction of calibration and maintenance efforts (up to 20%) (Chap. 9).
- Reduction of resource consumption (20–30%) (Chap. 9).
- Common look-and-feel (Chap. 15).

While these business advantages can be quantified, some others are very hard to quantify but nevertheless substantial:

- A feature can be developed for a single product and, when it is satisfactory, it can quickly be added to other systems in the product line. This is called *feature propagation.*
- Products that are derived from the same product line will exhibit a common look and feel. This eases the use of the systems by the clients, since the products act like other systems in the product line that they are familiar with. This considerably increases customer satisfaction.
- The quality of systems in a product line can be better guaranteed. Reuse implies many users, which leads to more environments in which the software is tested, and more reported and fixed bugs. For instance, this book shows that the product defect density can be reduced to 50% or less of what it was before (cf. Chap. 15).

Next consider architecture concerns. We emphasised some architectural aspects already in Sect. 1.6. Software product line engineering makes use of a reference architecture for all products. It needs continuous updates and maintenance, since in practice the platform is growing and improving throughout its lifetime. Variability is traced from requirements over architecture and design to testing, enabling reuse not only for the software assets, but also for those of requirements and test. Software product line engineering enables reuse of test cases by more than 50%. This reduces the test effort significantly.

The domain architects use the commonality and variability in requirements and their priorities to determine the commonality and variability of the reference architecture. Specific variability mechanisms have to be selected to enable resolving variability easily. It has to provide solutions for requirements interaction, including requirements that are in conflict with each other, and that are applicable to distinct systems. An important concern of the domain architects is to deal with qualities like flexibility, adaptability, maintainability and evolvability, that all need to be supported to keep the reference architecture stable.

The application architects specialise the reference architecture to the specific requirements of the application. This involves the selection and instantiation of reusable domain assets. For those requirements that are not covered, application-specific variants have to be determined, and placed in the configuration. Such application-specific variants may be candidates for promotion to the platform, and therefore a close co-operation between domain and application architects is important.

Next consider process concerns. We already discussed (Sect. 1.7) that a product line engineering approach relies on a two-life-cycle model, consisting of domain engineering and application engineering. Besides these fundamental development processes, additional co-ordination processes are necessary to effectively communicate between them. Software product line engineering usually takes place in organisations at CMMI level 2 or higher [139]. However, the domain engineering process often reaches level 3 fast.

Finally consider organisation concerns. The impact of software product line engineering on the organisation is often underestimated. While the two-life-cycle model does not necessarily imply a specific organisational structure, a similar grouping of personnel is often performed. In particular, we often see a single domain engineering group and several separate application engineering groups. This – as well as the larger organisational entities that are formed – typically leads to a diversification of jobs.

Domain engineerings develop high-quality software components, and maintain them afterwards to improve the quality even more. In large organisations, the reference architecture is maintained by a group of people, each of them is responsible for a specific aspect of the architecture, often a quality issue, like performance or safety. Of course, knowledge of variability mechanisms is crucial for domain engineers.

Application engineers are able to build applications fast, based on a given platform. They need to know how to use the variability mechanisms to configure systems.

Finally, collaboration specialists are needed with good communication skills that relate between aspects of domain and application engineering. In many cases, cross-functional teams are active. These are groups of specialists both in domain and application engineering groups. Together they decide on the introduction of the evolution of specific aspects that they are responsible for.

1.9 Summary

Software product line engineering enables major improvements in the software development process, in particular with respect to development costs and time to market. In terms of a software reuse program, it achieves levels of reuse that are so far unprecedented.

Software product line engineering is based on four major concepts:

1. *Variability management*: if there is a single core concept of product line engineering, this is it. Determining, modelling and implementing commonalities and variabilities lie at the heart of product line engineering. Throughout this book, we will focus on a modelling approach that relies on a variability model.
2. *Business-centric*: product line engineering is business-centric insofar as it needs to be well aligned with the strategies relevant to the underlying market. As individual components are built in order to go into the various products also in the long-term, it is important to keep product line engineering well aligned with the business strategy.
3. *Architecture-centric*: the reference architecture plays a key role in product line engineering. It is generally believed that the extremely high reuse

levels can only be achieved by means of a common architecture for the various products.

4. *Two-life-cycle approach*: product line engineering is subdivided into domain engineering and application engineering. These address development for reuse and development with reuse, respectively.

The impact of product line engineering on a company can be particularly well described by means of the four dimensions of the BAPO-model. This model will also be the basis for the next four chapters.

2

Business

Product line engineering has a tremendous impact on the business performance of companies. This holds both in the context of products the company is already producing and for new markets that it is about to enter. Successful alignment of product line engineering and business strategy can lead to a very strong market presence. In this chapter, we focus on the economics of product line engineering and how this impacts strategy definition and product management. The relevance of business aspects in product line engineering is explained in Sect. 2.1. Next, product line markets are examined, followed by a section on product line economics. Section 2.4 deals with product management and scope in a product line context. The chapter ends with a summary.

2.1 Motivation

While many software engineering techniques are introduced in order to improve with respect to business concerns like cost or quality, their impact in the other direction – from software engineering technique to business – is usually rather small. Not so for product line engineering. It aims at providing a platform for a whole set of products and is thus typically relevant for a whole market. As a consequence, the developed product platform determines the capability of the company to perform business in the market. Thus, strong links exist to the way an organisation does business and its overall market strategy.

Business concerns influence the answers to a large range of questions in product line engineering. The following are among these questions:

- Should product line engineering be started at all?
- How will product line engineering impact our business performance?
- Which products shall we develop as part of a product line?
- What shall be the characteristics or features of these products?
- What timing shall be chosen for the market entry of the individual products?

- How shall the products be produced?
  - Which functionality shall be developed as part of the product line, based on the platform?
  - What functionality shall be developed as individual functionality?
- How shall we introduce product line engineering in our organisation?
- How shall we evolve the product line over time?

The answers to these questions depend on the underlying product line goals and markets and require a model of product line economics. We will now discuss different types of product line markets and then we provide a product line economics model. Finally, we discuss specific decision-making procedures on this basis.

2.2 Product Line Markets

In order to explain the relationship between product line engineering and business, we must first discuss characteristics of markets that are relevant to product lines. We do so along four major dimensions:

1. Product definition strategy
2. Market strategy
3. Product line life-cycle
4. The relation of product line strategy and product line engineering

2.2.1 Product Definition Strategy

The product definition strategy describes how new products are defined. There are two main classes that can be distinguished: *customer-driven* and *producer-driven*. In a *customer-driven* situation, the specific products are mainly defined by demands from existing and future customers. The final products are individualised to the specific needs of the customer. We call this situation *mass-customisation* when there is a very large number of different customer-demands. In this situation, the specific requirements of individual products are very difficult to identify up-front. It is very important that the product line platform provides a flexible basis for further development of products. The opposite situation is called producer-driven. In this situation, it is mainly upon the producing organisation to define the products. This is usually the case when products are developed for *mass-markets*; where each product variant is sold to a large number of customers (often in the hundreds of thousands).

The producer-driven strategy can be further subdivided into *market-oriented* and *technology-oriented* strategies. In the market-oriented strategy the products that are used to form the product portfolio are determined based on an analysis of the potential market segments. New products are defined mainly to satisfy newly formed market segments or changing needs in established market segments. A technology-oriented strategy starts from technological capabilities that are developed by the company and brings them to the market.

The product definition strategy is one major input to determining the product portfolio, which defines the set of product types that are offered by a company.

In practice, product definition strategies are usually a mixture of the types explained above. For example, a company may realise that a specific market is best addressed by pushing additional technology, but because it is not available in-house, it first acquires a company that has this technology. Other examples of a mixed strategy are used by platform vendors. They provide a base for the development of end systems for broad market segments. The final customisation is done by partner companies. In specific situations, e.g. if new markets must be addressed, they may also support the end-customer directly. Finally, at certain intervals, the company becomes technology-driven in order to introduce a new platform technology into the market. The impact of such aspects is also discussed in [67].

While some markets lend themselves more easily to certain strategies, the specific product definition strategy is also a strategic decision of the company and is strongly related to other strategic decisions. Product line engineering can support all of these approaches, but its relative benefit varies in relation to the strategy (cf. Sect. 2.2.4).

2.2.2 Market Strategies

While the product definition strategy defines who has the major influence in defining the product portfolio, the market strategy determines how an organisation wants to be known on the market. A typical categorisation of market strategies is given by Porter [107], who differentiates three main types of strategy:

- *Cost leadership*: the company aims at providing the product at the lowest possible costs.
- *Differentiation*: the product sets itself apart from the competitors through a specific feature (e.g. service, brand name, etc.).
- *Focusing*: the company focuses on a specific niche.

According to Kotler [82], the differentiation strategy can be further subdivided into

- *Improving*: The company improves in certain aspects (from the point of view of the customer) over the offerings of its competitors. This may include cost improvement, quality improvement, accompanying services, breadth of possible products, etc.

- *Newer*: the ideas made available by the producer are new to the market. This implies that the company is strong on innovations, i.e. that it has good innovation strategies.
- *Faster*: new possibilities are made available to the customers quickly. As opposed to the previous strategy, this does not necessarily mean the company is the inventor of these concepts.

On a typical market, companies following each of these strategies exist and can reap their benefits from these strategies. It is a key decision for an organisation to determine the strategy it uses to address a specific market. Product line engineering can be combined with each of these strategies to a varying degree. A company may even use several strategies simultaneously in addressing a market and support this with product line engineering, as we discuss in Sect. 2.2.4.

2.2.3 The Product Line Life-Cycle

Individual product have a life-cycle on the market that is typically characterised by the following stages [106]:

- *Introduction*: a new product is launched. Initially sales are low as the product is unknown.
- *Growth*: the product – and its competitive qualities – becomes increasingly known on the market. As a consequence, sales increase and the profit turns positive.
- *Maturity*: the sales increase diminishes. Prices must be reduced to win market share.
- *Saturation*: the maximum sales are achieved. At this stage, hard competition is not unusual.
- *Degeneration*: the product is increasingly substituted by other products, perhaps from the same company. Profits strongly decrease.

This single-product life-cycle gives a view on an individual product. In a product line context, we need to take the combination of products into account. So, what is the relationship among the individual products in the product line? Here, we need to distinguish two perspectives: time and variation[1]:

- Different products from the same product line can be on the market at the same time fighting for market share. This leads to the so-called *product line cannibalisation* [90], i.e. they mutually reduce each other's market shares.
- Different products from the same product line supplant each other over time on the market.

Depending on the mixture of these two product line perspectives, the overall product line life-cycle can exhibit different forms of dynamism as shown

---

[1] These two perspectives are sometimes also called *variation in time* and *variation in space* [25]

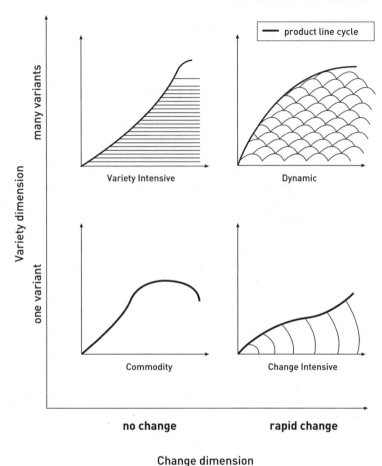

Fig. 2.1. Different possible product line life-cycles in terms of variety and change (based on [117])

in Fig. 2.1. These forms of dynamism can be categorised along two dimensions: product variety and serial change. The first dimension describes how many different products are available on the market at the same time. The second dimension describes how fast a new product is supplanted by a newer one. Along these two dimensions four categories can be identified: commodity, variety-intensive, change-intensive and dynamic.

The product line engineering approach can provide benefits to a development organisation.[2] When analysing a specific market in order to determine which kind of lifecycle is most appropriate, one needs to take into account that

---

[2] Except in the case of development organisations that focus on commodities. In this case, a product line is absent by definition

the characteristics of the market itself may change over time. For example, in a rather young market, the required variety is usually much lower than in a mature market.

2.2.4 The Relation of Strategy and Product Line Engineering

Most of the strategies that are used to capture a market can be supported by product line engineering, albeit by varying degrees. When analysing the relationship of the product line market strategy and product line engineering, we first need to appreciate that the two are different in the first place. In the past, companies realised all these marketing strategies with various development approaches, ranging from ad hoc reuse to single-system development. But product line engineering and a product line market strategy can start a fruitful symbiosis.

Product line engineering can support a product line marketing strategy. Product line engineering is able to strongly reduce the amount of effort – and thus cost – and the time to market required for a new product that fits within the product line. Mostly, these two factors enable product line engineering to support the strategies outlined above. The quality benefits of product line engineering usually play a secondary role.

Product line engineering is well suited for companies that choose a *cost leadership strategy*, as it enables them to produce their products at much lower costs (at least, if they produce more than two or three). The costs for an additional product are much lower[3] than with traditional development approaches. Thus, product line engineering also enables companies to use an approach of stronger differentiation as more products on the market can be cost-effective than with traditional development, despite product line cannibalisation. Due to the strongly shortened time to market in product line engineering, a stronger differentiation in the category "faster" is possible. Even for a company searching a focusing advantage, product line engineering enables it to produce its products cost-effectively, where traditional development approaches would fail.

Product line engineering and the market strategy must fit. Product line engineering aims at establishing a product line platform. This focus on a specific platform needs to be well aligned with the market strategy, as its existence makes it more difficult to develop products that do not fit the product platform well. As a consequence, it is of key importance for an organisation to strongly connect its market strategy and product line engineering. This is also known as *scoping* and, in a product line engineering context, this is the focus of product management. We will discuss this further in Sect. 2.4.

---

[3] The exact improvement with respect to cost reduction cannot be easily quantified. The reason is that the cost advantage of the product does not only depend on the production costs, but other costs like marketing, customer support, etc. dilute the development and maintenance costs advantages of product line engineering

2.3 Product Line Economics

In order to further clarify the relationship between product line engineering and business aspects, we now discuss in detail the economic aspects of product line engineering. We start with the key impacts of product line engineering on product and process qualities [121] and the impact this has on possible business strategies. In Sect. 2.3.1, we present a simple model of product line economics that also takes into account the issues of setting up a product line initiative. As the full range of issues that come up in product line economics would be beyond the scope of this book, we will only briefly illustrate some of them in Sect. 2.3.2.

2.3.1 Economic Results of Product Line Engineering

Any product that can be developed using a product line engineering approach can in principle also be developed without one. Although product line engineering does not necessarily impact the functionality of the products it delivers, it does influence certain other properties. These can be classified as *product qualities* and *process qualities* (cf. Fig. 2.2).

Product qualities are characteristics of product execution – like security, safety, reliability and usability, which can be experienced by using the products – as well as product development qualities, like maintainability and portability, which can be observed when developing and maintaining the system. Further, process characteristics like development effort (costs) and development time are strongly impacted by product line engineering. The following list gives an overview of key examples:

- *Development costs*: as large parts of the functionality of the systems are realised by the platform, the development of new products can substantially be reduced in size and complexity. As a consequence, development costs are often reduced on a similar scale.

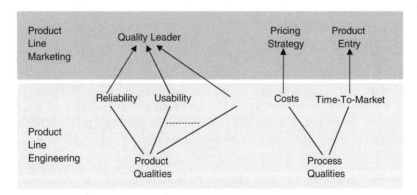

Fig. 2.2. Qualities in product line engineering and product line marketing

- *Development time*: as a consequence of the dramatic reductions of over-all effort, the development time for new product variants is reduced in a likewise manner.
- *Reliability of product*: product line engineering is not a reliability improvement strategy per se, but reusing proven components leads to product quality that is usually greatly improved over single system development.
- *Usability*: product line engineering may lead to strongly increased consistency among the various user interfaces, if the same components, implementing user interfaces, are reused across the product line.
- *Portability*: porting products across platforms can simply be seen as a form of variability. If the product platform is prepared for this, portability becomes a simple exercise.[4]
- *Maintenance*: product line engineering supports maintainability mainly in two ways. First, if the change has already been addressed as part of the platform, maintenance is simplified to product configuration. Secondly, even if explicit changes of the product line infrastructure must be performed, changes are usually greatly simplified because it is sufficient to maintain the platform as opposed to each individual product. Although changing a variable platform can be harder and more expensive than changing a single product, the benefits of the change are reaped by the entire product line.

Besides these fundamental impacts on qualities, product line engineering also reduces the *development risks*.[5]

As an organisation sets up a strategy for its product line development, it usually has one or more of the above goals as a basis for its introduction. These product line aspects have corresponding effects on the market view as shown in Sect. 2.4.

2.3.2 A Simple Model of Product Line Economics

As shown above, product line engineering has a large range of impacts on the economic situation of an organisation. However, most models of product line economics restrict themselves to the point of view of return on investment (ROI) with respect to costs. For certain companies, other issues (e.g. time to market reduction, quality improvement) might actually dominate this aspect.

Software cost modelling has been known for many years. The most well-known models are probably COCOMO and COCOMO II [24]. In a product line context, a cost model must describe the additional costs that are incurred that result from transitioning to a product line approach. A simple cost model

---

[4] Of course, preparing the platform can be hard work. On the other hand, a potentially large number of products benefit from it

[5] Where risk is defined as the probability of deviation from the intended result

has been presented in [23]. This model also provided the basis for describing product line transitioning in [106]. It distinguishes the following cost functions:

- $C_{unique}()$: describes the cost for developing software for use in a single product. A possible realisation of this model is given by models like CO-COMO [24].
- $C_{cab}()$: describes the cost for developing a core asset base that is suited to satisfy a particular scope (cf. Sect. 2.4.3). This summarises all costs of development for reuse.
- $C_{reuse}()$: describes the cost of reusing assets from the product line infrastructure when developing a new system.

As a consequence, we can describe the cost for developing the products in the product line as: $C_{unique} + C_{cab} + C_{reuse}$.

What does this mean in terms of numbers? Unfortunately, the situation with respect to precise data is still rather poor as we still lack a lot of thoroughly validated data. Most data on the economic impact of product lines is only available on a highly aggregated level, as we will see in Part II of this book. So far only little data exists on a detailed level [123].[6] The picture that emerges looks roughly as follows:

- The cost of building assets for product line reuse is higher than building assets for single system development. However, the precise overhead seems to be strongly dependent on several factors, among them the product line introduction approach and the specific functionality that must be generalised. In [123] a variation of a factor between roughly 1.1 and 10 was reported in otherwise identical circumstances, depending on the functionality alone. It seems, however, that for large systems an average factor of two to three is often realistic.
- The cost for reusing seems to be very low in a product line situation, much lower than for traditional reuse. The major reason is that traditional reuse approaches rely on adaptation of the reused component as part of the reuse step [108], while product line engineering does not.

In summary, product line engineering leads to additional set-up costs, while also enabling much more efficient production of the individual systems, thus recouping the efforts rather rapidly.

2.3.3 Advanced Aspects of Product Line Economics

The discussion of product line economics in the preceding section takes only costs into account. As we discussed in Sect. 2.3.1, product line engineering has further impacts on the business goals of an organisation, which should be quantified. Some of these aspects stretch into the area of market valuation. Only few models try to bridge this gap [121].

---

[6] Note that there is quite some data on reuse in general, but this can be applied to a product line situation to a very limited degree only

The following are some of the issues that the simple model does not address:

- Positive impacts like reliability, safety and usability.
- The reduction of time to market may lead to market advantages.
- Product line engineering provides additional flexibility for developing new products effectively.

Increases in quality achieved as a side effect of product line engineering bring about two kinds of benefits. First, the cost of development is reduced as the effort for defect detection and correction during development is minimised. Secondly, the quality of the products that are brought to the market is likewise improved. The first effect is usually included in the aggregated effort numbers; however, the effect on product quality stands out independently and can hardly be assessed by an economic model of software engineering alone, as adequate valuation of this fact must include aspects like higher market share due to better quality, reduced customer support costs, etc.

Shortening of the development time can be subdivided into two aspects. First, products can be brought to the market earlier. Depending on the market, this may lead to huge competitive advantages. Again, a market-oriented model is needed as a basis for valuation of a product line approach. The second aspect is of a more general nature. As product line engineering is usually set up to go over prolonged periods of time, an additional factor must be taken into account: *discounted cash-flow analysis*. The idea is that a euro today is worth more than a euro tomorrow. This is usually addressed by adding a discounting rate to the various expenses. Discounted cash-flow analysis starts to make a difference as soon as the modelled period exceeds two or three years.

Flexibility is a key issue that is mentioned over and over again, as organisations are asked for motivation for product line engineering. However, closer analysis reveals that flexibility is a two-edged sword. The key question is: flexibility to do what? Product line engineering provides a platform on which additional products can be built, but it does so only for some products. It does not provide any support for other kinds of products. Moreover, it might even prove to be a hindrance if basic assumptions of the platform do not fit to the product to be built. We can thus interpret the platform as a form of an option for building products.[7]

The key consequence of the search for flexibility is that product line engineering and the range of products that shall be developed must be well aligned. This is discussed further in the next section.

---

[7] Actually, we can use this interpretation also as a basis to build corresponding product line value models as shown in [53, 155, 121]

2.4 Product Management and Scoping

The advantages an organisation can reap from product line engineering strongly depend on how well the product line infrastructure and the actual products that the organisation is going to develop are aligned [67]. Thus, the integration of technical and marketing-oriented product line planning is key to successful product line development. This is also defined as *scoping*, i.e. bounding the product line. Scoping can happen on three different levels [119]:

1. *Product portfolio scoping* determines the range of products that shall be supported. This is mainly driven from market inputs.
2. *Domain scoping* identifies major functional areas (domains) that are relevant to the engineering of the product line [45, 134].
3. *Asset scoping* defines the precise functionality that reusable components should support.

The three different types of scoping can be seen as three different levels that build on each other. Thus, product portfolio scoping is a basis for domain scoping, which in turn provides the basis for scoping the asset base or product line infrastructure. Currently, no single scoping approach addresses all three levels. A rather comprehensive scoping approach is PuLSE-Eco [122]. It focuses mainly on domain scoping and asset scoping.

2.4.1 Product Portfolio Management

The definition and ongoing management of the product portfolio is at the heart of product management, especially in a product line situation. Product portfolio management depends strongly upon the definition of a product line market as discussed in Sect. 2.2. Only a focused market definition provides a basis for establishing a stable product line infrastructure. After a market has been defined, it is necessary to determine the relevant product types.[8] This defines the product portfolio. It can easily be characterised by a simple list of products along with their major features and functionalities. This is sometimes also called a *product map* [118]. In order to determine the right products, they need to be analysed according to their market position [106]. In particular, the decision should be made whether or not existing products will be continued on the new platform. This decision can be refined later, but a first cut should be made at this stage.

---

[8] We are interested only in the product *types*, as it is in general not meaningful – or even impossible possible – in a customer-oriented market to define the various customer *products* in advance. In a purely market-oriented situation, the two might actually be identical

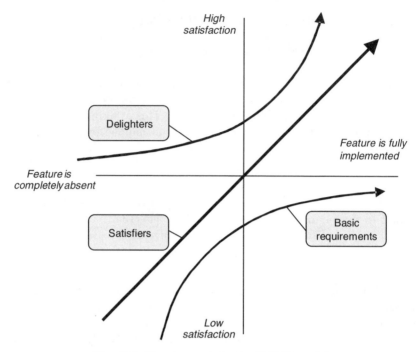

Fig. 2.3. Requirements in the KANO model

A widely used approach to defining new products is the KANO model. In this model requirements are subdivided into the following categories (cf. Fig. 2.3):

- *Delighters*: These go beyond standard customer expectations – and thus beyond the competition. In order to be successful, a product should have some delighters.
- *Satisfiers*: Customer satisfaction is roughly proportional to the degree of satisfaction of the requirement.
- *Basic requirements*: These correspond to fundamental expectations of the customers. As a consequence, these must be fulfilled in order for a product to be successful.

This distinction provides the basis for determining the chances of a product on the market.

In order to arrive at a full portfolio definition, we need to analyse the interrelation among its products. Different products within a product line may compete with each other (product line cannibalisation) or they might even support each other (e.g. an entry-level product designed to get people buy into the product line combined with higher-level products designed to make customers migrate along this line of products). Only when the various products are harmonised with each other can we accept the product portfolio definition as being appropriate.

An additional complication when defining a basic product portfolio is that the product line as seen from a marketing point of view and the engineered product line need not be the same [68]. For example, deviations may occur if the product line infrastructure is used in order to develop products for third parties (marketed under a different label) or if third party products make up for part of the own product line. All such additions and exceptions should be identified as input to product portfolio scoping.

2.4.2 Domain Potential Analysis

Domain potential analysis builds on the result of product portfolio scoping. It requires an input that describes the specific products and their requirements. These shall be built as a result of product line engineering. The core task of domain potential analysis is to perform an analysis of the reuse potential in a product line.

All modern approaches to domain potential analysis are based on the concept of an assessment [12, 120]. They assess the domain and the overall product line development based on a number of domains. As an example, we here provide the list of dimensions used in the PuLSE-Eco approach [122]. These are differentiated into two main categories: viability and performance dimensions.

The *viability dimensions* aim to determine whether product line engineering can be successfully established in the domain. This is not only dependent on the domain alone, but also requires additional information like organisational and resource constraints:

- *Maturity*: the domain must be sufficiently mature so that the necessary concepts are established and can be codified in an appropriate way.
- *Stability*: the domain must be sufficiently stable so that a product line infrastructure can be stable as well.
- *Resource constraints*: setting up a product line initiative requires an initial investment. The necessary resources must be available.
- *Organisational constraints*: the organisation must be appropriate for a product line – or at least the necessary flexibility must exist to make it appropriate.

The *performance dimensions* describe how successful a product line effort can be expected to be:

- *Market potential*: in order for a product line engineering initiative to succeed, the necessary market potential needs to exist. Ideally, this is already clarified in the product portfolio scoping phase. We further differentiate *external* and *internal* market potential. The external market potential describes the potential relative to customers who are not part of the organisation, while the internal market potential describes the potential that internally produced components are actually used in the final products.

- *Commonality / variability*: the presence of commonality and variability is a basis for a product line. However, the variability should be systematic to some degree, so that systematic reuse can be enforced.
- *Coupling / cohesion*: coupling and cohesion impact the ease with which adequate, reusable components can be built. If there is strong coupling with other domains, it becomes very difficult to develop reusable assets, as the assets will exhibit a lot of context dependencies.
- *Existing assets / legacy*: existing assets can give a product line initiative a serious head-start as they may provide a good basis for developing components in the product line infrastructure. On the other hand, existing products that predate the product line engineering effort but must be maintained from this basis in the future may require huge additional effort.

As a result of a domain potential analysis – regardless the approach – we can expect that the viability of product line engineering is established at this stage and that those areas that provide the best basis for product line engineering have been identified as well.

It might come as a surprise, but usually there are huge variations among domains with regard to serving as a basis for product line engineering. Some sub-domains might be well-suited while others might be so completely dependent on the individual customer situation that it does not make sense to provide any reusable components. It is one of the strengths of product line engineering that it still can take optimal advantages of these situations.

2.4.3 Asset Scoping

Asset scoping is still part of the business perspective, as it classically takes a return-on-investment perspective. But at the same time it bridges to the development of the software architecture, as the architecture is key in the definition of further implementation-oriented assets. Asset scoping provides initial aggregations of functionality that are defined based on a return-on-investment perspective and can be a starting point for the software architecture, but it does not introduce a technical or implementation perspective.

In the PuLSE-Eco approach, asset scoping is realised by the so-called *reuse infrastructure scoping component*. This component consists broadly of the following four steps:

1. Formalise the reuse goals as economic functions.
2. Identify (detailed) relevant functionality.
3. Characterise functionality in terms of economic characterisation functions.
4. Derive asset proposals from evaluation results.

In the first step, the economic goals for product line reuse are detailed and transformed into an economic model attuned to the specific organisation. The more precise these models are, the more precise the resulting evaluation will be. On the other hand, the models should not be made too complex as the base data already has significant impreciseness. As a result of this step, high-level benefits – like effort-saving – are broken down into elementary, directly measurable elements, like size of component or developer productivity. These elementary functions are called *characterisation functions* as they serve to characterise elementary functionality from an economic perspective.

The level of granularity of functionality required in this step is much finer than in the previous steps, as we want to identify the specific functionality that should be combined. This requires a more detailed identification of requirements than in the previous steps.

The next step aims at collecting values for the characterisation functions for individual requirements in order to perform the calculation of economic benefits. This often becomes the stumbling block for organisations aiming at such an approach. If there is little or no background knowledge and experience available on measurement programs, the organisation will have significant problems to estimate adequate values for the various characterisation functions. These deviations and errors may influence the final results.

Asset scoping is particularly relevant in case a new product line infrastructure is set up from scratch. It also makes certain demands on the organisation, like being able – at least to some degree – to perform measurement-based management. This is very often not the case in an organisation, so usually only the first two steps are performed. In these cases, the benefits of a quantitative analysis of reuse potential cannot be reaped.

2.5 Summary

Product line engineering strongly impacts the way a company is doing business. It provides a basis for the efficient development of products for whole market segments. As a consequence, the definition of the company's markets and business must be thoroughly aligned with its activities in product line engineering. Ideally, business strategy drives technological decisions and is influenced by technical opportunities and difficulties with little or no lag time in between.

Companies that effectively establish a product line engineering effort are able to reap substantial benefits that improve their market positions. While cost and time to market advantages are the most well known, quality improvements in terms of reliability or usability can as well provide a substantial market advantage.

In order to optimise the economic returns of a product line initiative, various models and approaches have been developed. Existing economic models of product line engineering still focus on cost issues, although some models look at the broader picture.

Optimally, aligning product line engineering with the business implies that an organisation has a well-defined flow from its high-level business perspective to its product portfolio and finally to the definition of specific components relevant to its product line infrastructure.

3

Architecture

The architecture is an important part of any non-trivial system. It roughly bounds the scope of functionality that a system can handle, and plays a big role in determining the system's quality attributes. A common architecture is essential for a set of products to efficiently share large parts of their implementation.

A product line architecture serves the needs of not one but potentially many different products. To that end it must capture the commonality of these products and deal with their differences in an effective manner.

In this chapter, we discuss the topic of architecture in a product line engineering context. The first section explains the reason for having a software product line architecture. In Sect. 3.2, attention is paid to the four primary elements of architecture: its requirements, concepts, structure and texture. The following sections describe how a product line architecture is designed, evaluated and evolved respectively. The chapter ends with a summary.

3.1 Motivation

The architecture of a system captures its high-level design decisions, including the organisation in components and their interaction, as well as principles and guidelines for implementing and evolving the architecture.

The shared architecture in a product line is called the *reference architecture*. The reference architecture describes a generalised architecture that provides a solution for the range of products in the product line. It contains the variability that is instantiated in product architecting, although not all of it is visible on the architectural level.

The reference architecture is a result of domain engineering. It is used as a common asset in application engineering, where it is instantiated and extended to create product architectures. Extensions happen in accordance with the variation points that were defined in the reference architecture.

Architecture is especially important in product line engineering because a shared architecture makes it easier for products to share assets. Reusable assets are created with the shared architecture in mind. This enables domain engineers to make assumptions about the architectural context in which the common assets that they create or develop will be used. As a result, creating assets becomes easier and cheaper. Further, incorporating also becomes much easier for application engineers as long as they adhere to the reference architecture.

3.2 Architecture Concerns

Architecture has four primary concerns [73]:

1. *Architecturally significant requirements*: those requirements that have an essential impact on the architecture.
2. *Conceptual architecture*: describes the key concepts of the architecture, abstracting from implementation details.
3. *Structure*: captures the decomposition of the system into components and their relationships.
4. *Texture*: a collection of rules for implementing the architecture and evolving it over time. These rules may be expressed as coding conventions, design patterns and architectural styles.

Each of these concerns is explained below.

3.2.1 Architecturally Significant Requirements

In theory, requirements engineering is a prerequisite to architecting, and thus requirements for the architecture will be established. In practice, architects often cannot afford to wait until a stable requirements specification is available to them. Instead, they have to deal with incomplete and changing requirements. Next to taking part in the 'normal' requirements engineering process as stakeholders, architects take the evolving set of requirements and dig up and document the architecturally relevant requirements: a small set of requirements that will really shape the reference architecture.

A reference architecture for a software product line has to deal with the requirements of many (planned) products. Requirements that are common to all should be satisfied by the reference architecture. Other requirements may be unique for certain products, some of them may be conflicting. The reference architecture must support such variability in its concepts, structure and texture.

Two types of requirements can be distinguished. *Functional requirements* determine *what* is realised. *Quality requirements* drive *how* it is implemented. Desired quality properties – such as those with respect to performance, safety, or reliability – are often decisive during the design phase of an architecture.[1] In product line engineering, variability is one of the most important architecture drivers.

3.2.2 Conceptual Architecture

The conceptual architecture describes the major concepts that govern how the system works, without going into implementation details. A conceptual model is a description of the concepts in the domain of interest, showing the most important concepts in the problem domain, and their relations. In a reference architecture, it captures the problem domain that is common to the entire product line. It serves as a "a mental model that allows one to understand and simplify the problem" [55] This makes the conceptual model a good vehicle for communication between and with stakeholders of the architecture.

3.2.3 Structure

The architectural structure is the decomposition of a system into its major components, and their relationships. A component is a unit of composition with contractually specified interfaces. The term can refer to both a high-level design unit and its physical implementation.[2] Interfaces describe not only the services that a component offers, but also the context that is required for its use. It can be deployed independently as a building block by others than its original developers and maintainers.

Components can be generic or application-specific. They can be designed and developed in-house, developed by a third party according to a given design, or bought as a commercial off-the-shelf product. In the latter case, some wrapping is usually required to fit the component in the architecture. Wrapping is also a means to reduce the dependency on an external party, even if it is technically not needed per se.

3.2.4 Texture

The texture of an architecture guides both designers and architects:

- Its guidelines and rules tell designers how to work out the architecture in detail, and how to implement it. It is used throughout the design of the system, ensuring a consistent approach to interpreting the architecture and solving recurring problems.
- It guides architects in evolving the architecture over time without destroying its core concepts. It captures the basic ideas (or philosophy) that lead to the architecture and that keeps it a coherent whole. This part of the texture is sometimes called *meta-architecture* [30].

---

[1] On the lower design levels, the main quality concerns deal with keeping the design and source code easy to understand and maintain

[2] The context of the text will make clear which interpretation is meant

The texture may contain such things as coding conventions, design patterns, architectural styles [133] and principles [156].

3.3 Product Line Architecting

Although architecting methods that aim specifically at product lines do exist,[3] they can all be used for single system development too. Vice versa, many existing single-system architecting methods have been used successfully for designing product line architectures, for example Attribute Driven Design [18], Bosch [25] and Bredemeyer [30].

The main challenge in designing a reference architecture is based on the fact that the architect has to deal with many different products at the same time. In some cases, especially in large companies, each product has many stakeholders. In practice, this means that communication becomes even more important than in single-system architecting.

Getting the requirements right for all the products is hard, especially since there will be conflicts between requirements for different products. These conflicts must be resolved in the architecture. Deleting products until there are no conflicts left would be an easy way out, but leads to a very meagre product line. Instead, support for variability must be an integral part of the reference architecture.

Variability is modelled in a variation model, as described in Chap. 1. The reference architecture must implement all the variation points of the product line to support the right scope of products.

3.3.1 Basic Variability Techniques

On an abstract level, there are three basic techniques to realise variation in an architecture: adaptation, replacement and extension.

In the *adaptation* technique, there is only a single implementation available for a certain component, but it offers interfaces to adjust its behaviour. Such interfaces may take the form of a configuration file, run-time parameterisation or even patches to the component's source code, to name some options.

In the *replacement* technique, several implementations of a component are available. Each implementation adheres to the component's specification as described in the architecture. In application engineering, one of the available implementations is chosen, or a product-specific implementation is developed instead, again following the given specifications.

The *extension* technique requires that the architecture supplies interfaces that allows adding new components to it. The added components may or may not be product-specific. The difference with replacement is that now

---

[3] See [91] for a comparison of five product line architecting methods: COPA, FAST, FORM, KobrA and QADA

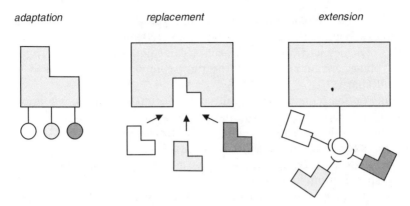

Fig. 3.1. Three basic techniques for realising variability in an architecture

only generic interfaces are available for adding components, allowing different types of components to be added. With replacement, the interface specifies exactly what the component should do, and only how it is done varies. Also, a number of components can be added using the same interfaces, whereas with replacement, a single (default) component is replaced by another one.

In some cases, the reference architecture covers only a sub-domain of a product. The reference architecture may then be a (small) part of the application architecture. From the domain engineering point of view, this would also be a case of extension.

Figure 3.1 graphically depicts these three basic techniques.

3.3.2 Concrete Variation Mechanisms

In the reference architecture, these techniques are deployed to model the variation points. The architecture's texture describes the implementation mechanisms that should be used to realise the variation points in the software assets. Examples of such mechanisms are as follows [9, 25]:

- *Inheritance* (adaptation): given a class and its implementation, a subclass is introduced that changes some of the default behaviour as needed by the application.
- *Patching* (adaptation): if the source code of a component is available, patching can be an effective way to change part of its behaviour without taking over the burden of maintaining the entire component.[4] The patch is maintained by the application engineering group, while the component itself is maintained in domain engineering.

---

[4] Popular in the world of open source software development, patching can also be applied within the boundaries of a single organisation as long as different development groups agree to share their source code. This is also referred to as *Inner Source*

- *Compile-time configuration* (adaptation): compilers may offer mechanisms to vary a component at compilation time. Pre-processors and macros are ways of achieving variability. Makefiles can compile a component into several binary variants, or select the right components to be linked to an executable.
- *Configuration* (adaptation): in this case, a component implementation has different variations internally, and provides an interface to choose among the possibilities. A simple configuration file may do the trick. Other examples are parameters in procedure calls.
- *Code generation* (replacement): a code generator reads some kind of high-level specification, for example a model, or a script, and generates the code required for a certain component or even a whole product. The complexity of generators varies. Sometimes, all that needs to be generated is glue code between a set of reusable implementations. In other cases, the code generator can be very complex and its development and maintenance a significant cost factor.
- *Component replacement* (replacement): the default implementation of a component is replaced with another one.
  In some cases, the reference architecture may provide only an empty implementation by default, because there is no common implementation available. The chosen implementation may be product-specific, or common for the whole or part of the product line. It may be developed in-house, either in domain or application engineering, or it can be a third-party component. In the case of a commercial off-the-shelf implementation, wrappers may be required to bridge the available interfaces to the desired ones.
- *Plug-ins* (extension): the architecture offers interfaces that allow plug-in components to be added to the system. The plug-ins provide certain functionality. Plug-ins may be common or application-specific.

3.4 Evaluation

Evaluation is an important step in every architecture design process. Informal evaluations are done most often, for example by going through use case scenarios at a whiteboard, making back-of-the-envelope performance calculations or programming out pieces of the architecture to test certain concepts. More formal evaluations are done less frequently. Examples are building proof-of-concept prototypes, performance modelling and evaluation workshops, for example ATAM, CBAM and SAAM[5] [37].

When evaluating a reference architecture, close attention should be paid to the variability support. Does the proposed architecture support all products in the product line? Or is it perhaps too generic, trying to solve too

---

[5] In full, Architecture Trade-off Analysis Method (ATAM), Cost Benefit Analysis Method (CBAM) and Software Architecture Analysis Method (SAAM)

many problems at once? Application architectures should be evaluated for their specific product requirements. Certain issues may be revealed that cannot be solved in application engineering, but are a problem in the reference architecture. Care must be taken such that feedback reaches the right people, for example by including product line architects in application architecture evaluation sessions.

3.5 Evolution

A successful architecture will inevitably face unforeseen requirements. In fact, its success may well depend on how it is able to cope with them. A well designed architecture can handle certain new requirements, mostly if the new requirements were more or less expected. Usually, the architecture will sooner or later face requirements that it cannot support in its current form, and therefore it must change in order to be able to. This is called *intentional evolution*.

The following are some sources of new requirements:

- The market demands new features or enhanced quality properties. This is rather common not only in many technology-intensive markets such as consumer electronics, but also in professional medical equipment. The features and properties may end up in new versions of existing products, or lead to a whole new product.
- On the other hand, features or products may become redundant. For example, most personal computers are no longer equipped with a floppy disk drive. Such changes may be a chance to simplify the architecture and cut off some dead wood.
- When a company acquires another company, a whole range of existing products may be added to a product line.
- Third-party components need to be updated. Support for deprecated technology can often be bought, but is usually expensive. It may be cheaper to evolve the architecture and its implementation, especially if it reduces maintenance costs.
- Technological advancement makes it attractive to introduce new technology. For example, a home-grown solution to a problem that was exotic at the time can now be replaced by a commercially available component.

When new requirements come up, the existing architecture must first be evaluated for its capability to deal with them. In most cases, unforeseen requirements will not be supported by the architecture. Still, the evaluation will give insight into how much the architecture must be changed to handle them properly.

Evolution also happens without purpose, in which case it is called *unintentional*. Even if a documented architecture remains stable, its implementation changes because of maintenance. If this process is not guided and monitored, it can lead to two problems: a mismatch between the documented architecture and its implementation, and architectural erosion, also known as software entropy or software rot.

Over time, the documented architecture and its implementation drift further apart. If nothing is done about it, at one point the gap will be so large that reading the architecture documentation does not help to understand the software anymore.

Architectural erosion means that the design of the software is unintentionally ruined by a series of small changes. This may start with innocent little shortcuts here and there. Given enough of them, these shortcuts make it impossible to understand the rationale behind the original design.

The architecture texture can play an important role in slowing these processes down. Its guidelines apply not only during the initial implementation, but also during maintenance.

Refactoring is another important way of fighting erosion [57]. Refactoring means that design is improved without changing the functionality of a system. Originally described for use on a detailed design level, it can be applied to all levels of design, including the architecture.

3.5.1 End of Life

The lifespan of an architecture depends on the problem domain that it serves. Some systems, like professional medical equipment, may be actively maintained in the field for decades, whereas others, like mobile phones, may have a new architecture every third year. In any case, no architecture lives forever.

An architecture can handle only so much evolution before it breaks. When evolving the architecture to support new requirements becomes too expensive or risky, the architecture has reached its end of life. This does not mean that it becomes worthless.

For one, there may be products in the field that were built on (an earlier version of) the architecture. Perhaps they are even actively maintained.

Moreover, the architecture represents a wealth of knowledge on and experience in the problem domain. Its requirements, concepts, structure and texture can be an important source of assets and inspiration for the new reference architecture.

3.6 Summary

The reference architecture is a key asset of a product line. It enables the efficient sharing of software-related assets. As such, it must reflect the scope of the product line, and support its commonality and variability.

The reference architecture can be adapted, extended or partially replaced to derive application architectures. The ways in which this can be done are captured in the texture of the reference architecture.

Given enough time of life, a reference architecture will evolve, even though it was designed with a range of planned products in mind. Care must be taken that the architecture and its implementation do not drift apart too far during the evolution. Intentional evolution is done to meet new requirements, for example stemming from the introduction of new products to the line. As the implementation changes, so should the documented architecture. Unintentional evolution is a normal part of software maintenance. Refactoring is crucial to keep the design and architecture understandable and effective.

An architecture has reached its end of life once it becomes more expensive to change the architecture than to create and implement a new one. The old architecture can serve as a valuable source of knowledge when creating its successor.

4

Process

Software product line engineering comprises two life-cycles: *domain engineering* and *application engineering*. During domain engineering, a common platform is developed and maintained. A set of reference requirements, a reference architecture, and a set of reusable components form the major parts of this platform.

The platform is the basis for application engineering. Application engineering develops the products in the product line. The platform needs to be flexible enough to support all planned products. It consists of assets that can be tailored to the needs of specific products through managed variation points.

In the rest of this chapter we explore the process dimension. First, we explain the importance of process in a product line engineering context. The following section describes a high-level framework for software product line engineering as a whole. Sects. 4.3 and 4.4 zoom in on the sub-processes in domain engineering and application engineering respectively. The chapter ends with a summary.

4.1 Motivation

It is widely accepted that the quality of a development process strongly influences the quality of the systems that it produces [140]. No matter how good the tool, it is useless without a proper way of using it. Software product lines are not different. They can be great for companies to make a range of related software intensive products, but one still needs a good process to make them work.

Jones and Northrop argue that process discipline is extra important when software product line engineering is considered [74]. More co-ordination, discipline and commonality of approach is needed than for single system engineering, and since the dependencies within the organisation are greater, predictability and quality become more critical. Disciplined process management and execution can help to improve these aspects and thus contribute to the success of a software product line.

4.2 The Software Product Line Engineering Framework

Figure 4.1 shows a framework for software product line engineering. The framework divides product line engineering into two life-cycles : domain engineering and application engineering. Domain engineering results in the common assets that together constitute the product line's platform. Application engineering results in delivered products. Within the two life-cycles, there are nine sub-processes. Eight of the engineering processes form four pairs: requirements engineering, design, realisation and testing are done in both domain and application engineering. These pairs of processes are strongly connected. The domain engineering sub-processes result in common assets that are used in their application engineering counterparts to create products. In return, the sub-processes in application engineering generate feedback that is in use in domain engineering to improve the common assets. This feedback loop is essential to ensure that the platform remains suitable for the efficient production of end products. In some cases, application-specific assets are reused in

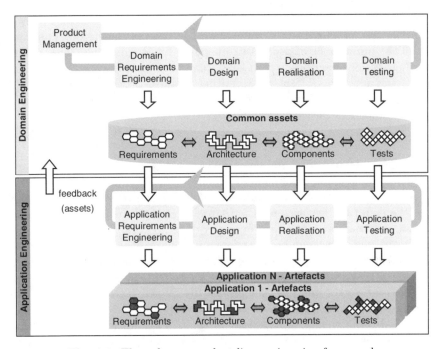

Fig. 4.1. The software product line engineering framework

domain engineering to become part of the platform, but that is a side effect – not a goal – of application engineering.

4.3 Domain Engineering

Domain engineering is the life-cycle that results in the common assets that together form the product line's platform. It is further responsible for scoping the product line, and ensuring that the platform has the variability that is needed to support the desired scope of products.

4.3.1 Product Management

Product management deals with the scope of a product line and its market strategy. The scope determines what the common and variable features of the product line are. Existing products and shared development assets are documented and a product roadmap describes future products and their planned release dates.

In some cases, application engineering also has product management processes. Obviously, domain engineering and application engineering strongly influence each other, and the processes must be well aligned to be effective.

More information on product management and scoping can be found in Sect. 2.4.

4.3.2 Domain Requirements Engineering

Domain requirements engineering is the process of creating and managing requirements for the reference architecture and its implementation. The resulting reference requirements should cover the requirements for all (foreseeable) applications within the product line scope. They include common requirements and the variation points that the product line architecture should support.

Requirements engineering has five basic phases [106]:

1. *Elicitation*: the analysis of the needs of users and other stakeholders.
2. *Documentation*: means writing those needs down as product requirements in a precise way.
3. *Negotiation*: stakeholders try to reach an adequate level of consensus on the requirements as they are documented. The way in which this is done depends heavily on company culture.
4. *Validation and verification*: it results in a set of requirements that are clear, complete, correct and understandable.
5. *Management*: it deals with maintaining the requirements throughout the development and the rest of the platform life-cycle. Often, the previous phases will be revisited during the management phase, as new requirements come in and existing ones change.

Stakeholders play an essential role in each of these phases. The end product stakeholders are typically customers and all kinds of users. They may be represented by internal departments, such as marketing, but they can also be involved directly. These stakeholders care about how the features and quality properties of the platform influence end products.

But domain engineers also have to take into account the users of the platform that they are creating. These platform stakeholders are the ones responsible for application engineering. They are interested in creating products as efficiently as possible. They want a platform that allows them to do this, leading to requirements regarding documentation, the quality of components, their testability and a simple but flexible reference architecture.

The platform requirements have to deal with the full range of products in the line. Some of these requirements are common to all products, others will vary. The domain requirements must take this variability into account, so that they can be used as templates in the requirements engineering processes for the applications.

The variability model, as discussed in Sect. 1.4, guides the variation in the requirements. As an example, Fig. 4.2 shows how variability can be captured in use case scenarios and diagrams.

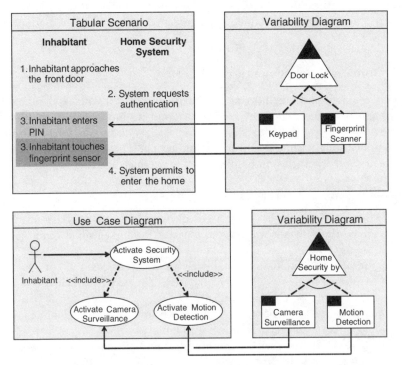

Fig. 4.2. Variability in use case scenarios and diagrams [106]

4.3.3 Domain Design

Domain design takes the reference requirements as input and creates a reference architecture for the platform. This architecture serves as the basis for designing products during application design.

The architecting process is described in Sect. 3.3.

4.3.4 Domain Realisation

In domain realisation, the common assets are designed and created. It can be worthwhile to use existing implementations instead of making them anew. For each asset, a *make/buy/mine/commission* decision is made, although often unconsciously [38]:

- *Make*: the asset is built in-house. The main advantage of this option is the level of control that it implicates. The organisation has full control over the specification and implementation of the asset, limited only by its own capabilities. This is especially valuable when the assets are distinguishing for the product line, for example because they enable an innovative feature.
- *Buy*: the asset is bought as an off-the-shelf product. Commodity assets that are readily available in the market are often cheaper when bought from others. Examples are not only operating systems (e.g. Windows, Linux), middleware software (e.g. J2EE, .NET), but also development tools and processes (e.g. RUP, CMMI).
- *Mine*: the asset is reused from an existing system within the company. In this case, the organisation opens its lumber room and searches its existing systems for an asset to be used. Their freedom is limited by the range of assets that are available, and how easy it is to adapt them to the platform. Especially if the system being mined has reached end-of-life or is out of use, getting high-quality assets out of it can take significant reverse engineering effort.

  In some cases, an application-specific asset can be taken and turned into a common asset. If the application engineering process responsible for the asset is still running, this can be relatively easy.[1]
- *Commission*: the asset is assigned to be built by a third party. The asset's specifications are created in-house, but it is left to a third party to implement it. This may well create a gap between the ones who make the specifications and the ones who implement it. This implicates the risk with it that the implementation does not meet the original intention of the asset. This risk should be addressed properly, e.g. by putting effort in creating very high quality specifications, or installing extra communication mechanisms and short feedback loops.

---

[1] Often, a series of related assets can be made reusable in one go, e.g. apart from a component's implementation, its design, use cases, documentation, end-user documentation, test, etc.

Usually, the common software in a product line is grouped in the form of components and the interfaces that they provide and require. The interfaces serve as a contract between a component and its context. *Provided* interfaces describe what the component offers, whereas *required* interfaces specify what the component needs to do its job.

A single component can have many different interfaces. A component may implement several interfaces that describe its major functionality, and others that deal with aspects such as logging or testing. A component's variability may be made accessible through a configuration interface, but it may also use a required interface to enquire about variability-related information from its environment and configure itself accordingly. To achieve variability, different components can implement the same set of interfaces. Other mechanisms for implementing variability have been described in Chap. 3.

4.3.5 Domain Testing

A product line platform ends up in many different end products. Errors in the platform may find their way to each of these products, which is why it is very important to make sure that the platform is of sufficient quality. Testing is crucial.

Software testing is the process of uncovering evidence of defects in software systems [93]. There are several types of tests [92][2]:

- *Dynamic testing* covers a range of tests. Unit testing for individual components and interfaces, integration testing for interactions between components and system testing for the whole executable platform.
- *Regression testing* is done to ensure that existing specifications are still met after a component has evolved. Some regression tests cover code that was not changed at all. This code may contain defects that will surface now that it is used in different ways by those parts of the component that did change.
- *Acceptance testing* is done for third-party mined and acquired components. Although mining and acquisition may lead to lower development costs, they usually result in increased test efforts. Acceptance testing may also be done for the platform as a whole, with the customers being those who use the platform for product development.

A major problem that has to be addressed during domain testing is variability. The variation mechanisms that make it possible to base many different products on a single platform also make it very hard to thoroughly test the

---

[2] Although non-executables cannot be tested, it is important that their quality is verified. Source-code can be checked for its conformance to programming rules, design and architecture during code inspections. Design and architecture can be evaluated, and validation and verification are essential to produce high-quality requirements. McGregor calls this *static testing* [92]

platform. Even a modest number of variation points will quickly lead to an immense number of possible configurations, making it impossible to test all potential products in a product line. Since future products cannot be predicted precisely, one cannot test the platform for each product in the scope in advance. This makes a brute force approach to testing – where all platform components are tested in all possible configurations – impossible. Instead, a limited number of configurations will be tested. The suite of tested platform instances requires careful consideration and management, since each costs effort to create, maintain and test on its own.

As an example, consider a reference architecture that has a plug-in variation mechanism. In this case, the software platform has gaps that need to be filled with product-specific components during application engineering. The required and provided interfaces for these components are precisely documented, but the final implementation will differ from product to product. To test the platform, the gaps must be filled somehow. This can be done by creating stubs: components that adhere to the interfaces but have a controlled dummy behaviour for test purposes. However, these stubs reveal their own problems [106]. They cost effort to create, maintain and also test since stubs can be a source of defects themselves. Moreover, they can never fully replace the real plug-in components that will be developed in application engineering.

4.4 Application Engineering

Application engineering takes the common assets of the product line and uses them to create products. Application engineers bind variability in the common assets to create instances that are fit for the products that they are developing. They combine these instances with application-specific assets that they develop themselves.

4.4.1 Application Requirements Engineering

Application requirements completely specify a particular product. The requirements come from the stakeholders of the product under development, for example end-users, product managers, customers or service engineers. The variability model and the common and variable domain requirements can be a valuable tool to elicit stakeholder requirements [106].

The requirement assets produced in domain engineering are a start, but they will not satisfy all stakeholder requirements completely. The gap between what is available and what is required must be analysed, and a trade-off decision taken for each unsatisfied requirement. The requirement may be satisfied by application-specific assets. Alternatively, the stakeholder may be able to adapt the requirement such that it can be satisfied by assets offered by the platform. Another option is to drop the requirement completely, or postpone it to a later version of the application.

If a requirement is shared by many applications, feedback may be given to the domain engineering life-cycle to achieve that the next version of the platform does satisfy this requirement. Any available application-specific solutions may then be generalised to become part of the platform, or an entirely new asset can be created. Later, the application-specific assets are replaced by the solution offered and maintained as part of the platform.

4.4.2 Application Design

In application design, a product architecture is derived from the reference architecture. Its variation points are instantiated to create an architecture that deals with all the requirements of a certain product. The resulting architecture is extended with new components and interfaces, or particular components are replaced, in order to satisfy all application-specific requirements that are not covered by the reference architecture. Chapter 3 describes the relationship between reference and application architectures.

4.4.3 Application Realisation

The goal of the application realisation process is to implement products. The common assets delivered by the domain realisation process are used to minimise the effort and time needed to do this.

Domain interfaces can be reused without changes, but variable components have internal variation points that must be bound. To this end, the components offer mechanisms such as parameter bindings and configuration files.[3] Often, a number of domain components need to be similarly configured in a single application. Repeating the same configuration by hand for each of them is error-prone and costly. Specialised configuration components or tool support are two options to do this more efficiently.

In application realisation, common assets are complemented by application-specific components. In many cases, such components will provide interfaces that are specified by the domain architecture. A plug-in framework, for example, will prescribe interfaces to register a plug-in component and allow it to hook to the framework in a number of ways. Apart from this, creating application-specific components is done in almost the same way as in single-system development.

4.4.4 Application Testing

Application testing is performed to ensure that an application is of sufficient quality. Although the common components were tested in domain engineering, this does not mean that they should not be tested again. The domain components have internal variability that was bound to make them useful in

---

[3] A list of variation mechanisms is given in Sect. 3.3

the application at hand. Section 4.3.5 shows that it is impossible for domain engineers to predict and test all possible combinations of configurations in advance. Therefore, the configured domain components must be tested again in the context of this specific application to chase out more bugs.

For those application requirements that are identical to domain requirements, domain tests can be repeated. Other tests will contain variation points that must be bound to match the application. For application-specific requirements, new tests must be developed and executed.

4.5 Process Maturity: CMMI

A capability maturity model is a reference model of mature practices in a specified discipline. It can be used to improve and appraise the capability of an organisation to perform that discipline [140].

The Capability Maturity Model Integrated (CMMI) was created and is maintained by the Software Engineering Institute (SEI). The SEI developed its first capability maturity model in the 1980s: the CMM for software engineering. Several CMMs for other disciplines followed, until recently they were integrated in the CMMI.

The CMMI is a framework of capability models in several disciplines: software engineering, systems engineering, integrated product and process development, and supplier sourcing. The CMMI models for specific disciplines can be combined as needed by their users. It is recommended to combine the software engineering and systems engineering models, as they are similar. The resulting model is called CMMI-SE/SW.

The CMMI framework can be extended to suit the needs of other disciplines through the introduction of discipline amplifications. Discipline amplifications are model elements that contain information relevant to that particular discipline. Each amplification is associated with a specific practice. In Chap. 6, we describe amplifications for the CMMI that make it suitable for software product line engineering.

4.5.1 Maturity Levels

CMMI models describe discrete levels of process improvement.[4] Each higher maturity level builds on its predecessor. There are five levels:

1. *Initial*: an immature organisation with an undefined process. Results are unpredictable and the organisation cannot be expected to repeat past successes.

---

[4] Actually, the CMMI models come in two flavours: *continuous* and *staged*. This is done to enable the integration of certain CMM models. Here we will focus on the staged models

2. *Managed*: the organisation has enough discipline to retain existing practices even during times of stress. Requirements are managed, processes are planned, performed, measured and controlled, on a per-project basis.
3. *Defined*: the organisation has a set of standard processes that are tailored to meet the needs of individual projects.
4. *Quantitatively managed*: processes are managed based on quantitative objectives that meet the needs of customers, end-users and internal stakeholders. Detailed performance measures are collected and analysed to support fact-based decision-making.
5. *Optimising*: this level focuses on continuously improving the performance of the organisation. The organisation sets quantitative process improvement objectives and uses them to manage process improvement.

These levels are incremental: an organisation at level 3 satisfies the goals of both levels 2 and 3 (level 1 comes for free and has no goals).

4.5.2 Structure of CMMI Models

Figure 4.3 shows that each maturity level has a number of *process areas*, for example 'product integration'. A process area is related to a set of *goals*, like 'ensure interface compatibility'. When an organisation satisfies all goals of a process area, it is considered to have made significant process improvement in that area. For each goal there are *practices* that should be performed to satisfy the goal. 'Review interface descriptions for completeness' is a practice that helps ensure interface compatibility.

The CMMI-SE/SW has 22 process areas in the following four categories:

1. *Process management* deals with cross-project activities such as planning, deploying and improving processes.
2. *Project management* covers project-related activities, e.g. planning and monitoring projects.
3. *Engineering* is concerned with development and maintenance activities of both software and systems engineering. Examples are requirements management and verification.
4. *Support* covers supporting activities such as configuration management, and measurement and analysis activities.

Table 4.1 shows the process areas for CMMI-SE/SW by category and maturity level. More detailed information on the CMMI models and related products, such as the SCAMPI appraisal method, is available from the SEI [39].

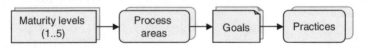

Fig. 4.3. Elements of CMMI models

Table 4.1. Process area categories and maturity levels

Category:	Process Areas per maturity level:
	Level 1
	Level 2 - Managed
	Level 3 - Defined
	Level 4 - Quantitatively Managed
	Level 5 - Optimising
Process Management	Organisational Process Focus
	Organisational Process Definition
	Organisational Training
	Organisational Process Performance
	Organisational Innovation and Deployment
Project Management	Project Planning
	Project Monitoring and Control
	Supplier Agreement Management
	Risk Management
	Integrated Project Management
	Quantitative Project Management
Engineering	Requirements Management
	Requirements Development
	Technical Solution
	Product Integration
	Verification
	Validation
Support	Configuration Management
	Process and Product Quality Assurance
	Measurement and Analysis
	Decision Analysis and Resolution
	Causal Analysis and Resolution

4.6 Summary

The two main life-cycles of software product line engineering are domain engineering, in which the common assets are developed, and application engineering, where the common assets are used to create products.

Both domain and application engineering have sub-processes for requirements engineering, design, realisation and testing. These pairs of sub-processes are strongly connected, exchanging assets and feedbacks.

The repeating challenge in each of these processes is how to deal with variability. In domain engineering, the right scope of variability must be supported in the right way. In application engineering, the right choices must be made to bind the variability.

The CMMI is a framework of capability maturity models that can help organisations to improve and assess their processes. The CMMI can be extended to the needs of unsupported disciplines by adding amplifications to its process areas. In the next chapter, we will show how to do that for the software product line engineering discipline.

5

Organisation

The organisation provides the actual mapping of activities, roles and responsibilities to people and organisational structures. Reflecting the processes, the organisation has structures and responsibilities for domain and application engineering and for collaboration and co-ordination roles. Persons and structural units may play more than one role, and roles may be performed by more than one person or organisational unit.

This chapter discusses the organisational aspects of software product line engineering. We first discuss the importance of setting up a good organisation to achieve success with product line engineering. In Sect. 5.2, we describe the product line specific roles and responsibilities that the organisation has to deal with. Next, we discuss several ways how these roles can be accommodated in an organisational structure. Sect. 5.4 describes the consequences of geographically distributed organisations. An important aspect of any organisation is the way people collaborate together, and we discuss several collaboration schemes useful for software product line engineering in Sect. 5.5. The chapter ends with a summary.

5.1 Motivation

The organisation executes software product line engineering. Activities and roles in the development process are assigned to organisational units and to people in these units. The precise mapping of the activities and roles in the organisation is important for the following reasons:

1. It determines the amount to which people work together. People in the same organisational unit are more inclined to work together than those that are distributed over several units.
2. It determines accountability and funding. This goes via the hierarchical structure of the organisation.
3. It determines the decision hierarchy.

The structure of the organisation plays a predominant role in structuring the practice of people and what they need to communicate about. The tasks people have to work on, the problems they have to tackle, etc. are strongly influencing the mindset of people as they will determine whether considering product line issues are also the best solution for the individual. As a consequence, the structure of the organisation has a strong impact on *whether people will be able to see the product line*. If product line engineering is not taken into account in structuring the organisation, the structure may work against it, leading to an efficiency reduction.

The following problems can occur:

1. The same role is distributed over many places, leading to work that is done at several places in the organisation.
2. Local profit optimisations of a department may be harmful.
3. Decision-making involves too many people, and thus takes too much time.

The severity of these problems depends on the size of the organisation. In small organisations, persons have several roles that complement each other. Often people are working close to each other. This enables a clear distribution of work, few accountability roles and short decision-making times. In larger organisations, the structure of the organisation and the determination of enough roles are crucial to get the work done efficiently. Larger and smaller restructurings of the organisation take place frequently. This is usually inspired by the aim to better balance the different requirements to the organisation, satisfying the demands above. Such reorganisations are not easy. There is often resistance in the organisation to the adaptations. As a consequence, reorganisation should be planned and executed carefully in order to reduce these problems.

Experience shows that having the right organisation structure is crucial for product line engineering. The dominating success factor for product line development is the mindset of people, i.e. the interpretations people give to their experiences as well as to their personal motivations and goals.

For software product line engineering, the organisation involves structures and responsibilities for executing domain and application engineering and for supporting and co-ordinating roles. This involves the normally available software development roles within both domain and application engineering. Domain engineering jobs are for people that are able to develop high-quality software components, and maintain them afterwards to improve the quality even more. Application engineering jobs are different. These are for people that are able to build applications fast, based on the given platform. They need to know how to use the variability mechanisms to configure systems.

Especially in large companies, activities are often distributed. Specific groups are responsible for a part of the activities. In particular, we often see a single domain engineering group and several separate application engineering groups. Collaboration specialists are needed with good communication skills that relate between aspects of domain and application engineering. There are many shared responsibilities to facilitate agreements over subjects ranging from the reference architecture and testing to a common way of communicating with each other. This involves *cross-functional teams*. These are groups of specialists in both domain and application engineering groups. Together they decide on the introduction or evolution of specific aspects that they are responsible for. The cross-functional teams form a secondary organisation structure in addition to the primary structure that is determined by managers and reporting structures.

The organisation is responsible for the execution of the processes. There is a tension between product- and process-oriented drives to the organisation. The product-oriented drive assigns related activities to people that are close to each other, preferably in the same organisational unit. The process-oriented drive combines people with same discipline, leading to organisations that have units not only for architects, development and testing, but also for sales and strategy. The organisation has to find a good balance for these conflicting drives.

In a product line organisation, this leads to the placement of domain engineering people close to each other. Keeping disciplines together may result in different solutions for application and domain engineering processes. Application engineering may have separate development units, but it may also be the case that application engineering is done by the domain disciplines. This is partly dependent on the relative weight of the two processes. If application engineering involves much work, it is better to assign to a separate organisation. If domain engineering is dominating, application engineering may be done as an additional activity in the domain engineering organisation.

5.2 Roles and Responsibilities

In this section we go into the roles and responsibilities required for software product line engineering. A role combines a set of responsibilities in relationship to other roles. Each role and responsibility can be assigned to one or more people in the organisation. Typically, we find that in large organisations there are groups of people that are assigned a single role. In small organisations a single person may play several roles. In medium-sized organisations we may have a mix of both, and roles that are assigned to a single employee only.

In Fig. 5.1 the roles of software product line engineering are mapped on activities. In the following we discuss all the roles and responsibilities.

5.2.1 Product Manager

The role of the product manager in software product line engineering involves the planning and evolution of the complete range of products, the portfolio management. This involves planning of present and future products in the product line, their features and their business value. The business value is

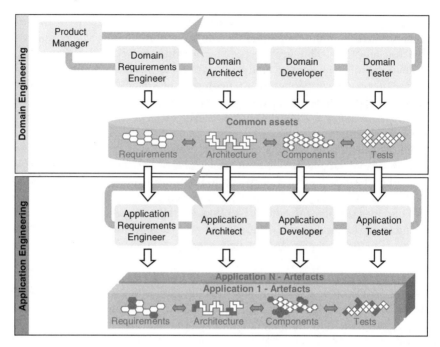

Fig. 5.1. Roles in software product line engineering (adapted from [106])

important for the *business owner*. It involves the planning of the costs and profits of present and future systems on offer. The business owner is also interested in the costs and profits of the present and future variability in the product line. The features of present and future products are important for *marketing and sales*. The planning of systems on the market has to be clear in terms of the available features. The *domain requirements engineer* is interested in the evolution of features, their commonality and their variability. This is necessary to plan the requirements of the platform and features. The *product manager* initiates the first step in new application developments. The relationship with the *application requirements engineer* involves product definitions and the selection of application requirements.

5.2.2 Domain Requirements Engineer

The domain requirements engineer deals with the development and maintenance of all requirements that are relevant to the complete range of products. This involves the development of common and variable requirements, including an underlying variability model. These requirements are prepared in agreement with the roadmaps and plans of the *product manager*. One of the tasks of the domain requirements engineer is to provide feedback on the feasibility and cost of features. The actual common and variable requirements and the underlying variability model are the main input to the *domain architect* who has to maintain the product line architecture. The *domain tester* needs the same inputs. They are used to provide test cases for domain assets. The *application requirements engineer* uses the domain requirements for specialisation to the application at hand. Finally, like for all other domain engineering roles, the common and variable requirements are provided to the *domain asset manager* who performs management on variants and versions.

5.2.3 Domain Architect

The domain architect involves the development and maintenance of the reference architecture for the complete range of products. In the first place, the reference architecture is a technical solution for the domain requirements, including commonality and variability, and is prepared in collaboration with the *domain requirements engineer*. In particular, the domain architect has to provide feedback on feasibility and cost of features, and the involved variability. The common and variable parts of the architecture are provided to the *domain asset manager* who performs management on variants and versions. The reference architecture is an important input to the *domain developer*. It includes the selection of reusable domain components and interfaces. The commonality and variability, available in the domain requirements is refined towards the reference architecture, based on technical possibilities. An important task of the domain architect is to validate whether the designs of reusable assets fulfil the reference architecture. To facilitate configuring, the domain architect determines configuration mechanisms to be used to build the end products. The *application architect* uses the reference architecture, its commonality and variability and the set of reusable domain assets to derive application architectures. The domain architect plays a role in the validation of the application architectures, namely to ensure that they adhere to the domain architecture.

5.2.4 Domain Developer

The role of the domain developer involves the development and maintenance of reusable components and interfaces for the complete range of products. In addition, configuration mechanisms must be provided to support the variance of systems in the product line. This involves further refinements of commonality and variability to implementation mechanisms. The *domain architect* determines the design of these assets, and the domain developer develops them according to the reference architecture. In addition, the domain developer has the responsibility to provide feedback on the feasibility of their development. The *domain tester* uses the assets to be configured and tested. The *application developer* reuses the domain assets and their configuration mechanisms to realise applications. The common and variable parts of the design and implementation are provided to the *domain asset manager* who manages variants and versions.

5.2.5 Domain Tester

The role of the domain tester involves the development and maintenance of reusable test assets for the complete range of products. In addition to the traditional testing tasks – involving the testing of integrated products – the domain tester must perform integration and systems tests on domain assets, and he must prepare common and variable test assets to be used by the *application tester*. As a consequence, the domain tester is responsible for the domain testing strategy that explains what can be tested at domain level and what has to be tested at application level. The domain testing strategy is also important for the other roles in domain engineering. This strategy determines the domain and application testing costs, which is important for the *product manager*. In addition, it determines the possibility to test domain assets at the domain level. Execution of such tests provides important feedback towards the *domain architect* and the *domain developer*. The domain tester has an important role in the feedback towards all other domain engineering roles in so far as he provides information on the testability of requirements and design choices. The common and variable parts of the test assets are provided to the *domain asset manager* who performs management on variants and versions.

5.2.6 Domain Asset Manager

The domain asset manager is responsible for maintaining versions and variants of all domain assets for the complete range of products. All assets produced by the domain engineering are placed under version control. In addition, traceability has to be in place to relate the assets of the different development roles. Towards the application engineering roles the domain asset manager has the responsibility to maintain valid versions and configurations of domain assets and the traceability among the assets. Application engineering puts actual application configurations under version control. This is used for determining valid configurations.

5.2.7 Application Requirements Engineer

The role of the application requirements engineer involves the development and maintenance of the requirements for a single product. This encompasses the selection of variants of reusable requirements for the application at hand, according to the roadmaps and plans from the responsible *product manager*. The application requirements engineer provides feedback to the *product manager* on the feasibility and cost of the specific feature selection. In cases that specific domain requirements are lacking, application-specific ones must be developed and maintained. These requirements can be assigned as being candidate domain requirements, but this must be decided together with the *domain requirements engineer*. If problems occur with application requirements that can be traced back to domain requirements, these must be reported back to the *domain requirements engineer*. The *domain asset manager* gets the actual selection of requirements as input for configuration management. Towards the *application architect* and the *application tester*, the *application requirements engineer* has the normal responsibility of providing the actual selection of requirements as input for architecture and testing.

5.2.8 Application Architect

The role of the application architect involves the development and maintenance of the architecture for a single product. This architecture is a specialisation of the reference architecture. Problem reports on the reference architecture are communicated to the *domain architect*, who is also informed of the actual set of reusable domain assets that are used and candidate domain architecture elements. Towards the *application requirements engineer* the application architect has the normal roles of providing the application architecture as technical solution for the application requirements, and feedback on requirements feasibility and costs. Towards the *application developer* the application architect provides the application architecture and the configuration of domain components and interfaces and configuration mechanisms to be reused. This determines the selection of application-specific components and interfaces to be developed.

5.2.9 Application Developer

The role of the application developer involves the development and maintenance of application-specific components and interfaces. This involves the reuse of domain components and interfaces and their specialisation towards the application. Problem reports on reusable domain components and interfaces and configuration mechanisms are reported to the domain developer. Components and interfaces that can be promoted to the domain are reported. Towards the *application architect* and the *application tester* the application developer has the normal roles of providing an implementation for the application at hand, fulfilling the application architecture and ready for testing.

5.2.10 Application Tester

The role of the application tester involves the testing of single applications. This implies the use of the domain testing strategy and the reusable domain test assets provided for by the *domain tester*. Towards the other application engineering roles the application tester has the normal roles of performing application integration and system tests.

5.3 Organisational Structures

The roles and their mutual responsibilities are the basis for determining the organisational structure. We focus on the situation of large companies, with groups of people sharing product line roles. In smaller organisations the structure is less complex. A single person in a small organisation can do similar work as departments in large organisations. As a consequence, certain lower-level departments do not exist, or are not made explicit. However, the basic principles for the choice of the organisation structure are the same for large and small organisations.

The way that people interact with each other can be captured in communication patterns. Such patterns determine what kinds of mechanisms are used for which communication and by whom. The communication patterns are partially determined by the organisational structure, as they influence what information needs to be communicated to which person. The organisational structure determines who is concerned with which part (functionality-wise) and aspect (life-cycle perspective) of the product line. The organisational structure provides constraints on the overall communication patterns. An organisation that focuses on product line development needs to have communication structures that mirror its product line [40].

Organisational structures for product lines arise from the consideration of roles and responsibilities. We see the following structures[1]:

- Domain engineering and application engineering each perform a software development life-cycle. Note that in many cases several application engineering developments happen simultaneously.
- Interactions between domain and application engineering are mainly "functional", i.e. at requirements, design, realisation or test level.
- The tester has interactions with most other phases in the same development.
- Domain asset manager is a specific role. It interacts with most of the domain engineering roles and with some of the application engineering roles as well.
- The product manager has a special role, in which he provides the input for domain engineering, and is the initiator of application engineering.

Based on these observations, the structure of organisations is mainly influenced by domain engineering, application engineering and their interaction. Product management, testing and asset management lead to an additional structure.

We identify three basic structures: product-oriented, process-oriented and matrix organisations. We discuss these forms in the following sections. Moreover, adaptations of these structures for involving testers, asset managers, and product managers are discussed from Sect. 5.3.4 onwards.

---

[1] An overview of different organisational structures that are used in the context of product line engineering is given in [26]

5.3.1 Product-Oriented Organisation

We can take the separation between domain and application engineering units as a guiding principle. Each such unit has a sub-structure according to the different development phases: requirements, design and realisation. We call this the *product-oriented* organisation [94]. The organisation is distributed over domain and application engineering units. This is the most common way to structure the organisation for software product line engineering (Fig. 5.2).

Often, there is a single unit responsible for domain engineering, and several units for the development of distinct applications. But if domain engineering grows in scope, it may become too big for a single unit. In that case, domain engineering may be split over several units, each taking care of a part of the reusable assets.

The advantage of separate domain and application engineering units is that it clearly distributes the main responsibilities and accountabilities. The domain engineering unit is responsible for the delivery of a platform consisting of high-quality reusable assets. The application engineering units are responsible for obtaining income for the company by serving a part of the market. Closely related software engineering activities are in the same unit, which improves the communication about these developments.

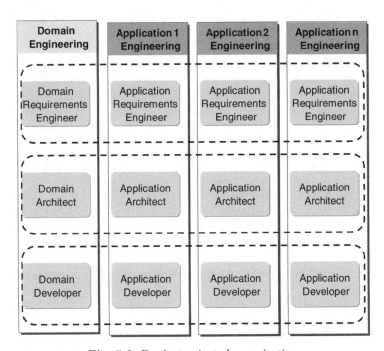

Fig. 5.2. Product-oriented organisation

Two main challenges exist for this kind of organisation:

1. Funding of the domain engineering unit.
2. Functional interaction between developers of different units.

We discuss both challenges separately, and present ways of dealing with them.

Funding the Domain Engineering Unit

The application engineering organisations generate income from the products they sell. However, the domain engineering unit has internal customers only: the application engineering organisations. Payment has to come from these units. This means that the domain engineering unit is seen as an internal provider by the application engineering organisations. The drawbacks of taking this customer role too far are

- The budget of the domain engineering unit is under pressure, as application engineering organisations demand more value at lower prices.
- Application engineering organisations may (threaten to) seek to use an external provider instead.[2]

A shortage of domain engineering resources can make it impossible to develop a high-quality platform. In order to deal with the second threat, the domain engineering organisation may be seduced to focus its resources on a few specific applications in an attempt to keep them on board. Ignoring the needs of the product line as a whole, this tactic may have serious repercussions on future return on investment.

Both cases have severe business consequences for the domain engineering unit, disabling it to do its work properly, leading to low-quality domain assets, and endangering the long-term profit of the whole organisation. A good business plan, supported by higher management, is necessary to provide enough and stable income for the domain engineering unit.

Functional Interaction Between Developers of Different Units

Each unit aims to maximise its profit. The communication with people in other units is easily considered overhead, which should be avoided as much as possible. This holds for both domain and application engineering units. As a consequence, the necessary communication between requirements specialists, architects and developers does not take place, or it is not enough. This reduces the added value of the domain engineering unit that as a consequence may

---

[2] This is especially true at the earlier phase of deploying a software product line, when investments are painfully real while the returned value is still a promise. In a mature, successful product line, application engineering organisations will not be able to find any external platform that is so well suited to their needs for the price they pay as the platform

build the wrong assets for their customers. This problem can be solved by the introduction of a secondary structure, according to the functional areas, see the dashed areas in Fig. 5.2. This secondary structure is meant to initiate meetings over unit borders. The functional teams have a responsibility for improving the communication along the functional axis. Such a secondary structure only succeeds if organisation has the right culture. Higher management commitment is crucial to make this happen. The "overhead time" has to be accepted as being an important part of normal work.

5.3.2 Process-Oriented Organisation

Another way of structuring the organisation is by taking the functional hierarchy prime (Fig. 5.3). In this way, the functional interaction within software product line engineering is facilitated. Organisations like this need to ensure communication and co-ordination between the different development phases to get the right products out in time. External guidance, e.g. by the business owner, is needed. An advantage of this kind of organisation is that people can be allocated flexibly to the different developments upon need, in particular between domain and application engineering. As the same people are charged with developing similar functionality for different products, this leads to two important effects:

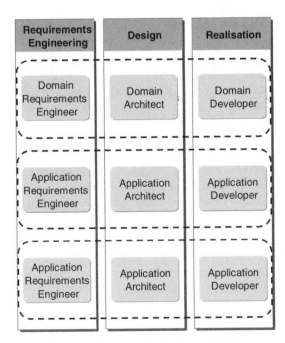

Fig. 5.3. Process-oriented organisation

1. It becomes easier to ensure the integrity of the architecture as the same person responsible for a part of it also makes changes to it.
2. People experience a personal benefit in their work by focusing on reusability aspects.

The advantages of this organisational mode on the mindset are clear: it becomes the personal benefit of the developer to focus on reuse as he will benefit again from any preparations for reuse. Many developers are involved in several products and in domain assets. As a consequence, it is less of an issue to get domain activities funded in this kind of organisations: it is a normal part of the daily work.

This organisation has as the drawback that the different phases of engineering are not close to each other, and thus communication is more difficult. A more severe disadvantage is that conflicts have to be escalated high in the hierarchy to be solved. Accountability for the production of the right applications and domain assets is not assigned clearly. In many cases, this can be solved by a secondary structure that deals with the development of separate applications. Domain engineering is distributed over the organisation, and appears only in the secondary structure that is depicted by the dashed regions in Fig. 5.3. This is similar to the product-oriented situation. Only the relative emphasis between the product and the functional axis is shifted.

We see this structure more often in small organisations than in large ones. In small organisations the communication problem is less of an issue.

5.3.3 Matrix Organisation

In order to compromise between both the functional and the product demands, certain organisations have a matrix structure (Fig. 5.4). Each developer has a product and a functional responsibility towards different managers in the two dimensions of the matrix: product-wise and functionally. This can be a good basis for software product line engineering, since it institutionalises the virtual structure. However, in this situation the management structure can be very complex and problems are not always solved in the right way. Care should be taken that the functional hierarchy executes the necessary software product line work.

5.3.4 Testing

Because it relates to all other engineering activities, testing has a special role in the organisation. In principle, it can be treated like other engineering activities, and placed similarly in the organisation. Thus, in a product-oriented organisation, testing is distributed over the domain and application development organisation, with an emphasis to test the own development. The intense

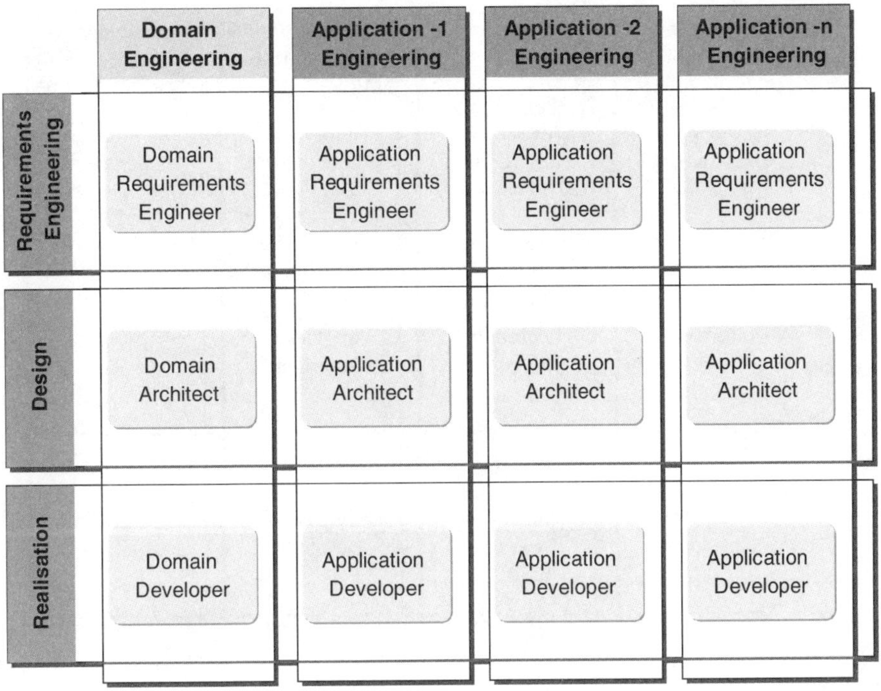

	Domain Engineering	Application -1 Engineering	Application -2 Engineering	Application -n Engineering
Requirements Engineering	Domain Requirements Engineer	Application Requirements Engineer	Application Requirements Engineer	Application Requirements Engineer
Design	Domain Architect	Application Architect	Application Architect	Application Architect
Realisation	Domain Developer	Application Developer	Application Developer	Application Developer

Fig. 5.4. Matrix organisation

collaborations with the own development can be managed within the unit itself. Active management is needed to co-ordination testing across the product line. In a process-oriented organisation, testing will get its own department. This eases the reuse of test assets, and planning of product line testing. In this case, collaboration with the other developments has to be managed carefully. It is easy to communicate products to be tested, and problem reports. It is more difficult to have early communication on testability and test planning. In a matrix organisation, testing may get an additional testing row in the matrix.

Certain organisations choose a hybrid approach with regard to testing. The engineering is organised according to domain and application engineering units. The testing department is a separate functional unit (Fig. 5.5). The main reason for such an organisation is the fact that testing is a final quality check before the products go to the clients. Testing is seen as a specialised discipline that best can be managed within a single unit. In this case, the testing department takes any product to be tested as input. These may not only be the applications, but it can also be the platform. The main advantage of this set-up is the internal co-operation between domain and application testing, and the planning of test asset reuse. The disadvantage is that this situation may lead to a very late involvement of testing in development

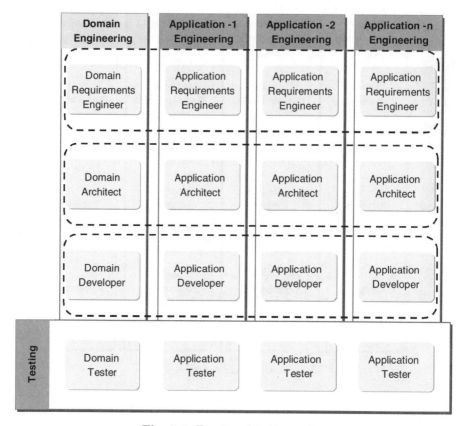

Fig. 5.5. Functional testing unit

cycles. The involvement will start only as soon as the first integration tests are performed. The problem reports are the only feedback expected from the department. As a consequence, testing may take too much time, and reuse of test assets may be very low, since it may not be clear in time what the reuse in the product line is at all. However, if the testing department is involved in the complete software development life-cycle, these problems can be reduced. The already-mentioned disciplinary interrelationship among testers severely eases the reuse of test assets within the development.

5.3.5 Asset Management

Asset management mainly relates to domain engineering. It has to interact with all activities within domain engineering. It manages the versions and variants of the assets that are created by domain engineering. Application engineering only interacts with asset management through the retrieval of reusable domain assets. As a consequence, asset management is mainly considered as a part of domain engineering.

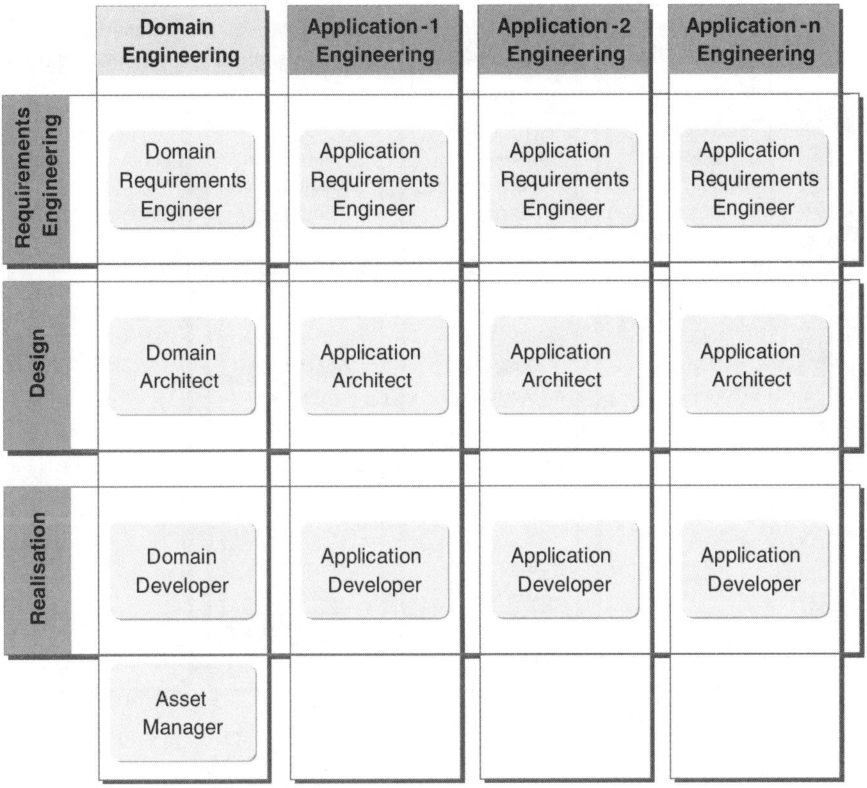

	Domain Engineering	Application-1 Engineering	Application-2 Engineering	Application-n Engineering
Requirements Engineering	Domain Requirements Engineer	Application Requirements Engineer	Application Requirements Engineer	Application Requirements Engineer
Design	Domain Architect	Application Architect	Application Architect	Application Architect
Realisation	Domain Developer	Application Developer	Application Developer	Application Developer
	Asset Manager			

Fig. 5.6. Asset management in the domain

In product-oriented and matrix organisations, asset management can be added as an additional discipline in the domain engineering unit (Fig. 5.6). Communication between asset management and domain engineering is easy in this way. Application engineering units have to comply with the environment set up by asset management and can access the reusable assets they need (Fig. 5.7).

Certain organisations have a separate department that is responsible for the software engineering environment; this often involves asset management. This leads to a uniformity, and eases communications over unit borders. Since managing the environment is a special discipline in itself, this can be a good choice. A disadvantage of this situation occurs when the software development environment department optimises the tool support in such a way that the other developments do not get the best tools they need. Sub-optimal choices can be made because

- All tools must be acquired from a prescribed vendor.
- Ignorance of new tools prohibits progress.

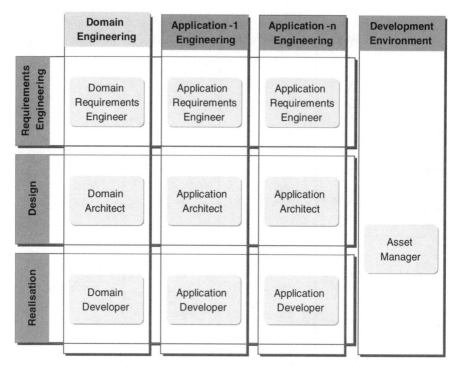

Fig. 5.7. Functional asset management

- Unawareness of special requirements for software product line engineering development, such as
  - reuse over department borders
  - long life-cycles of assets
  - management of other assets than documents and code
  - communication needs over department borders
  - separation between versions and variants

5.3.6 Product Management

Product management strongly interacts with domain engineering, since it determines what is common and what is variable in the product line. Therefore, it is often placed in the domain engineering unit (Fig. 5.8). However, application engineering is initiated by the roadmap of product management, and thus there is interaction between product management and application engineering. This has to be explicitly managed for application engineering to provide the needed applications. Another disadvantage is that domain engineering is far from the customer. Application engineering units deliver products and are much closer to the customer. As a consequence of this, product management

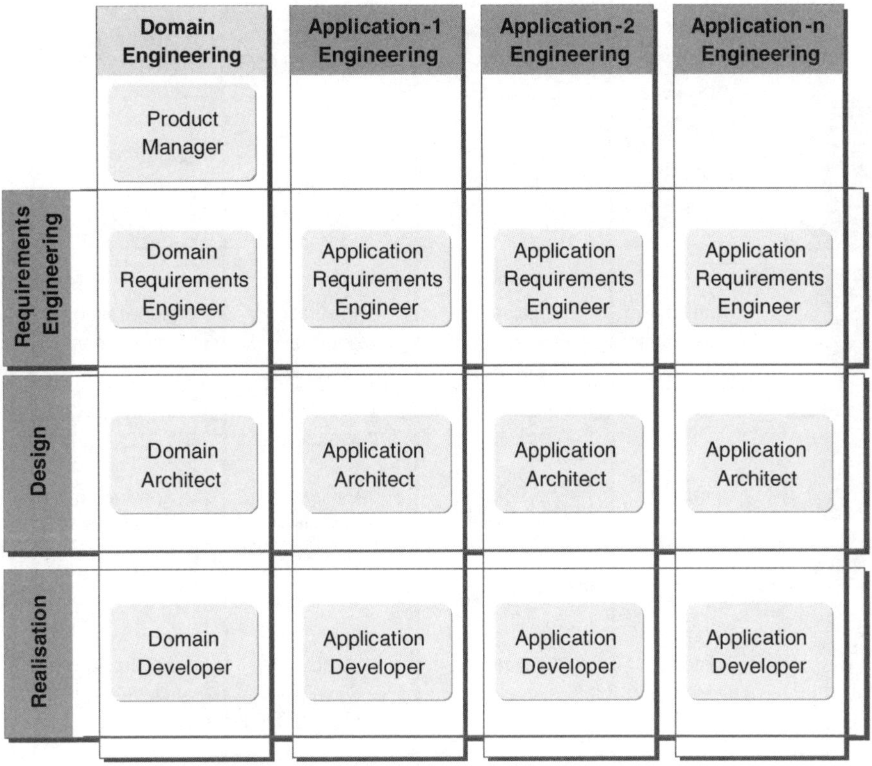

Domain Engineering	Application-1 Engineering	Application-2 Engineering	Application-n Engineering
Product Manager			

	Domain Engineering	Application-1 Engineering	Application-2 Engineering	Application-n Engineering
Requirements Engineering	Domain Requirements Engineer	Application Requirements Engineer	Application Requirements Engineer	Application Requirements Engineer
Design	Domain Architect	Application Architect	Application Architect	Application Architect
Realisation	Domain Developer	Application Developer	Application Developer	Application Developer

Fig. 5.8. Product management in the domain

may give the wrong priorities to features and products, and the market will not be served well.

To deal with this situation, product management can be placed closer to application engineering. Often it is distributed over several application engineering units. Application product management mainly plans a range of applications, and there is no global responsibility for software product line product management. By adding a new role of domain product manager this responsibility can be served (Fig. 5.9). The domain product manager has the responsibility of the planning of domain assets. Communication with the application product managers is needed to be able to set the priorities right and to determine what is common and what is variable.

Note that in a process-oriented organisation this problem does not occur. Product management is a separate discipline that gets its own unit that plans all developments of the other units. Again, the communication has to be managed well, but at least product management has a clear position in such an organisation.

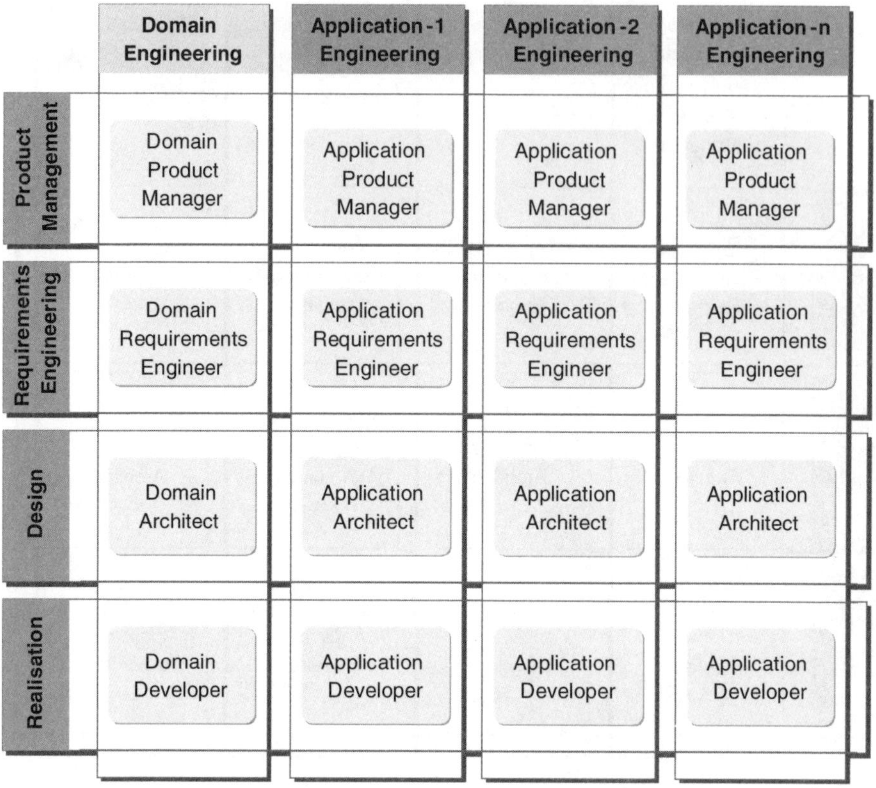

	Domain Engineering	Application-1 Engineering	Application-2 Engineering	Application-n Engineering
Product Management	Domain Product Manager	Application Product Manager	Application Product Manager	Application Product Manager
Requirements Engineering	Domain Requirements Engineer	Application Requirements Engineer	Application Requirements Engineer	Application Requirements Engineer
Design	Domain Architect	Application Architect	Application Architect	Application Architect
Realisation	Domain Developer	Application Developer	Application Developer	Application Developer

Fig. 5.9. Functional product management

5.4 Geographical Distribution

Many of the organisations that have embraced software product line engineering are large and complex. Their software development is distributed over different departments that are located at different sites and even in different time zones. They involve other companies that are specialised in doing a part of the work, e.g. through outsourcing. This situation leads to a demand for a product line organisation structure that can deal with the difficult communication originating from this distribution. In any case, communication has to be managed very explicitly, otherwise it will not happen. People in different locations often do not know each other, and have different communication cultures.

The easiest solution is to have complete parts of the matrix involving connected process and product responsibilities together. Then the communication to other sites can be treated as special cases of communication with other departments. In many cases, however, this solution is simply not an option. For instance, different departments have responsibilities for the same piece of work because of historical reasons, and they have to communicate very often. Moving the responsibility to a single site may lead to loss of knowledge and to friction with the personnel. There is a danger that some people with specialised knowledge are not willing to move. Another risk is that certain departments do not trust assets developed by departments at other sites, the infamous not-invented-here-syndrome. A solution for this situation is to gradually move towards a structure that improves the mapping of the elements of the organisation on the different sites. In the mean time, extensive communication is necessary, both through face-to-face and virtual meetings such as telephone conferences and video meetings.

5.5 Collaboration Schemes

Collaboration schemes are another part of the organisation concerns. Collaboration is the glue among the people working in the organisation. Dependent on the kind of collaboration scheme used in the organisation, it is possible to work together on a single software product line. Specific types of information must be communicated with specific people depending on their needs and interests. These communication patterns are partially determined by the overall work organisation, as they influence what information must be communicated to which person. Several collaboration schemes support such communication.

Software product line development requires a large group of people in the organisation working together. To do this well, the right collaboration schemes are needed. Collaboration schemes support the way people are involved with and convinced of the need for product line engineering. They can make the benefits and the organisation of the product line clear. They make it easier to find options to improve reuse and spread good engineering practices [124].

Collaboration can take on several forms, and many mechanisms can be used (Table 5.1).

People use different collaboration *mechanisms* depending on their information needs, but to have a good collaboration, all *forms* are necessary. If one or more of the forms is lacking, it may be a sign that collaboration is not optimal.

Collaboration can be done in the vertical direction, involving people with management, and horizontally, involving people in the same or different departments. The vertical axis is important to keep people informed about the product line and its evolution. The horizontal axis is necessary to enable the different roles to work together well. Especially when there is a secondary structure, people need to collaborate over department borders using the different mechanisms mentioned above. In many cases, special roles are recognised for people in the organisation to facilitate collaboration. This may be a chairperson of certain meetings or people responsible for the collaboration platform.

Table 5.1. Collaboration forms and mechanisms

Form	Example mechanisms	
Meetings	Real, virtual	Several people together discussing the same subjects
Bilateral conversations	Face to face, by telephone, via collaboration platforms	Two people work together to deal with a subject that is important for both
Asynchronous collaboration	Document exchange via e-mail, wiki, or normal mail	Several people inform each other and adapt information actively
Workflow	Workflow systems, manually	People get the documents that they need to work on and pass their results on to others (semi-) automatically

5.6 Summary

The right distribution of *roles and responsibilities* is an important aspect of the organisation of software product line engineering. Extensive communication is needed both in the process-oriented direction and in the product-oriented direction. Although a matrix organisation copes with this situation, the management of such an organisation is often not easy. We more often see that the communication in the product dimension is in many cases more important that in the process direction. This leads to a product-oriented organisation with a secondary structure in the process dimension. In cases where product line engineering is set up in such a way that application engineering takes much less work than domain engineering, the process-oriented organisation may be prime.

In any case, the communication must be managed very explicitly. Someone must be responsible that this occurs over department borders, and even over the different sites, if necessary.

In the case of small organisations, the structure does not matter so much. A person takes the responsibility of one or more departments, as described in this chapter. This means that (part of) the communication can be removed, which simplifies the structure considerably.

6

The Family Evaluation Framework

The Family Evaluation Framework (FEF) is a consolidated result of six years of European co-operation projects with industry and academia. These are the ESAPS, CAFÉ and FAMILIES projects.[1] Companies within these projects mainly work on a large variety of embedded systems including medical imaging, mobile phones, flight control software, utility control, supervision and management, financial services and car electronics. During these projects, the terminology in use was "software product family" or "system family" instead of "software product line". This terminology is also reflected in the name of the final project in the series and in the name of the FEF.

This chapter gives an overview of the FEF. Section 6.1 describes the purpose of the framework. Next, its basic structure is described (6.2). The FEF is based on the four concerns of the BAPO model, leading to four dimensions in the evaluation framework. Sects. 6.3–6.6 describe these dimensions in detail. Then, the application of the FEF is discussed, including its use in complex organisations. As an illustration, we present the evaluation of a fictitious company as an example. In Sect. 6.8, we describe the FEF's relation to other evaluation approaches and end with a summary.

6.1 Motivation

The purpose of the FEF is to evaluate the performance in software product line engineering of organisations, including departments, business units, divisions and even complete companies. It does not evaluate single system software engineering practices but focuses on the aspects that are specific to software product line engineering. In particular, it emphasises the main aspects of product line engineering:

- The execution of both domain and application engineering.

---

[1] For more information about the collaborating partners and the results, see the publications [143, 144, 106] and the websites of the projects [49, 35, 51]

- The comprehensive management of variability.

There are diverse reasons for executing an FEF evaluation. For instance, a company may use the FEF to assess how well a certain department is doing software product line engineering to prove that it is on the right track. Alternatively, it may use the FEF as a benchmark tool to compare with other companies' software product line engineering capabilities. A third reason is to use the FEF as a decision tool to find the best way to improve software product line engineering within one or more departments.

6.2 Structure

The BAPO model covers the main concerns of software engineering. These concerns are used as the four dimensions of the Family Evaluation Framework (cf. Fig. 6.1).

Each dimension is divided into five levels and has three to four evaluation aspects assigned to it.

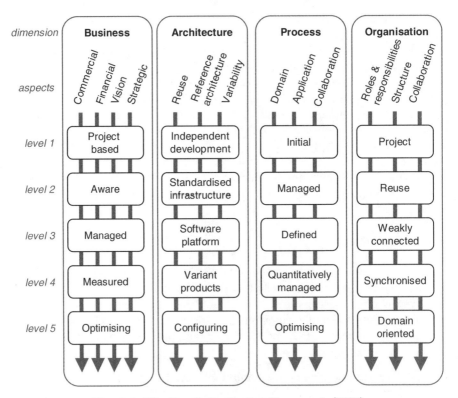

Fig. 6.1. The Family Evaluation Framework (FEF)

The *levels* reflect the way in which organisations deal with each of the concerns of product line engineering. The levels are incremental; to reach a certain level, an organisation must satisfy the requirements of all lower levels, too. The FEF measures an organisation's level in each dimension, but it does not prescribe ways to reach a certain level.

The organisation is evaluated for three to four *aspects* per dimension:

- *Business* measures the business involvement in software product line engineering and variability management. It deals with the business relationships between domain and application engineering and the costs, profits, market value and planning of variability.
- *Architecture* deals with the relationship between domain and application architectures and how they are related via variability. Important architecture concerns deal with the right variation mechanisms and how the reference architecture influences the application architectures and vice versa.
- *Process* measures which software product line processes are used and what is their maturity. The processes can be subdivided into domain, application, and collaboration and co-ordination processes. Each of them can be evaluated using a maturity model such as CMMI.
- *Organisation* measures the effectiveness of the distribution of domain and application engineering over the organisation. The organisation has structures and responsibilities for domain and application engineering and for collaboration and co-ordination roles. In particular, the organisation distributes responsibilities between platform, applications, collaboration and co-ordination and determines the relative importance of them.

The result of an FEF evaluation is an *evaluation profile* consisting of four values, one for each BAPO dimension. The framework allows different results in the different dimensions, as may be the case in companies where one BAPO concern receives more attention than another. This means that an organisation has a separate, independent evaluation level for each of them. Having separate dimensions guarantees attention – and potentially different ratings – for each of them, but in practice, the BAPO concerns themselves are not completely independent. The relation between business, architecture, process and organisation becomes obvious as soon as one studies the effects of changes. Changes in one dimension will virtually always have consequences for the other dimensions as well. In the end, all BAPO concerns have to be taken into account in order to improve. A low score in one dimension may hamper the achievement of reaching a high score in another dimension.[2] Actions to improve the evaluation result for one concern may reduce attention for the other concerns, leading to lower evaluation results for some of these.

---

[2] This may mean that we may get a high score for the architecture dimension and low for the others. Such scores may be defendable in certain situation. However, in many cases, this is a sign to have less attention to architecture and more to business, organisation and process

Although evaluation and improvements can be addressed separately in each dimension, the overall picture should be kept in mind while doing so.

There are many ways to implement software product line engineering in the organisation. Similar to the philosophy of the CMMI, the FEF evaluation does not deal with specific ways to perform a certain activity, modelling, structuring, responsibility or task.[3]

6.3 Business Dimension

The business dimension deals in general with profits, costs, strategy and planning. Business management has several techniques to influence the development process and improve marketing and sales of the products. The FEF deals with those business issues that are unique to software product line organisations, involving investment decisions, measuring the costs and profits of product line engineering and funding of domain engineering. The business dimension also deals with managing variability. That means measuring costs and profits generated by variability in the product line engineering and using this information to plan prices and marketing strategies for the product portfolio.[4]

The following aspects play a role in the business dimension of software product line engineering (Fig. 6.2):

- *Commercial*: how is marketing, sales and product management involved in and influenced by the software product line?
- *Financial*: how does software product line engineering influence budget and investment decisions?
- *Vision and business objectives*: how well does the organisation aim for a future involving software product line engineering?
- *Strategic planning*: how well does the organisation plan long-term product line development and its business aspects?

In the following sections, each of the business dimension's levels is discussed in detail.

6.3.1 Level 1: Project-Based

This is the basic level. The business is arranged for project-based single system engineering. Domain engineering results and variability – if they exist at

---

[3] The ESAPS, CAFÉ and FAMILIES projects have delivered a large amount of such methods, tools and techniques [49, 35, 51]. These are best practices and can be applied in software product line engineering. They provide a good insight of what is necessary in the different BAPO dimensions, but none of them is obligatory

[4] There exist a few initial economic models for measuring the success of software product line engineering [58, 125]

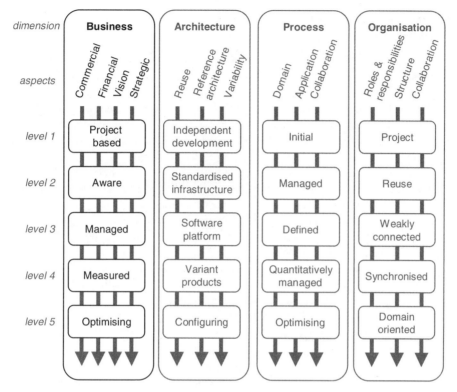

Fig. 6.2. Business dimension

all – are not visible at the business level. None of the aspects covers software product line engineering. With regard to the business concerns, we see the following typical situation:

- *Commercial*: there is no, or little, involvement in software product line engineering by the business. Systems are planned, sold and marketed on a single system basis.
- *Financial*: there are no specific budgets for domain engineering. Instead, budgeting is done on a per system basis.
- *Vision and business objectives*: they do not mention the existence of software product line engineering.
- *Strategic planning*: the business planning does not consider relations among systems.

6.3.2 Level 2: Aware

At this level, the business is aware of the benefits of software product line engineering for the company. It provides some context in which software product line engineering can be done. However, a clear management of software product line engineering is not available. This level shows the following typical situation:

- *Commercial*: the sales force, marketing and product management are aware of the opportunities of software product line engineering. It is expected that managed variability will lead to a greater variety in sold systems and that production costs will decrease. The mere fact of supporting more variants is seen as an additional benefit for the customer. However, there is no clear strategy available for using the software product line engineering in marketing, sales and product planning.
- *Financial*: the business invests in domain engineering activities to support a repository for reusable assets. There are budgeting consequences to encourage the use of the domain engineering results.
- *Vision and business objectives*: there is commitment from top management to do software product line engineering. However, there is no clear vision on its use for the company.
- *Strategic planning*: the planning is still committed to single system development. However, the results of domain engineering are taken into account in an opportunistic way in product roadmaps.

6.3.3 Level 3: Managed

At this level, software product line engineering is part of the business strategy. Management takes control of the execution of corresponding activities. It recognises the benefits and drawbacks of software product lines.

- *Commercial*: the expected return on investment drives the marketing, sales and development of software product line products. Marketing addresses the user values of having a large amount of variability for low costs.
- *Financial*: software product line engineering is influencing the investment decisions. There is a well-defined budget for domain and for application engineering activities. There is an institutionalised mechanism to generate budget for domain engineering by the sales of systems produced by application engineering. There is an awareness of the costs and profits of variability and how that generates a return on investment.
- *Vision and business objectives*: the top management strongly supports software product line engineering. The organisation's vision and business objectives incorporate in a qualitative way the software product line, its value for the organisation and its evolution. The software product line engineering strategy is visible to the organisation.
- *Strategic planning*: there are separate plans and roadmaps for domain and application engineering. The plans are related, and commonalities in applications provide the basis of the domain engineering plan.

6.3.4 Level 4: Measured

At this level, the business measures the effects of software product line engineering to improve the strategy. A typical situation:

- *Commercial*: the costs, profits and return on investment of software product line products and managed variability are measured. The results influence the marketing and sales strategy. In addition, the product management strategy is guided by measured return on investment.
- *Financial*: the costs and savings of reuse and variability and software product line engineering are measured and reflected in the budgets.
- *Vision and business objectives*: the top management knows the effects of software product line development on their organisation. The business objectives incorporate in a quantitative way the software product line, its value for the organisation and its evolution. The advantages of software product line engineering appear in the vision and business objectives. The drawbacks are recognised, and measures are planned to diminish their effects. The software product line engineering strategy is visible outside the organisation, for example to clients or investors.
- *Strategic planning*: the plans and roadmaps are co-ordinated to get the best business value out of software product line engineering.

6.3.5 Level 5: Optimised

At this level, the business strategy involves optimisation of software product line engineering.

- *Commercial*: marketing and sales know the costs, profits and return on investment of software product line engineering and use this knowledge to improve the business strategy.
- *Financial*: there is an accurate integration of financial information with the forecast of sales, costs and savings of software product line products.
- *Vision and business objectives*: they are influenced by software product line development upon a well-understood basis.
- *Strategic planning*: the plans and roadmaps are used strategically to get the best business value out of software product line engineering.

6.4 Architecture Dimension

The architecture dimension deals with the technical means to build the software. It determines the technical realisation of the products in the software product line. The architecture is split over domain and application architectures, which are related via variability. The evaluation in the architecture dimension mainly deals with the relationship between the reference architecture and the application architectures. It takes into account how variability is modelled in the reference architecture. The following aspects play a role in the architecture dimension of software product line engineering[5] (Fig. 6.3):

- *Asset reuse level*: the extent of the use of domain assets in products.
- *Reference architecture*: the extent to which the reference architecture determines the application architectures.
- *Variability management*: the explicit use of variation points and supporting mechanisms.

In the following sections, each of the architecture dimension's levels is discussed in detail.

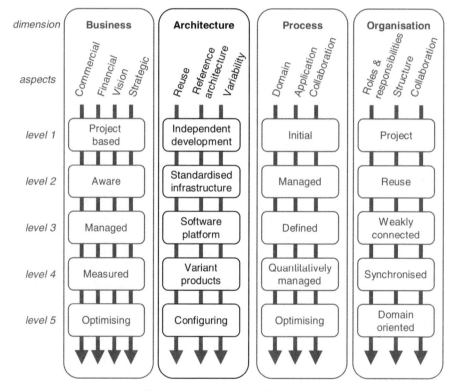

Fig. 6.3. Architecture dimension

---

[5] This is an adaptation of a model of software product line architectures presented in [28]

6.4.1 Level 1: Independent Development

This is the basic level. There are only architectures for single systems. Reuse is not visible in these architectures. With regard to the architecture concerns, we see the following typical situation:

- *Asset reuse level*: there is no or only unsystematic reuse.
- *Reference architecture*: there is no software product line architecture.
- *Variability management*: variability is not managed.

6.4.2 Level 2: Standardised Infrastructure

At this level, reuse is focused on third-party infrastructure. Common software infrastructure (such as middleware) is defined. There is no formal reuse of domain-specific assets.

- *Asset reuse level*: there is a common third-party infrastructure defined and in use. There is only ad hoc reuse, mainly based on the repository of the third-party products.
- *Reference architecture*: the software product line architecture is derived from the third-party infrastructure. It only enforces the use of this infrastructure.
- *Variability management*: only variability offered by the third-party infrastructure is somewhat limited. The remainder of the variation is open to be determined by the application architecture.

6.4.3 Level 3: Software Platform

At this level, domain commonality is captured and implemented in a software platform. There is a reference architecture available for all applications, mainly determining the use of the platform. This configurable platform is used for various products. Nevertheless, there is no variability support for configuring. A typical situation looks like this:

- *Asset reuse level*: there is a common platform defined as a collection of common assets in a domain repository. Reuse is restricted to this platform and by architectural constraints.
- *Reference architecture*: it is in use for the applications. It contains rules and determines the use of the platform. This incorporates the common use of certain quality solutions as offered by the reference architecture.
- *Variability management*: the reference architecture determines which configurations of domain assets are allowed within applications. It determines explicit variation points, where application-specific variants may be bound.

6.4.4 Level 4: Variant Products

At this level, the domain commonality and variability is captured and a reference architecture is specified for the complete software product line. Domain assets include support for deriving products. Variability management is explicitly addressed in the software product line architecture.

- *Asset reuse level*: there is systematic and managed reuse based on an asset repository, with explicit variability in the assets.
- *Reference architecture*: there is an explicit reference architecture that determines where application architectures may vary. Many quality solutions are incorporated in the software product line architecture.
- *Variability management*: the software product line architecture determines which configurations are allowed for application architectures. The reference architecture determines variation points and restricts the allowed variants for most of these variation points. It determines rules that application-specific variants have to obey.

6.4.5 Level 5: Configuring

At this level, the reference architecture is dominant and application architectures divert only marginal from it. Products can be derived automatically, using scripts, tools and very high level languages. Application development consists mainly on configuring within the borders of the reference architecture. As a consequence, automated configuration of products is possible.

- *Asset reuse level*: there is systematic reuse based on an asset repository, with explicit variability in the assets and their configuration mechanisms.
- *Reference architecture*: it determines the application architectures completely. There is automated configuration support to derive specific applications. Quality is supported through the managed use of specific variation points.
- *Variability management*: it is fully integrated in the architecture. Variability is described in models or languages that are semantically and syntactically standardised within the organisation. Variants are derived automatically.

6.5 Process Dimension

The process dimension deals with the roles, responsibilities and relationships within a software development organisation. For software product line engineering, distinct processes can be identified for domain, application and collaborating processes. CMMI can be applied to domain and application engineering separately. Because application engineering processes must be coordinated with domain engineering and with other application engineering processes, additional collaboration processes must be implemented.

The following aspects play a role in the process dimension of software product line engineering (Fig. 6.4):

- *Domain engineering*: these processes guide the domain engineering work.
- *Application engineering*: these processes guide the application engineering work.
- *Collaboration*: these processes guide the collaboration activities between domain and application engineering.

The levels for the process dimension of software product line engineering are based on the CMMI levels [139] but they contain amplifications, i.e. specialisations or extensions, for CMMI practices at the same level.

In the following sections, each of the process dimension's levels is discussed in detail.

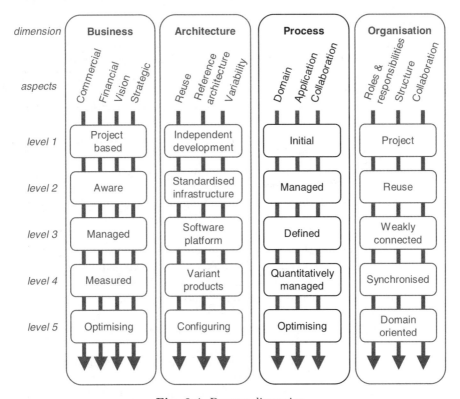

Fig. 6.4. Process dimension

6.5.1 Level 1: Initial

This is the basic level. Domain and application engineering and collaboration processes are performed at CMMI level 1.

- *Domain engineering, application engineering and collaboration*: if present at all, performed at CMMI level 1.

6.5.2 Level 2: Managed

At this level, basic software product line project-management is in place. For software product line engineering, domain and application engineering projects are synchronised.

- *Domain engineering*: performed at CMMI level 2. Amplifications are necessary for the following process areas:
  - *Requirements Management (RM)* manage software product line requirements. Maintain traceability between variation points and variants.
  - *Project Planning (PP)* define variability. Involve application engineering as stakeholder for reusing the domain assets. Define a policy of communication and co-operation with application engineering.
  - *Project Monitoring and Control (PMC)* monitor the usage of reusable assets per application.
  - *Measurement and Analysis (MA)* take global product line view into account.
  - *Configuration Management (CM)* pay attention to baseline created and released for reusable assets.
- *Application engineering*: performed at CMMI level 2. Amplifications are necessary for the following process areas:
  - *Requirements Management (RM)* is management of application requirements, both as reused domain requirements and as application-specific requirements.
  - *Project Planning (PP)* reuse domain assets and bind variability. Analyse the risk of dependency on domain engineering. Involve domain engineering as a stakeholder for developing reusable domain assets. Consider the influence of domain engineering on the scope of application projects.
  - *Project Monitoring and Control (PMC)* monitor the usage of reusable assets.
  - *Measurement and Analysis (MA)* measure use of common assets by application engineering activities.
  - *Configuration Management's (CM)* reusable assets provide a basis for the identification of configuration items.
- *Collaboration*: performed at CMMI level 2. Amplifications are necessary for the following process areas:

- *Requirements Management (RM)* maintain bi-directional traceability between software product line and application requirements and use it to identify inconsistencies.
- *Project Planning (PP)* asset life-cycles live longer than projects. Synchronise between domain and application engineering. Monitor the involvement between domain and application engineering.
- *Project Monitoring and Control (PMC)* monitor and control the synchronisation points between domain and application engineering.
- *Configuration Management (CM)* change requests regarding application-specific variants of reusable asset variants may lead to change requests on the reusable assets themselves. Synchronise application and domain configuration management.

6.5.3 Level 3: Defined

At this level, processes are aligned across the organisation, and engineering is performed in a disciplined way over the organisation. For software product line engineering, this means there is control over variability and reusable assets, both in creation and in use.

- *Domain engineering*: performed at CMMI level 3. Amplifications are necessary for the following process areas:
  - *Requirements Development (RD)* develop requirements for multiple products in a market segment. Define the scope of the software product line. Identify the products to be built. Identify commonality and variability.
  - *Technical Solution (TS)* variability must be included in operational concepts and scenarios for the domain. Develop a platform architecture and the relevant common product derivation support must be defined and implemented. Consider multiple origins and destinations for interfaces.
  - *Verification (VE)* ensure that application engineering makes the proper intended use of domain assets.
  - *Validation (VA)* in application engineering is a stakeholder of the domain validation process.
  - *Organisational Process Focus (OPF) and Organisational Process Definition (OPD)* include the platform for a given domain, procedures of use of this platform, methodologies, reusable components and guidelines. Consider multiple products in a market segment. Use the scope of the software product line.
  - *Organisational Training (OT)* add training on products, application processes and application project groups.
- *Application engineering*: performed at CMMI level 3. Amplifications are necessary for the following process areas:

- *Requirements Development (RD)* considers a single customer or market segment. The software product line's variability and capabilities are used in the communication with the customer. Reuse product line process requirements, bind variability and develop application-specific requirements.
- *Technical Solution (TS)* reuse domain assets, bind variability and develop application-specific assets. Specialise the platform architecture for the application and use the common product derivation support.
- *Validation (VA)* validate both domain and application work products. Staff must be especially trained to know what use they may make of the domain assets. Domain engineering is a stakeholder of the application validation process.
- *Organisational Training (OT)* add training on the platform, asset usage, domain processes and domain project groups.

- *Collaboration*: performed at CMMI level 3. Amplifications are necessary for the following process areas:
  - *Requirements Development (RD)* identify application requirements as potential software product line requirements.
  - *Technical Solution (TS)* determine selection criteria for and co-ordinate the inclusion of application assets in the platform. Communicate existing and planned application and domain assets. Identify application assets as potential domain assets. Co-ordinate make, buy or reuse decisions.
  - *Product Integration (PI)* maintain a roadmap of future products and product enhancements. Determine the actual transfer protocol of deliverables and the timing of the product transfers. Support the integration of domain and application assets.
  - *Verification (VE) and Validation (VA)* develop a domain verification environment, procedures and criteria concurrently and iteratively with the application verification environment. Communicate verification results and corrective actions between domain and application engineering. Share a policy of planning between domain and application engineering.
  - *Organisational Process Focus (OPF)* determine the organisation's performance objectives over the whole software product line process. Synchronise action plans between domain and application engineering.
  - *Organisational Process Definition (OPD)* assign responsibilities that cover several projects and products.
  - *Integrated Project Management (IPM)* communicate existing and planned application and domain assets. Identify application assets as potential domain assets.
  - *Risk Management (RSKM)* ensure that the risk management strategy and risk mitigation plans cover both domain and application engineering.

– *Decision Analysis and Resolution (DAR)* ensure that alternative solutions' evaluations cover aspects from both the applications and the domain.

6.5.4 Level 4: Quantitatively Managed

At this level, processes are managed and measured within the organisation. For software product line engineering, this means that there is quantitative control over variability and reusable assets, both in creation and in use.

- *Domain engineering*: performed at CMMI level 4. Amplifications are necessary for the following process area:
  – *Quantitative Project Management (QPM)* integrate the related application engineering sub-processes in the project statistics.
- *Application engineering*: performed at CMMI level 4. Amplifications are necessary for the following process area:
  – *Quantitative Project Management (QPM)* integrate the related domain engineering sub-processes in the project statistics.
- *Collaboration*: performed at CMMI level 4. Amplifications are necessary for the following process area:
  – *Quantitative Project Management (QPM)* measure the dependencies between domain and application engineering and the behaviour of their synchronisation activities. Communicate the influences between domain and application engineering. Negotiate improvement actions on performance of bottleneck projects. Co-ordinate stakeholder identification over application and domain projects.

6.5.5 Level 5: Optimising

At this level, processes are continuously optimised for their effectiveness for the organisation. For software product line engineering, this means a combined improvement of domain and application engineering together.

- *Domain engineering, application engineering and collaboration*: performed at CMMI level 5, and software product line processes of level 4 are performed.

6.6 Organisation Dimension

The organisation dimension deals with the actual mapping of roles and responsibilities to organisational structures. Within software product line engineering, this dimension measures the effectiveness of the distribution of domain and application engineering over the organisation. It involves structures and responsibilities for domain and application engineering separately and for

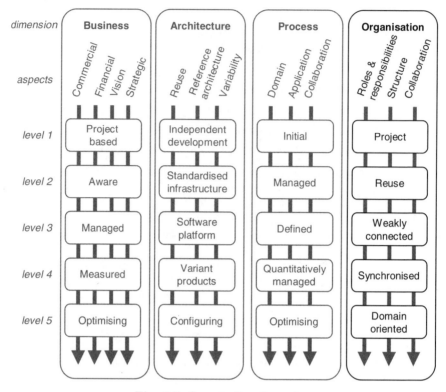

Fig. 6.5. Organisation dimension

supporting and co-ordinating roles. In particular, the responsibilities for domain engineering, application engineering and their internal co-ordination are identified.

The following aspects play a role in the organisation dimension of software product line engineering[6] (Fig. 6.5):

- *Roles and responsibilities*: how does the organisation manage the distinct responsibilities and relationships occurring in software product line engineering – are they undifferentiated or are there specific roles for product line engineering?
- *Structure*: this deals with the organisation structure that puts the roles and responsibilities into practice. It involves both the primary structure as shown in the organisation chart and the secondary structure that is not visible in the organisation chart. This aspect is also relevant to small organisations, which have usually less structure than large organisations. People's tasks will distribute the personnel over virtual departments, some exist of one or a few persons, and persons may be member of several virtual

---

[6] This is an adaptation of a model on organisational structures in [27]

departments. In small organisations, the structure is partially determined by roles and responsibilities.

- *Collaboration schemes*: this involves the co-operation in primary and secondary organisation structures and the extent of shared values.

In the following sections, each of the organisation dimension's levels is discussed in detail.

6.6.1 Level 1: Project

This is the basic level. The organisation is arranged for project-based single system engineering. With regard to the organisation concerns, we see the following typical situation:

- *Roles and responsibilities*: only the application engineering roles, which are the traditional software engineering roles, are defined.
- *Structure*: it is organised around project-based single system development.
- *Collaboration schemes*: the organisation is internally focused, human resources may be shared among projects, but software assets are usually not shared.

6.6.2 Level 2: Reuse

At this level, application projects drive reuse in an opportunistic way. First, certain common assets are identified and then refactored to reusable components that are shared between projects.

- *Roles and responsibilities*: there are no explicitly defined domain engineering roles. The application engineering experts collaborate over project borders to identify and share common assets.
- *Structure*: it is focused on doing projects. Certain senior resources are allocated to reusable component identification and development.
- *Collaboration schemes*: it is based on negotiations and information sharing among projects.

6.6.3 Level 3: Weakly Connected

At this level, there are one or more separate domain engineering organisations and multiple application engineering organisations There are simple interactions between them at early and late phases of domain and application engineering life-cycles. In small organisations, the different sub-organisations may be less visible.

- *Roles and responsibilities*: there are both domain and application engineering roles and responsibilities defined. There are responsibilities defined for separate domain and application engineering organisations.

- *Structure*: the domain and application roles are distributed over the organisation. There is a separate domain engineering department. Both domain and application engineering have mostly project-oriented structures. In small organisations, there are people that are explicitly responsible for the development of domain assets and application aspects. Although certain persons are responsible for both, this is not the normal situation, and domain and application tasks have separated descriptions.
- *Collaboration schemes*: it is document-based, mostly in exchanging requirements and shared management of change requests and problem reports between domain engineering projects and several application engineering projects.

6.6.4 Level 4: Synchronised

At this level, there are multiple interactions between domain engineering and application engineering, an institutionalised secondary structure for early problem prevention and co-ordinated planning of domain engineering and application engineering.

- *Roles and responsibilities*: there are co-ordination roles between domain and application engineering and across domain engineering organisations. Domain engineering has a major role in software development.
- *Structure*: there is a secondary structure that incorporates cross-functional teams. The primary structure follows the major sub-structure of the reference architecture. Functional domains, which are important for the reference architecture, determine the secondary structure in the organisation. In small organisations, there are people that are explicitly responsible for the development of domain assets and application aspects. Most persons are also responsible for certain functional domains, extending both over domain and application engineering. Domain and application tasks have separated descriptions.
- *Collaboration schemes*: there is a strong co-operation of domain and application engineering projects in cross-functional teams, task force groups, etc. There are regular meetings of people fulfilling collaboration roles.

6.6.5 Level 5: Domain-Oriented

At this level, the functional domains determine the primary structure for mainly domain engineering. Application engineering now determines a secondary structure.

- *Roles and responsibilities*: the responsibilities of the people in the organisation are related to the functional domains in the architecture, like in level 1 organisations. However, the most important focus is on domain engineering. Many people in the organisation have explicit determined application responsibilities in addition. Application engineering roles take only a small part of the time of most people.

- *Structure*: it is driven by disciplines in domain engineering. Specific application engineering is within the secondary structure. Application development teams are formed over the organisational borders. In small organisations people are explicitly responsible for certain functional domains, extending both over domain and application engineering. Few people are responsible for domain or application engineering only. Functional domain tasks in domain engineering have separated descriptions, in addition there are the application task descriptions.
- *Collaboration schemes*: persons can assume domain and application engineering roles as needed.

6.7 Applying the FEF

There are three main ways to use the FEF. It can be used to assess the organisation to get information how well the organisation is doing. It can be used as a benchmark tool to compare organisations. And it can be used as an improvement tool to plan the improvement of the organisation.

The result of an FEF evaluation is a profile consisting of a level for each of the BAPO dimensions. Figure 6.6 gives an example profile, discussed in more detail in Sect. 6.7.2.

The optimal profile for a given organisation depends on the situation. In general, having the maximum on all axes may not be optimal. There are several reasons to prefer a less than maximal profile. A particular organisation needs to determine from an investment perspective which profile would be adequate for it. Achieving higher levels may just not be worthwhile.

For example, in immature domains or domains with short system lifecycles, a less than maximal score may be preferred in at least the B and O dimensions since fast responses may be needed. Another reason may be that a company that is a business follower may not need to reach more than the lower business dimension levels contrary to a company that shapes a business.

6.7.1 Complex Organisations

Software product line organisations are often complex. Development may be distributed over different departments that are located at different sites and even in different time zones. Third parties may be involved that are specialised in doing a part of the work, e.g. through outsourcing. Such situations call for a practical approach to evaluation.

Applying the FEF to the complete organisation at once would probably take too much time. Moreover, the lowest common denominator of the sub-organisations would dominate the profile, obscuring the results of higher-scoring departments.

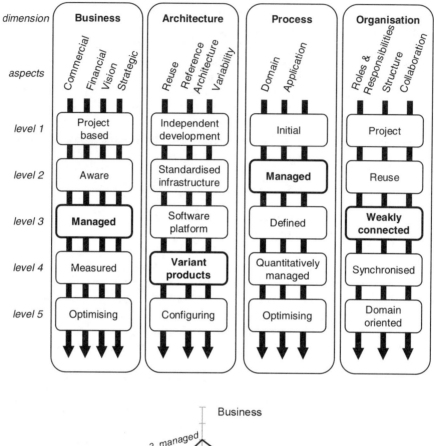

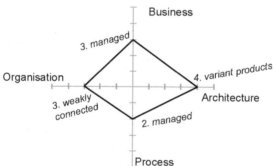

Fig. 6.6. Example company profile

A better idea is to apply the evaluation to units of manageable size. Such units may be departments, divisions, sub-contractors, or even virtual parts of a group of organisations. Restricting the evaluation to such units means that only parts of the software product line engineering aspects are evaluated. For instance, it may happen that a unit is only involved in domain engineering.

In that case, the aspects related to application engineering are not applicable, but the collaboration aspects are still important.

In some organisations, the software product line is structured as a hierarchy or as part of a population [148] (Fig. 6.7). A hierarchy exists if there are several product lines that use a single common infrastructure that is modelled as a product line. In a population, several product lines reuse different parts of a very broad platform. Usually no or only few systems use all assets of the platform.

Applying the FEF to parts (units) of complex organisations gives rise to the following observations:

- *Business* involves business relations internal to the complex organisation as well. In particular, the business relationships of the department that is assessed with the remainder of the software product line engineering parts of the organisation. External business concerns mainly apply if the given part of the organisation is dealing with that concern.
- *Architecture* concerns apply to that part of the architecture that the specific unit is responsible for either in creating it or in using it.
- *Process* concerns only apply for those that the unit is performing.
- *Organisation* concerns only apply for internal organisation of the unit and to its role in relationships with other parts of the organisation.

In a hierarchical situation, application engineering for the generic platform is domain engineering for a single software product line. In the case of populations, it may happen that a department is responsible both for a specific software product line and for parts of the domain. Although this may complicate an FEF evaluation, the principles remain the same. Each unit can

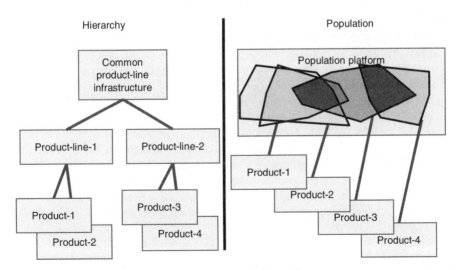

Fig. 6.7. Hierarchy and population

be evaluated for each of the different families in which it is involved and in the interplay between them in the overall product line process structure. The evaluation has to be applied separately to each of the roles that a development unit plays. This means that a single unit may get a separate evaluation for each of its roles, for example as a platform developer and as a user of a (larger-scale) platform. These evaluations may result in different profiles. Similar to the situation in complex organisations, this may mean that only parts of the FEF can be applied to each role.

6.7.2 Example

As an example, we introduce ProtAct – an imaginary company that provides security systems for office buildings and business plants. It delivers observation rooms, cameras, sensors for intrusion, fire and water, and all kinds of alarms. It provides door locks operated by keypads and other kinds of authentication mechanisms. Since the systems are sold in many countries, many languages are supported. Each client has his or her own configuration of the system, and there are many possible configurations available. Therefore, ProtAct develops its software using product line engineering. Now, ProtAct wants to assess itself to find the best ways to improve this development in the future in order to reduce software cost to a minimum level and keep lead-times of new developments as short as possible. It wants to know what are the best improvement actions to be taken. Initially, the expectation is that the architecture and organisation dimensions are satisfactory, but that the business and process may need improvement. Applying the FEF will indicate whether this intuition is right.

Business

ProtAct has an internal tax system that deducts money from departments that sell products, to fund serving departments. The departments that do domain engineering are examples of departments that get funding. The business uses a fixed amount of about 40% of the development budget to be used for domain engineering. Product management uses a roadmap that plans the future variants of their products. The roadmap indicates when new variants are to be built, and it gives feedback to marketing and sales on when these variants will be available. The roadmap is prepared using feedback from development on the distribution of new requirements over generic and specific software. ProtAct management pushes to make as many generic assets as possible and tries to reduce the cost of specialised developments since it is aware that costs are too high. In particular, the management put limits on development budgets to reduce the total development costs.

ProtAct has the following business evaluation:

- *Commercial*: marketing and sales are aware of the software product line. Product management keeps an eye on features that are needed in the future and is in contact with development to determine when such features may be available. The marketing department uses this information to determine which features can easily be supported and which are difficult to build, or take some time to be finished. The former ones are priced lower than the latter ones. As there is no specific measurement of the costs and profits of variability, this aspect is satisfied at level 3: Managed.

- *Financial*: an internal tax system deducts money from departments that sell products, to fund domain engineering. A fixed amount of the development budget is reserved for domain engineering. The costs and savings of product line engineering are not yet measured. This aspect is evaluated at level 3: Managed.
- *Vision and business objectives*: ProtAct's management pushes to make as much as possible generic and reduces the cost of specific developments, since they are aware that costs are too high. There are limits on development budgets to reduce the total development costs, and the management advocates this to the organisation. Again, product line engineering is not yet measured; therefore, also for this aspect, the evaluation is satisfied at level 3: Managed
- *Strategic planning*: product management uses a roadmap to plan the future variants of the product. It involves new variants that are to be built, and it gives feedback to marketing and sales when these variants are available. The roadmap is prepared in agreement with development, obtaining feedback on the distribution of new requirements over generic and specific software. Co-ordination among different roadmaps is not done. Thus, this aspect's evaluation is also satisfied at level 3: Managed.

Combining the results, the ProtAct Company is evaluated in the business dimension at level B3: Managed.

Architecture

ProtAct has a reference architecture for the complete software product line. The reference architecture defines a layered structure. Each layer has a framework of components that have to be present in each product. The lower layer consists of the operating system and database that are used in all applications. Variants are defined by adding plug-in components at interfaces that are specially designed for them. Thus, a single application architecture consists of a collection of fixed framework components and a configuration of plug-ins. A plug-in component may be specifically built for the application, but many plug-in components are shared by several applications and are therefore part of the platform.

ProtAct has the following architecture evaluation:

- *Asset reuse level*: important reusable assets are the architecture, the framework components and the frameworks themselves. A single application consists of a collection of fixed framework components and a configuration of plug-ins. A plug-in component may be specifically built for the application, but many plug-in components are shared by several applications and are therefore part of the platform. The requirements and test cases – both regression and integration tests – are reused over the whole software product line. As some plug-ins are application-specific and some of them have their own architectural rules, level 5 is not reached. This leaves ProtAct at level 4: Variant products.

- *Reference architecture*: there is a layered reference architecture for the complete software product line. Each layer has a framework of components that have to be present in each product. The lower layer consists of a single operating system and database that are used in all applications. Variants are built by adding plug-in components at interfaces that are specially designed for them. Thus, application architectures consist of the collection of fixed framework components and a configuration of plug-ins. A plug-in component can be added using specific interfaces only. Plug-in components embody the variation points of these interfaces. They have a configuration interface that is used to select the right variant in the applications. However, some parts allow plug-ins that are not completely determined by the architecture, and so the software product line architecture is at level 4: Variant products.
- *Variability management*: variation is managed in requirements that determine the configurations and plug-ins that have to be built or used. Reusable components have standard interfaces to select a variant, as prescribed by the reference architecture. Variability management is satisfied at level 4: Variant products.

Combining the results, ProtAct is evaluated for the architecture dimension at level A4: Variant products.

Process

ProtAct has separate processes for domain and application engineering. Domain engineering follows parallel tracks to iteratively develop separate parts of the architecture. A refactoring track is available for keeping the architecture in shape. Most application engineering departments follow a waterfall model to produce a single product. Collaboration and co-ordination processes deal with the following:

- The selection of reusable domain assets in the application.
- Collecting feedback of problem reports and application priorities from application engineering towards domain engineering.
- Determining the standard interfaces between domain engineering frameworks and the plug-in components.
- The promotion of application-specific components and interfaces towards domain engineering.

ProtAct Company has the following process evaluation:

- *Domain engineering*: it follows several iterative developments for separate parts of the architecture. A separate track is available for keeping the architecture in shape. The domain engineering department is at CMMI level 3. In addition, the domain engineering amplifications are performed. Therefore, this leads to an evaluation of level 3: Defined.
- *Application engineering*: these departments usually follow a waterfall model to produce a single application. Most departments have CMMI level 3, although some of them are still at level 2. Certain level 3 application engineering activities are performed, such as the technical solution and validation activities. In total, the evaluation leads to a level 2: Managed.
- *Collaboration*: these processes are mainly organised by domain engineering, and they are performed at CMMI level 3. They involve the communication of reusable assets between application and domain engineering. The feedback from application engineering towards domain engineering involves problem reports and application priorities. Not all level 3 collaboration activities are performed though, and the evaluation leads to a level 2: Managed.

Combining the results to the lowest of the levels measured, the company is evaluated in the process dimension at level P2: Managed.

Organisation

Domain engineering is performed in a department separate from several application engineering departments. Collaboration is supported through many cross-departmental groups that have the responsibility for one or more of the collaboration subjects, such as roadmaps, global architecture issues, interfaces, problem reports and maintenance, and making application-specific assets reusable.

ProtAct has the following organisation evaluation:

- *Roles and responsibilities*: the domain and application engineering roles and responsibilities are defined, and people are assigned to these roles and responsibilities. Although there are co-ordinating roles defined between domain and application engineering, they do not play an important role. In particular, domain engineers do not play a major role in application development. As a result, the evaluation for this aspect results in level 3: Weakly connected.
- *Structure*: domain engineering is performed in a department separate from several application engineering departments. A secondary structure is defined through many cross-departmental groups that have the responsibility for one or more collaboration subject. Domain engineering does not determine the primary structure. The evaluation for this aspect results in level 4: Synchronised.

- *Collaboration schemes*: it is supported through cross-departmental groups. However, collaboration mainly results in reports between domain and application engineering projects. As a result, the evaluation for this aspect results in level 3: Weakly connected.

Combining the results to the lowest of the levels measured, ProtAct is evaluated for the organisation dimension at level O3: Weakly connected.

Application of FEF results

ProtAct wants to go to levels *B4, A4, P4 and O4*. Therefore, they need to know what improvement actions must be taken. The expected profile was *B2, A3, P2 and O3*. Use of the FEF pointed to *B3, A4, P2 and O3*. This means that the business and the architecture are closer to their targets than expected. Because of this, the company decides on an improvement plan to reach levels *B3, A4, P3 and O3* first. This means that the process dimension will be addressed to reach level P3. Each application department will have to move to CMMI level 3, and level 3 collaboration amplifications have to be put in place. For instance, the identification of application assets as potential domain assets has to improve.

With all these improvement actions, care has to be taken that the business stays at level 3 and the architecture stays at level 4. This means that the business and the architecture need attention to stay healthy and to keep their present quality. It is expected that this will take less effort than what will be needed in the other dimensions.

The next goal is to go to levels *B4, A4, P4 and O4*. For the business dimension, this means that several measurements have to be introduced, e.g. for costs and profits of variability. For the process dimension, this means that CMMI level 4 has to be reached in the organisation. In addition, the quantitative project management amplifications have to be introduced. For the organisation, this means an improvement of the secondary structure that deals with collaboration over the organisation.

6.8 Connection to Other Approaches

The FEF is not the first model to evaluate software development. In particular, in the area of software development processes, there are several capability evaluation models. The most prominent process improvement framework is the Capability Maturity Model (CMM). It was developed by the Software Engineering Institute (SEI) and published in 1993 [50]. Later, the model was adapted to be applicable for systems engineering in general and renamed CMMI (see also Sect. 4.5) [140, 139].

In the field of software product line engineering, the SEI published a Framework for Software Product Line Practice [38] that distinguishes 29 practice areas, divided into three categories:

1. *Software engineering*: to apply appropriate technologies to create and evolve platforms and products.
2. *Technical management*: to engineer the creation and evolution of platform and products.
3. *Organisational management*: for the synchronisation of all software product line activities.

The SEI's Product Line Technical Probe is based on this framework. It allows one to examine an organisation's ability to adopt or improve in software product line engineering. The product line practice framework serves as a reference model for collecting and analysing data of an organisation. The results of applying the technical probe include a set of findings that characterise the organisation's strengths and challenges relative to a product line effort and a set of recommendations.

The SEI approaches have influenced the FEF. The CMMI's basic model of five maturity levels was adopted for the entire framework. The levels in the FEF's process dimension are extensions of the CMMI levels. Software product line concerns are reflected in amplifications[7] of CMMI practices, mainly in levels 2–4. These amplifications deal with the separation of domain and application engineering and with co-ordination activities. An FEF evaluation is similar to a CMMI assessment: for each of the dimensions, an incremental questionnaire leads to an evaluation result. The FEF differs from the Framework for Software Product Line Practice as it is differently structured (for example business is a primary dimension), and its process dimension is explicitly aligned with the CMMI.

Unlike CMMI – which has a single scale for a single dimension: process – the FEF has a scale for each BAPO dimension. Most importantly, the FEF is focused on software product line engineering. The separation into two processes and the explicit management of variability are the main concerns in the evaluation. As such, it is complementary to the CMMI, which is used to evaluate the single system software engineering process.

6.9 Summary

This chapter gives an overview of the Family Evaluation Framework for the evaluation of software product line development units. The FEF improves existing approaches by systematically distinguishing the four BAPO concerns: Business, Architecture, Process and Organisation. Each of these concerns is evaluated separately, and each leads to its own evaluation value. In the evaluation, only software product line development issues are covered. Other software development issues are treated elsewhere and are not part of the

---

[7] An amplification is an adaptation of a CMMI practice by specialising it to product lines

framework. In particular, the framework relies on process maturity models, like CMMI, for normal software development process issues.

Each dimension of the framework has a collection of aspects that are to be considered in the evaluation. Dependent on the evaluation in these aspects a level from 1 to 5 can be obtained. At level 1, no software product line engineering aspects are dealt with. At level 5, all these aspects are satisfied. Level 5 is not an ideal situation that does not allow improvements any more. We consider it unrealistic to have an ideal situation as highest level, since such a situation is unreachable, and because it differs from company to company and may even shift in time; there is not a single best profile that fits every situation.

The result of an evaluation is a profile that can be used for several reasons, such as assessing a department, benchmarking with other departments or companies, or as a starting point for improvement actions.

For software product line engineering organisations that are distributed over several sites or time zones, evaluations can be performed per department. Since a department will only perform part of the software product line engineering process, the evaluation must be adapted to suit this situation. Likewise, when the product line is structured, the evaluation may be performed for several roles separately.

This chapter provides a first public version of the FEF. A steering committee has been established to guarantee the continuous improvement of the FEF, based on company experiences.

The evaluation levels for the *business* dimension are project-based, aware, managed, measured and optimised. At the initial level, there is no real business involvement in software product line engineering. The business deals with a project-based organisation, and all projects are treated in a similar way by the management. The business dimension of the FEF deals with the following aspects:

- *Commercial*: from an unaware state, product management, marketing and sales force get aware of the possibilities of dealing with managed variability. In the higher level, the marketing and sales grow to use variability management in such a way that the product planning supports the expected sales, and marketing supports the variants that are available in the software product line.
- *Financial*: initially, there are no specific budgeting or investments available for software product line engineering. At the next level, the management is aware of possible benefits, but the best way to deal with this is still to be decided. With support from top management, initial investments are made to fund domain engineering. In the higher level, budgets and funding of domain engineering get more sophisticated and support the position of domain engineering within the organisation. Domain engineering earns its own budget through a solid internal business model.

- *Vision and business objectives*: initially, the vision is carried only by the people doing software product line engineering. Next, the management gets aware and incorporates the managed variability in their vision and objectives for the future.
- *Strategic planning*: from an initial stage, where software product line engineering is not visible in the plans, it becomes an important driving force in the planning at the higher levels.

The evaluation levels for the *architecture* dimension are independent development, standardised infrastructure, software platform, variant products and configuring. At the initial level, there is no domain architecture available, each product gets its own architecture and reuse is unsystematic and ad hoc.

- *Asset reuse level*: from an initial level of unsystematic reuse, this aspect grows via a common infrastructure to larger parts of the architecture that is reused, ending in a level where reuse is managed through variation points.
- *Reference architecture*: from an initial level where no domain architecture is available, this aspect grows to a situation where a reference architecture governs all applications, greatly simplifying the application-specific parts of product architectures.
- *Variability management*: from an initial level with no variability management, the aspect grows to a level where variability is fully integrated in the architecture and variants are configured.

The evaluation levels for the *process* dimension are based on CMMI: initial, managed, defined, quantitatively managed and optimising. At the initial level, there are no software product line processes available. Domain engineering and collaboration are almost absent. The process dimension of the FEF deals with the following aspects:

- *Domain engineering*: from being absent, this grows to be the dominating process. It starts with the determination of commonality and variability within the reusable platform and ends with the planning and definition of policies for all application engineering processes.
- *Application engineering*: from being the only development process, this aspect grows to processes at a high-maturity level, reusing not only technical assets, but all kinds of guidelines and rules as well.
- *Collaboration*: from being absent, this becomes an important set of mature processes supporting the co-ordination between the domain and application engineering processes. It involves activities that align other processes and that communicate available assets between the different projects.

The evaluation levels for the *organisation* dimension are project, reuse, weakly connected, synchronised and domain-oriented. At the initial level, there are no organisation structures available for doing software product line engineering. If at all, it is done within a single department, invisible to the remainder of the company. The organisation dimension of the FEF deals with the following aspects:

- *Roles and responsibilities*: from a state where they are non-existent, the organisation creates more and more domain engineering roles, up to the point where they become the most visible engineering roles in the organisation.
- *Structure*: from a state where the structure is defined by a project-based product organisation, domain engineering grows to define more of the structure. At first, this happens mainly in the secondary organisation, but eventually in the primary organisation too.
- *Collaboration schemes*: from a situation where there is no organised collaboration, the co-operation moves from an internal focus to a co-operative one.

Part II

Experience Reports

7

Experiences in Product Line Engineering

No matter how ingenious a software engineering technology sounds, no matter how well it is theoretically proven, this does not predict in any way its real-world success. In this respect, product line engineering is no exception to the rule. Only practical experience can show whether and how product line engineering works. In this part, we focus on exactly these practical experiences and demonstrate that product line engineering does indeed work in practice. In particular, we also show how it works in industrial settings and which adaptations must be made to the basic approach to account for different environments.

Compared to other kinds of software engineering techniques, product line engineering is actually rather difficult to analyse. The reason is that it is not a single technique – like inspections – which can be studied during a very short time-span, strongly limiting the number of influences that must be taken into account. Rather it is a life-cycle encompassing approach. As a consequence, it is necessary to evaluate the success of product line development in realistic organisational contexts: in full-scale case studies.

In the following chapters, we discuss different real-life case studies. In Part III, we compare and analyse them in order to highlight the different approaches and success factors they exhibit. Each of these case studies demonstrates very specific characteristics, which are required by the wide range of different development contexts.

In the remainder of this chapter, we introduce the very core of this book, namely a wide range of experiences on software product line engineering. We discuss in Sect. 7.1 some of the basics of experimental software engineering. This is followed by an overview of other work on experimentation and case studies in product line engineering. The basics of the case studies in this book are discussed further in Sect. 7.3 before we give a brief overview of the various case studies in Sect. 7.4.

7.1 Experimental Software Engineering

Software engineering supports the *real-world* production of software in terms of efficiency of the production (e.g. costs, time to market) and in terms of quality of the resulting product (e.g. reliability, portability, innovative functionality). Thus, the ultimate test for any software engineering approach is only possible *in the real world.* Only if proposals can be substantiated by real-world experience, we can accept that we are making progress towards a more professional level of software engineering [13].

The paradigm of experimentation in software engineering is a major factor in the concept of this book. Software product line engineering is still a rather new approach in software development. Even in organisations that already strive to perform product line engineering, the full potential of the approach is not yet achieved as only part of the relevant practices are truly performed. Investing in a full adoption of product line engineering requires a fundament of trust in an organisation and a good understanding of the key practices and their relevant benefits. This understanding can only be achieved by analysing experiences that are drawn from a large number of environments and development contexts.

An experimental approach to software engineering is also very important from a different angle: only feedback from actual experience can close the learning loop, which is very important to continuously improve software engineering approaches.

The importance of experimentation in software engineering has already been recognised some time ago [16]. Actually, it has been fundamental to such software engineering efforts as the Software Engineering Laboratory at NASA [14].

The core of experimental software engineering is the distinction of different types of experiments. This is shown in Table 7.1.

Table 7.1. Types of experiments in software engineering [13]

	One project	More than one project
One team	Single project (case study)	Multi-project variation
More than one team	Replicated project	Blocked subject-project

The various approaches to experimentation have different trade-offs. For example, case studies are the most detailed and most realistic opportunities to gain real-world experience. Thus, they enable the most profound results on the practical relevancy of the analysed approach. This is also called the *external validity* of the analysis. However, shortcomings of case studies are that the transfer of the gained experience to new situations is rather difficult, as each new situation is certainly different from the precise situation described in the case study. Thus, it is necessary to generalise beyond the single case study, by identifying commonalities among the results of a sufficiently large set of individual case studies. This book provides a first major step into this direction.

The other extreme of experimentation approaches are experiments with a large amount of replication (e.g. replicated project or blocked subject-project, Table 7.1). They enable to assure that the underlying observations are not merely accidental and they support the quantification of relations to such mitigating factors as experience, use of specific programming language, etc. This is also called *internal validity*.

In an ideal world, different approaches to experimental validation are used synergistically in order to provide an optimal validation of product line engineering. In this book we will focus on case studies:

- This book has its roots in the ESAPS, CAFÉ and FAMILIES projects. These projects aimed at the large-scale application of product line engineering in industry. This provided an unprecedented opportunity to collect product line engineering experiences on full-scale projects. This wealth of real-world projects actually provides a basis for cross-sectional analysis.
- Experiments on individual techniques and approaches have already been performed in other contexts. We do thus rely on this experimental data and present it where adequate, but we do not strive to fully reproduce it here.
- We are aiming for the practitioner. The analysis of full-size, real-world projects is most telling to practitioners as this matches most closely personal concerns and difficulties.

Case studies have the major advantage that they are firmly grounded in the real world. Thus, they are most relevant to the practitioner who seeks answers to such questions like the following:

- What activities should I perform in order to improve my reuse level?
- Which key success criteria do I need to address to achieve sustainable product line engineering?
- Does product line engineering impact other parts of my organisation – and if so – what is required from them?

This book provides a comparison of a rather large number of different case studies (multi-project variation) in order to ensure that the overview is not biased by a specific context. The presented case studies were mostly conducted in the context of the FAMILIES project. Besides this overall project context, the various case studies have very little resemblance. They come from all kinds of different companies: small and large; information systems and embedded.

Before we discuss the various case studies described in this book further, we now briefly survey some of the major case studies that have been described in the product line literature.

7.2 Experience Reports on Product Line Development

Product line engineering has always been a practice-oriented approach. The approach itself mainly originated in industrial practice and the analysis of industrial case studies has always been a significant part of the work in this area. However, especially during the early stages of product line development, the case studies were typically single case studies (i.e. without multi-project variation).[1] Most of these early case studies had in common that they described a rather revolutionary approach to product line engineering. Over time, more evolutionary approaches to product line engineering were described as well [34, 141] illustrating the fact that there is more than one way to start with software product line development in practice.

Today, the single case study approach is still the backbone of experience collection in software product lines. As a consequence, further case studies are continuously described [129, 136]. This approach is also institutionalised by the product line hall of fame as a continuous experience-collection approach for the community [104].

Only with an increasing focus on product line engineering more cross-sectional analysis was performed. However, these studies are usually restricted to a certain aspect. A rather large subset of studies focuses on technical and architectural issues. A common misconception of development for reuse is that the resulting generic solutions are less performing than those that are specifically developed. Zhang and Jarzabek show that this is an inappropriate conception based on a reengineering case study [157]. Svahnberg and Bosch provide an analysis of characteristics of the evolution of product lines. As a result, certain guidelines are provided to support the technical evolution [137].

Niemela even provides a cross-sectional analysis of 17 different small and medium-sized companies to determine strategies for the systematic configurability of product lines [98]. Along the same lines a study of Raatikainen et al. analysed the success factors of purely configurable product lines [111].

Besides domain engineering issues, the application engineering problems that arise from the increasing complexity of the product line infrastructure were also subject to case studies. Several guidelines were derived from an analysis of two case studies [44].

A very specific subset of product line engineering approaches is formed by those who rely on the formation of domain-specific languages for describing the resulting applications. Tolvanen and Kelly discuss success factors and approaches for modelling a domain in terms of domain-specific languages based on several case studies they performed [142].

This book provides a cross-sectional analysis of a rather large number of different case studies of product line engineering. As opposed to most

---

[1] Typical examples of this kind are [17, 43, 47, 88, 126]

proceeding cross-sectional analysis, the aim is to cover all major aspects of product line engineering as defined by the BAPO model, which we introduced in Part I.

7.3 Case Study Basics

The various case studies described in this book are based on a common approach, which provides a basis for comparing the various case studies. This section provides an overview of the principles the case studies largely adhere to. The following sub-section discusses the major information that was attempted to collect in the case studies.

7.3.1 Setting Up Case Studies

From a scientific point of view, it would be optimal to have each and every case study thoroughly prepared in advance and to have a measurement program that accompanies it and systematically analyses its details. Unfortunately, reality is not always fully compatible with rigorous scientific approaches. Product line engineering is not different from other areas of software engineering.

The ITEA projects ESAPS, CAFÉ and FAMILIES [143] provided the basis for the BAPO model and the Families Evaluation Framework (FEF). As a result, the various case studies that were part of these projects provided the basis for our analysis of these frameworks and most of the case studies described in this book are actually derived from these projects. However, the actual case studies and the Families Evaluation Framework were developed in parallel. Thus, the projects could not yet use the FEF as a basis for their development. As a consequence, all descriptions of case studies in this part of the book are based on a thoughtful posterior analysis of the projects.

The various case studies aim to cover each of the dimensions in detail. However, they were performed in different contexts. This lead to different focuses with respect to both comprehensiveness of process coverage (not all case studies addressed all life-cycle phases) and on the different dimensions (e.g. some organisations focused strongly on process concerns, while others mostly neglected this issue). Despite these restrictions, each of the different case studies aims to describe the experiences in sufficient detail to support the understanding of an evaluation along all of these dimensions.

Going from a non-product line organisation towards a product line organisation is a major transition. Processes, attitudes and technologies, sometimes even the business model, change in this transition. Thus, the case studies aim to cover both the initial situation in terms of BAPO – and in particular what caused the transition – and the new situation that was achieved after the transition was made.

Of course, it is important for the interested reader to know the results of product line development. What are the benefits to be expected? What aspects were instrumental in achieving them? But sometimes it is even more interesting and enlightening to see what did *not* work; the mistakes that should be avoided and the costs (in terms of effort and otherwise, necessary changes, etc.) that had to be imposed on the organisations. The various case studies are based on this rationale.

7.3.2 The Case Study Format

In order to simplify the understanding of the case studies and to ease their comparison, we describe all case studies in a comparable manner. While some deviations had to be made here and there, overall, the case studies are pretty much homogeneous.

All case studies start with a description of the company and end with a summary with the major findings and of BAPO aspects covered. Internally, they are structured as far as possible based on the BAPO model. In particular, the case studies aim to answer the following questions.

Motivation

- What motivated the transition to a product line approach in the first place? Why did the companies embark on such a profound change of their software development? Was it supported by adequate foresight and analysis?
- How was the transition planned? What difficulties were expected? Which occurred? What measures were taken to protect against the difficulties – before and after their occurrence?
- What were positive surprises? Things that just went right, or at least much better than expected?

Approach

- What did the development approach look like before the transition – what did it look like afterwards?
- What was the initial context? How was business performed?
- How can development situation, company context and technology be characterised in terms of the BAPO dimensions?

Business

- How did the business situation and the transition to product line development correlate?
- How did it impact – and in what way was it driven – by other departments in the organisation besides software development? What was the impact on sales? On marketing and branding? What was the impact on the overall business position?
- Was it possible to align the software development product line strategy and the marketing product line strategy? Which was the stronger driver?

Architecture

- How was the architecture created – or evolved – into its present state?
- How is variability represented in the architecture? How is new variability introduced and outdated variability removed?
- What mechanisms are in place in order to enforce the architecture and the accompanying variability mechanisms? What level of freedom do specific projects have to customise the architecture? How are deviations from the architecture handled?
- Was it possible to take advantage of existing assets like designs, components, or even complete software frameworks? Or was transfer restricted to domain knowledge?

Process

- How is the differentiation between domain engineering and application engineering realised? What exactly is the difference between the two in the specific organisation?
- If a standard process model is in place, did this help or hinder the effort? Which adaptations had to be made? How were adaptations made and to which processes?
- In particular, how did requirements management, project management and configuration management change? Which measurement programs were set up in order to validate any improvements?

Organisation

- Which roles, specific to product line engineering, were introduced? How was allocation of these roles to people handled?
- Was a real differentiation into a domain engineering and an application engineering unit introduced? What effects did this have on the overall organisation dynamics?
- What were the main concerns that governed the organisational change? To which degree were they satisfied?

Results

An important contribution of the individual case studies is, what results have been achieved and what would be done differently in the future?

- What was the major impact of the product line introduction? What were the major obstacles?
- What impact did product line engineering have on the overall business performance? What improved and what became worse?
- What are the limits to product line engineering that are currently seen?

Lessons Learned

- What are the major lessons? What went good? What bad? Which good ideas turned out to be false alleys?
- What would be done differently next time around?
- What recommendations are perceived that they can be generalised beyond the current situation?

7.4 Overview of the Case Studies

Ten case studies are presented in this part of the book, a considerable number. This section provides a brief overview of these case studies and their respective focus:

The case study on *AKVAsmart* (Chap. 8) describes the result of a major reengineering effort that aimed at the migration of several individual software products into a single product line. This aimed at easing development and maintenance of the products and providing a homogeneous look-and-feel to the products. The integration of the individual products resulted in a reduction of the overall code size by more than 70%.

The case study on *Bosch* presents the experience from setting up a large-scale product line engineering effort at Bosch Gasoline systems (Chap. 9). Besides capturing major improvements in terms of cost and time to market, the effort also resulted in reducing calibration and maintenance effort for resulting systems.

DNV started its product line effort in the context of the planned setup of a new product platform (Chap. 10). The major goal of the product line effort was to integrate the overall development and through the integration of the underlying structure reduce the total effort.

Of all case studies, *market maker* provides the best example for a very small organisation that successfully applied a product line approach and was able to scale it to an extremely high number of successfully delivered products (Chap. 11). This success was accompanied with a very high reuse rate that resulted in very short development cycles for the final products.

Nokia Mobile Phones is very well known for its mobile phone products. It delivers an extremely high number of different mobile phones, differing not only in the respective model type, but also with respect to the localisation, the supported network types, etc. (Chap. 12). Nokia can be regarded as quite the opposite to the market maker experience. Here, the organisational size was about 1,000 developers.

Nokia Networks provides networking technology, particularly in the area of mobile infrastructure. Modern communication technology infrastructure is extremely complex. Thus, the product line efforts at Nokia Networks are not only driven from attempts to save costs and improve time to market, but more from a general desire of dealing with complexity (Chap. 13).

Philips Consumer Electronics set up a product line in the context of television systems (Chap. 14). This effort aimed at managing the explosion of the software size within television systems. Due to the introduction context, the chapter nicely presents a case were reengineering both on the software and on the organisational side were required.

Philips Medical Systems (Chap. 15) again provides an example of successful product line engineering in a very large organisation of more than 1,000 developers. In this case, the product line approach was carefully planned from a strategic perspective. It is built on an existing asset base. The approach had a strong impact on the business competitiveness of the organisation, leading to an effort reduction of 50–25% per reused component with the corresponding time-to-market reductions.

At *Siemens* the focus within product line engineering was mainly on test optimisation (Chap. 16). Thus, product line engineering was only conducted partially. Within testing the organisation gained about 57% reuse, leading to an overall acceleration of the tests of about 75%.

The case study of *Telvent* is situated in the area of a TV-software platform (Chap. 17). This study focuses mainly on the architectural measures that were taken to provide the necessary degree of flexibility. This architectural evolution was aligned with a corresponding business strategy.

The very breadth of case studies we discuss in this book already illustrates a very important point: product line engineering is an approach that can – with suitable tailoring – be applied in a wide range of organisations and domains. Thus, no matter in what kind of organisation you are currently working, product line engineering can most likely improve the performance of your software development significantly.

AKVAsmart

with Magne Johnson
   Magne Syrnstad

Company facts of AKVAsmart ASA

Organisational size: 6–10 developers.
Starting Mode: Replacement of legacy systems.

Experienced improvements:
- Large reduction of code size by more than 70%.
- Uniform look-and-feel.
- Common technological platform and code style.
- Easier reuse, maintenance and integration.

Business: AKVAsmart management supports the product line engineering approach and uses it in the planning of new products.

Architecture: There is an enforcing architecture, involving a framework and plug-ins for the product line.
The domain is well known and mature, and the variation points are well known.

Process: The software process is defined but flexible, using elements from such different process models as the Unified Process, extreme Programming and SCRUM.

Organisation: The software development part of the organisation is too small to have separate units. Most of the work is done on general components that will be configured into specific products. Some customers get special functionality developed.

8.1 Introduction

AKVAsmart ASA[1] is the result of a merger in 2003 between the three leading companies in feed control and farm management software for the fish-farming industry. It is the leading supplier of technology and software to the fish-farming industry. The company is divided into two divisions:

1. *Information Technology and Consulting (ITC)*: primarily supplies biological Enterprise Resource Planning (ERP) software for control, traceability, quality, planning and budgeting.
2. *Farm Process Technology*: supplies hardware like camera technology, feeding technology, feed sensor technology, feed control software, barges and more.

AKVAsmart is present in all major industrialised fish-farming countries, with a focus not only on the salmon industry, but also on emerging species. It has offices in Norway, Chile, United Kingdom and Canada. The company has approximately 100 employees, 25 of whom work in ITC. The revenue for 2004 is approximately €15 million.

8.2 Motivation

8.2.1 Case Description

Fish-farming involves a lot of embedded equipment that has to co-operate. Figure 8.1 shows a marine fish-farm site with some examples of AKVAsmart technology. It shows an optimised fish-farm. The top left part of the figure shows the office staff working with the biological ERP software (Superior Control[2]). The top right part of the figure shows the head office, supplied with the decision support software Superior Manager. Down to his left a Doppler sensor is shown. This is a pellet sensor using sound waves to measure the amount of feed passing through the water. This technology is used together with feed control software. At the bottom left, the figure shows a sensor measuring stream and direction of the water. Next to this figure is a pellet counter in the form of a funnel and photocell. At the bottom right, the picture shows an operator controlling feeding using the feed control software and cameras.

AKVAsmart FPT supplies equipment and technology, mainly on the market for marine production, and in some degree on freshwater production.

---

[1] From here on, the term 'AKVAsmart' is used as a short hand for 'AKVAsmart ASA'

[2] AKVAsmart ITC supplies farm management software under the Superior Software banner

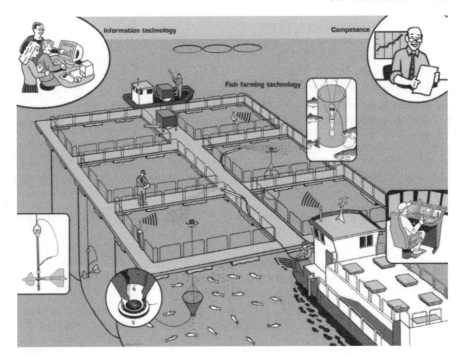

Fig. 8.1. Farming site with AKVAsmart technology

Figure 8.2 illustrates salmonoid production from eggs to the sale of the finished product. AKVAsmart provides equipment for the Freshwater and Ongrowing/Marine stages of the production chain. This equipment includes the following:

- Feed barges (with feed silos and feeding systems for farming).
- Central feeding systems for feed distribution into the cages.
- Feed quality control (automated feeding sensors based on Doppler or pellet counter technology).

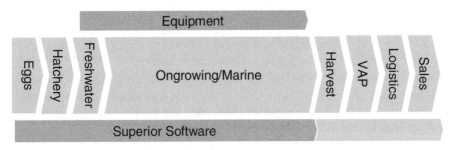

Fig. 8.2. AKVAsmart activities in the fish-farming market

- Sensors (stream, temperature, oxygen and more). Different sensors are needed to determine a feeding strategy and to measure environmental hazards for the fish. Colour camera technology can be used to visually study the fish.
- AkvaControl software is the feed control software using the sensor information as input, providing optimal feeding strategy to the feeders.
- Biomass estimation is a stereo camera solution used to measure the average weight of the fish.

The Superior Software for farm management covers the production chain up to the harvest phase. Plans exist to extend this support further. The current software consists of the following main categories:

- *Production planning*: short- and long-term production planning from eggs to sales.
- *Production control*: the main product, where all biological production information is recorded and stored. It consists of a range of integration points to control among others software and governmental portals.
- *Documentation, traceability and food safety*: this is one of the main focus areas in food production, and it is fully covered in the product portfolio.
- *Budgeting/cash-flow management/cost analysis*.

The farm management software is currently the most important software to most fish-farming companies. The complete product cycle (three years for salmon) means that the value of the company depends heavily on having correct information about the biological status of its products.

The topic of this case study are the software products of AKVAsmart ITC. The company is developing a product line with a flexible architecture that satisfies the needs of its different products. The goal is to reimplement all legacy products to a common platform. This common platform has to provide general as well as domain-specific services to the applications. This means that a large range of different products within the value chain is being merged into a single product line, while keeping in mind

- variation and configuration management
- common and variable needs in the different products
- the ability to select and configure parts of the platform by application engineering
- a common look-and-feel for the applications
- the applications must be able to change and extend existing behaviour.

The expected benefits of product line development are nothing too original in a product line setting. A major goal is to increase productivity, and shorten the time to market for new products, including variants covering new species and variants of existing products.

8.2.2 Market Drivers

Different species have different characteristics regarding growth, feed utilisation, life-cycle etc. Figure 8.1 presents a typical salmonoid production farm. Differences occur for other species. Different kind of seafood like shrimps and shellfish have a distinctly different biology, and this is reflected in the way they are grown. In the end, no matter what the species is, it is the quantity harvested that is most important.

There are different production types, among others land-based production, seawater production and pond production. Each type provides different requirements for environmental registration. Different countries have different governmental requirements for fish-farming. Considering the market requirements we see a clear distinction between small and large customers. Small customers often have a small production farm on the side. They employ just a few different users for their system. In the end, biomass control is most important to them. Larger customers may have hundreds of sites, in several countries on three continents. Their main request is for workflow support. As the software is used in different parts of the world, it supports many languages, among others Norwegian, English, Spanish and Japanese.

Several licensing-related limitations of system functionality are supported, including the availability of plug-ins, number of users and production size. Access rights, role and personal preferences determine what a system looks like to a particular user. The bandwidth that is available for communication between the equipment varies a lot per area. Currently, certain areas only have satellite links, providing expensive and narrow bandwidth connections, although that is rapidly changing.

8.3 Approach

At the start of the project, Microsoft .NET was chosen as development platform with C# the programming language. For the adoption of product line technology, an evolutionary strategy was selected. Development of a first framework release coincided with the development of the first product in the product line: Superior Manager, which is a small reporting product. At the time of Superior Manager's completion, the framework covered little more functionality than what was needed to run this first application. The framework was extended in parallel with the development of Superior Control, the second and major product. Superior Control was released together with the second, and current, version of the framework. This strategy of parallel development of framework and applications will continue in the future. The framework will be extended as additional functionality is required by the applications, but releases of the framework will be limited to major product releases. The reason is simply that releasing a new version of the framework is a costly operation.

This release strategy is likely to create conflicts in the future. In some cases, a new plug-in may require extra functionality in the framework. This plug-in may therefore have to incorporate functionality that logically belongs to the framework, at least temporarily until the next version of the framework is released.

8.4 Architecture

The product line architecture is a layered plug-in framework based on the client–server paradigm (Fig. 8.3). The business layer is separated from the presentation layer. The business layer typically runs on a server with multiple clients on separate computers. Communication between clients and server is done through standard .NET remoting mechanisms.

The framework has different flavours specific to clients and servers, each offering some additional functionality. Business data is stored in a database accessible to the business layer. The framework provides services that hide the separation of the client and server parts from plug-in developers. It also includes the main layout of the database.

Most plug-ins have a client (ALP) and a server part (BLP). In addition to this, a plug-in may extend the database (DBLP). Some plug-ins have no presentation part, like BLP_2 and $DBLP_2$ in Fig. 8.3. Typically, these plug-ins are available upon request to provide some services to presentation layer plug-ins, for example integration with an external system. Other plug-ins are representations of loose couplings to external services, like ALP_3. They merely include an external service in the user interface. An example of such a loosely

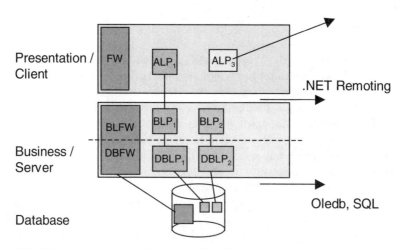

Fig. 8.3. Vertical plug-in architecture. The lines indicate parts belonging to the same plug-in or framework

coupled application is the integration to a web browser automatically showing the weather forecast for a site.

8.4.1 The Framework

The main task of the framework is to provide the plug-ins with facilities such as loading, communication between plug-ins and communication between the client and server parts of plug-ins. For the client side, there is also GUI functionality available to facilitate a standard way of building up user interface screens.

When the user signs on, the framework has the responsibility of checking accesses, licenses and to configure the application according to the user's role and preferences. The framework also provides the functionality needed to run certain standard tasks at specific times. Functionality is available that allows users to share their generated reports and data.

Besides this generic functionality, the framework also supports tracing, which is more domain-specific. By nature of the trade, fish is handled by groups, and may be moved about quite a bit. This means that tracing is a necessary part of handling (historic) data regarding a group of fish, such as calculation of growth. Tracing is used by many plug-ins, and adding it to the framework is a logical step. Because tracing is a challenging task with respect to performance, it is physically located close to the database, on the server-side flavour of the framework.

Plug-ins are highly independent of each other. This makes it easier to provide multiple variants of a product, and to sell functionality in pieces. A major feature of the product line is that it is product-independent. The plug-ins are set up in such a way that almost any configuration of them works, although some would make no sense. This means that while product planning decides which features are to be made, the exact size and shape of the products are unimportant to the developers.

To reach this, all communication between plug-ins goes through the framework, either as broadcasting or via direct connection through framework interfaces. An example of the use of the broadcasting mechanism is populating a right-click menu on a site. The contents of the menu list depend on the available plug-ins. A broadcast is made for plug-ins that have menu items to add. Plug-ins do not have to worry about what other plug-ins are available for the site: this information is collected on-the-fly by the framework. Broadcasting is also used to check if multiple plug-ins are editing the same data concurrently.

The alternative to broadcasting is direct communication through special determined interfaces. Direct communication is used in cases where broadcasting is unfeasible. This may occur, for instance, if a task involves very frequent communication of large volumes of data. Like broadcasting, direct communication is handled by the framework, but it is set up at sign on. This scheme allows for the same flexibility with respect to combinations of plug-ins

in a product, with options becoming unavailable when the targeted plug-in
is not there. In this case, however, communication is set up once in advance,
rather than on-the-fly each time that it is used.

The described set-up allows new plug-ins to be integrated and removed
in an easy and fail-safe way. Although it is possible to break the rules of the
architecture by making direct references between plug-ins, doing so is cum-
bersome and requires special code in both plug-ins to work. The architecture
is enforced by making the right way the easy way.

8.4.2 Examples of Plug-ins

To give a better idea of what plug-ins can be, we describe two examples.

The first example deals with two plug-ins that are frequently used to describe a part of an organisation (Fig. 8.4). One plug-in is called MyOrganisation. When initialised it registers itself on the main menu in the top left-hand
corner of the window. When the plug-in is activated a tool window is shown
on the left. Here, the user can navigate the tree structure of his organisation.
In addition to this presentation layer part, the plug-in also has a business layer
part, which is responsible for fetching organisation data from the database.
The other plug-in is called SiteStatus. This plug-in shows the status for a site,
and occupies the main part of the screenshot as a tab control. This plug-in
is activated by right-clicking a site in the organisation view on the left and
selecting "Show Status". Again, the plug-in has a business layer part to fetch
the data from the database. These plug-ins are unaware of each other, and the
framework does not know about either of them until they register themselves.

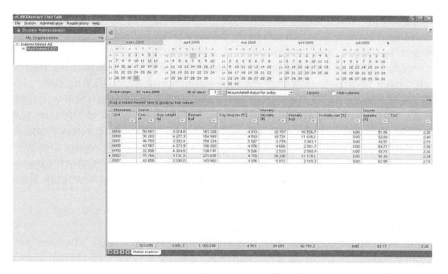

Fig. 8.4. Organisation view

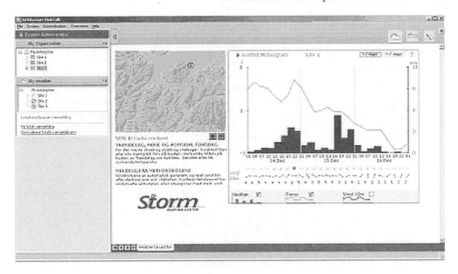

Fig. 8.5. Weather forecast

At start up, MyOrganisation asks to be placed in the "Administration" folder of the main bar, and so becomes available to the user. SiteStatus registers itself to be shown when a site is right-clicked, regardless of where this happens. MyOrganisation is unaware of the context of the right-click menu as it is populated at run-time. Thus, removing one or two of these plug-ins will reduce the functionality of the system, but will not confuse other parts as they are independent of each other.

The second example deals with the Weather Forecast plug-in that integrates weather information into a system. Weather data is bought from an external company. The plug-in has a business part that collects site data (mainly locations), and provides the left site browser (Fig. 8.5). The main part of the window is a web page wrapped into the application, delivered from the Storm Weather Center. Some wrapping is done to make it look more integrated than it really is. The main work of the plug-in is to allow for enabling and cancelling subscriptions of weather data for different sites. As this data has a monthly fee, many companies subscribe to it only during springtime when boat activity is high. Although in this example the weather browser is a separate part of the user interface, the architecture does allow a set-up where weather info is available for display on the right-click of any site.

8.5 Results and Impact Evaluation

The first product that was based on the new platform is Superior Manager, which was released in April 2005. The next product is Superior Control.net, which was released in August 2005. With it, version two of the framework

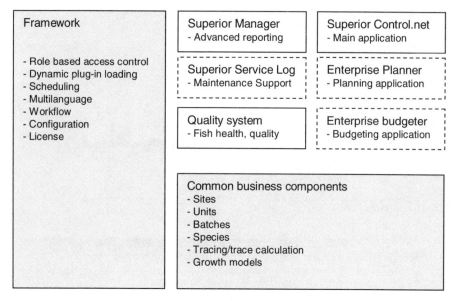

Fig. 8.6. Product line applications

was shipped. This required small changes in Superior Manager. Each of the products may be considered a small product line of its own because customer-dependent variants are delivered.

The complete set of products, shown in Fig. 8.6, forms a marketed product line called Fishtalk. The white boxes are the core AKVAsmart products. Superior Service Log is a purchased third-party maintenance system. The dashed boxes of Enterprise Planner and Enterprise Budgeter are planned products, and may be developed in-house or bought from external parties.

The old version of the products had evolved without much focus on design. As a consequence, it consisted of a lot of copy and paste code, and contained well above a million lines of code (excluding blank lines and comments). Although the current code base covers slightly more functionality,[3] it is less than a third the size of the original (cf. Table 8.1).

Proper design shrinks code.

The framework drives efficiency in application development through reuse of commodity functionality. The flexibility of the framework makes it possible to extend the product line in the direction of new species through simple extension and configuration mechanisms. This way, a larger part of the market can be covered. Moreover, products are well integrated. The reuse of crucial skills between projects is another way to increase productivity.

---

[3] Some features were left out, some others were added. Overall, the new systems offer more functionality than their pre-product line counterparts

Table 8.1. Platform and applications code size

Product / component	Codesize (kloc)	#Files	#Classes
Framework	70	1,020	1,577
Manager	40	705	793
Superior Control.net	125	1,930	2,300
Imports	25	310	385
Various	30–50		
Total	290–310	> 3,965	> 5,055

8.6 Lessons Learned

Time passes. The development time of the product line is longer than anticipated. While the architecture and framework mechanisms have not caused any problems, the development of content to match the old products have taken much more time than planned.

The plug-in architecture delivers what was expected of it. The main mechanisms of the framework survived without major changes. Most changes that did occur were extensions. For the completed products, the plug-in architecture and the independency between plug-ins have shown their value in the easy deployment of bug fixes.

Requirements remain an issue, though. AKVAsmart is still learning how to cope with them easily. The requirements for the first release of Superior Control.net have been in a flux. The main reason for this is that the first version was limited, targeting a dynamic group of selected customers. As discussions continued and feedback from development arrived, it happened that a company was taken out of the group. This meant that this customer's requirements were no longer valid for the first release. Similarly, other companies would be added to the group, bringing their own requirements with them.

8.7 Outlook

Framework releases are planned to happen rarely. They will normally occur only when a new product or a major new version of an existing product is released. Due to this, patches to the released framework will be avoided. Releasing new or updated plug-ins is easier and will happen much more frequently. It may be necessary to mask framework bugs in plug-ins. This has actually happened when a bug in the framework was exposed by a single plug-in. Code was added to the plug-in to hide the bug in such a way that the fix does not trigger if it is run on a corrected framework. The developing framework was patched, and will be released with the next version of the framework, when the next product ships.

9

Bosch Gasoline Systems

with Christian Tischer
Birgit Boss
Mirjam Steger
Juha Kuusela

Company facts of Bosch Gasoline Systems

Organisational size: $\sim$ 1,000 developers.

Starting Mode: Strategic focus, based on existing assets.

Experienced improvements:
- Reduction of calibration effort (–20%) and maintenance.
- Reduction of the resource consumption (20–30%).
- Product line definition reflecting market variance.

Business: Addressing new business challenges was a major driver. Three market segments were identified as a starting point.

Architecture: A new software architecture was developed, but assets were derived from the existing asset base.

Process: Bosch works on CMMI level 3. Systematic process engineering provided an important basis for product line development.

Organisation: A restructuring of the organisation was necessary to reflect the different roles in a product line organisation.

9.1 Introduction

Robert Bosch GmbH is one of the largest automotive suppliers. The company was founded in 1886 and works in the areas of automotive and industry technology. In 2005 the company had about 251,000 employees in more than 140 countries.

Within Robert Bosch GmbH the division for gasoline systems is one of the largest organisations with more than 1,000 developers. As basically every new engine control leads to a new variant, the total number of produced variants is already in the range of thousands, thus providing a good basis for the introduction of a product line engineering approach.

9.2 Motivation

Today's automotive software systems must deal with a set of requirements that is unique in the software community. While requirements on cost-efficiency and variability are addressed in today's software solutions, new challenges like standardisation, software sharing and growing system and organisational complexity must be faced. These changes require new approaches to find a trade-off to satisfy these needs.

Figure 9.1 illustrates the increase in complexity of an engine control unit in terms of resources, system components, features and software parameters over the last 10 years.

In the past, the approach of Bosch Gasoline Systems[1] to offer "best in class" solutions was based on the development of a very powerful platform that

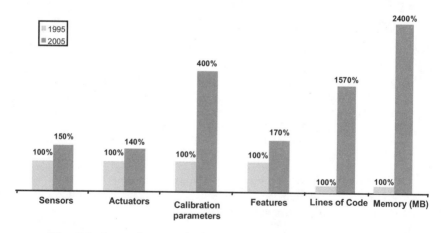

Fig. 9.1. Increasing complexity of gasoline engine control systems

---

[1] From here on, the term 'Bosch' is used as a short hand for 'Bosch Gasoline Systems'

included a broad range of functionality. With increasing product complexity and product variants, the strong focus on a platform-based development shows critical risks:

- High resource consumption
- Complex software integration and calibration procedures.

These risks may result in less competitive project and product costs.

The challenge of mastering increasing complexity at low costs, with high quality and with shorter time to market was the main driver for starting improvement initiatives for process and product excellence. To improve the process maturity of the organisation, Bosch started a CMM-based process improvement program in the year 2000, resulting in the achievement of CMM Level 3 in the year 2002. With respect to product excellence, the company investigated product line engineering in a parallel technology project. This project aimed at evaluating product line engineering in the engine control domain.

With respect to the automotive business context, the following characteristics had to be considered:

- Car manufacturers are competent and demanding customers in terms of functionality, quality and cost in a highly competitive market.
- Due to the specific customer relation (business to business), software requirements have to be negotiated carefully for every product. The goal of Bosch is to achieve an efficient implementation of the product requirements. The ability to sell predefined solutions is limited, depending on the market segment, as the solutions are defined to a large degree by the customer.
- The need of customers for differentiation from other manufacturers leads to a great amount of customer-specific software. Increasingly, customers require software sharing on object code level to protect their specific know-how.
- Innovation by adding or improving functionality faster than competitors is essential for car manufacturers. This leads to a continuous flow of change requests from customers in all project phases.
- Engine control systems must cover a tremendous range of variants. As a result, hundreds of program versions per year must be handled.

Product line engineering offered a comprehensive, systematic concept to analyse and improve business strategies, product development processes as well as technical solutions within the products.

The product line practice areas as defined in the product line practice framework provided helpful guidelines for a common understanding of strategies throughout the organisation [38]. This supported the required customisation of product line engineering to the engine control domain. This helps to achieve the demanding goals in line with the mid-term vision:

Software is built from a common architecture and set of components using a product line approach so that high-quality individually tailored products can be built easily and predictably, using as few hardware resources as possible, thereby reducing overall development costs.

These goals are as follows:

- *Competitiveness*
  - Reduced hardware resource consumption (e.g. scalability)
  - Reduced time to market for new features
- *Development efficiency*
  - Reuse
  - Easy configuration of software products
  - Increased planning accuracy
- *Quality*
  - Interface integrity
  - Reuse of core assets
- *Customer needs*
  - Differentiation by individual software solutions
  - Clear feature-cost mapping

The experiences presented here are specific to Bosch, but they confirm some essential general prerequisites for product line development such as strong leadership, high management commitment and high process maturity.

9.3 Approach

Introducing product line engineering affects several practice areas of both management and engineering. The interdependencies of the practice areas require parallel change and improvement.

This section details the experiences concerning the influence of product line engineering on the following aspects:

- Consideration of business strategy
- Consequences for the work products: software architecture and software components
- Consequences for processes and methods
- Consequences for the tool environment
- Consequences for the organisation

9.3.1 Business Strategy

Market requirements were analysed in the context of strategic product portfolio planning, leading to the definition of different market segments. Accordingly, the former strategy of "one platform for all" was changed in a strategic product line definition:

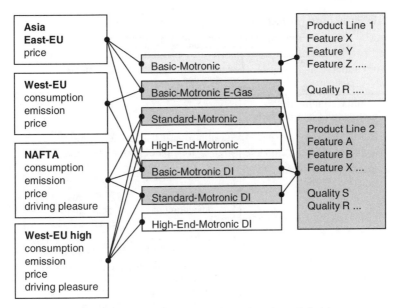

Fig. 9.2. Market segments and product line definition

- One product line for basic engine control systems
- Another product line for standard systems
- Single product development for high feature systems

Each product line has clearly defined features and qualities like hardware resource restrictions or the sharing of software. For each product line, standard software, standard options and customer-specific software options were defined. Some features will be sold separately as software product options. This definition has strong influence on quotation and development activities.

Figure 9.2 shows the mapping of market, market segments and product lines.

Other goals of the business strategy are common software for gasoline and diesel systems and software sharing with customers.

These aspects have a strong influence on the software architecture and process definition. They require exchange of data formats (MSR [151]) and mechanisms, e.g. for know-how protection or interface management.

9.3.2 Work Products: Software Architecture

This section describes the development of a software architecture and the design of software components that fulfil the product line definition, the qualities and address the business goals.

Figure 9.3 shows, in outline, the evolutionary path from the existing software to the new platform. Starting point for the activities is the analysis of

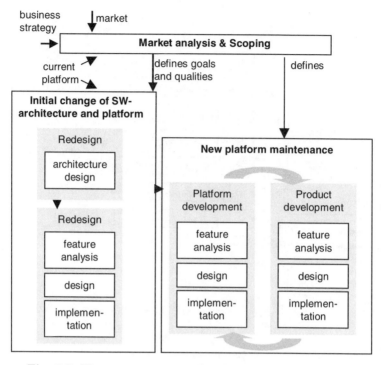

Fig. 9.3. The way to a new product line software architecture

market requirements and existing platform solutions. Driven by the product line definition and the prioritised qualities, there is an initial phase that includes both the design of an adequate software architecture and a redesign of the software components. The new architecture and the redesigned software components provide the basis for product line maintenance.

The development was largely based on the existing asset base. Most of the software components had to be restructured to fit into the new architecture. This restructuring took three years. It had also positive side effects. It has substantially reduced the resource consumption of the software (between 20% and 30%) and has also proven to decrease the maintenance costs.

In the past, the engine control domain was mainly driven by functional requirements. Consequently, non-functional requirements (qualities) were not explicitly considered in the software architecture.

For the development of the new software architecture for the EDC/ME(D) 17-generation, the non-functional requirements were analysed, prioritised and considered as main drivers for the design [66]. One of the main results of the software architecture design is the static view shown in Fig. 9.4.

Some of the most important qualities and the design decisions used to support them are listed below:

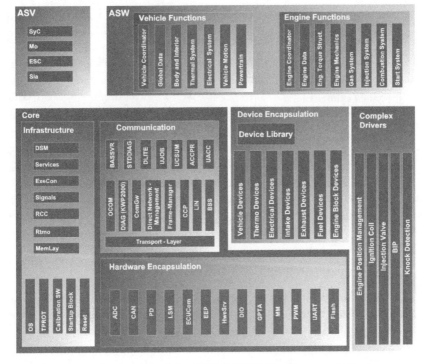

Fig. 9.4. Static view of the EDC/ME(D)17-software architecture

- *Resource consumption* (RAM, Flash and run-time) is very critical in embedded systems due to its cost relevance. The main approach to achieve resource reduction is the redesign of software based on feature analysis using suitable variability mechanisms.
- *Distributed development* requires thorough interface management to achieve stable and lean interfaces.
- *Software sharing* with car manufacturers is supported by the adoption of layers in the software architecture. As a result, a software component in the application layer is independent of how a sensor or actuator or the micro controller works.
- The *reuse goals* are reflected in the architecture in several ways:
  - The "Application Software (ASW)" can be used across different system generations.
  - The "Core" software is highly configurable and may be reused across projects without software changes as only the configuration must be changed.
  - The "Vehicle Functions" can be used in the gasoline engine domain as well as in the diesel engine domain.

- The adoption of a layered software model with hardware encapsulation, device encapsulation and application layer supports reuse of software components.
- The *standardisation of architecture* gains increasing importance. Structuring the application software according to the domain model and the adoption of appropriate layers qualify the architecture as a good basis for standardisation efforts. Bosch introduced their experiences in developing a software architecture for an automotive domain into standardisation initiatives, especially AUTOSAR [8].

To evaluate the new software architecture the Architecture Trade-off Analysis Method (ATAM) [37] was used to check the architecture against business goals, non-functional requirements and to identify risks and non-risks. The risks have been used as a basis for continuous risk management. The experiences show that ATAM predicts future problems fairly well.

9.3.3 Software Components

The redesign of existing software components focused on the qualities reuse, simplification of calibration, optimisation of resource consumption and stable interfaces. We will now describe the main activities in the redesign phase (see Fig. 9.3).

- *Analysis of existing software* (feature analysis [54])
  - Identify and document implemented features and variability in a feature tree.
  - Check on the necessity of these features in the product line definition. Eliminate these features or make them configurable. Document these decisions in the feature tree.
  - Document feature interdependencies (required, exclude) in the feature-tree.
- *Concept development and design of software components* (software component design)
  - Use simpler physical concepts that fulfil the requirements sufficiently.
  - Use a suitable variant mechanism to implement configurable features.
  - Shift from functionality-driven to architecture-driven component structures.
  - Document relations between features and implementations to support ease of configuration and product derivation.
  - Define interfaces (as stable as possible).
  - Document the interfaces of the software component as the basis for interface management and consistency checks.
  - Provide an "overview documentation" for the software component and provide tailored documentation for the selected variant to give easy access to the functionality.

- Baselines for different variants of software component (reference configuration):
  - Document baselines for variants of the software component. These baselines are helpful for product planning, product configuration and integration.
  - After the initial development of these work products, it must be ensured that they are kept up-to-date and are used in the development process (e.g. interface management, product derivation and calibration).

9.3.4 Processes and Methods

The improvement of processes and methods was mainly motivated by the cost and technology challenges. The product line engineering model [38] was used as a systematic approach, a framework and a kind of "checklist" for existing and future product improvement activities. It was not intended to cover all product line engineering practice areas.

Although Bosch has had some form of platform development for years, design and reuse were not systematic or driven by the business strategy. The organisation had to become aware of the difference between this initial approach and the product line idea.

There were three phases:

- *Phase 1*: investigate and customise product line engineering.
- *Phase 2*: design and pilot adequate processes and methods.
- *Phase 3*: roll-out and institutionalise in standard development process.

Phase 1: Investigate and Customise Product Line Engineering

The investigation and adoption of the product line engineering ideas was one of the main tasks in the first phase of the project. Bosch applied the Product Line Technical Probe to identify the starting point in terms of organisation readiness to adopt product line engineering (strengths and challenges). The probe gave valuable feedback about the organisational status, a comprehensive analysis across roles and hierarchy levels and provided helpful recommendations for the next steps. There was reluctance to accept certain results: details of the analysis must often be known to judge the results, and in contrast to CMM assessments, the Bosch staff was not part of the technical probe evaluation team.

Phase 2: Design and Pilot Adequate Processes and Methods

Methods and processes to address the challenges were designed and piloted. One important step was to explicitly separate the tasks and work products for platform- and customer-specific development. Consequently, the following engineering process steps and technical management activities were introduced.

The following are the new engineering process steps:

- Feature-analysis
- Software architecture design
- Interface management
- Software component design
- Packaging / reference configurations

The following are the new technical management activities:

- Scoping
- Initial measurement for product line engineering-goals

Phase 3: Roll-Out and Institutionalise in Standard Development Processes

For the roll-out and institutionalisation phase, it was necessary to enable the organisation to live the new process steps.

Strong management commitment and attention was a key factor for success in this phase. Other important enabling elements are shown in Table 9.1.

The roll-out of the new processes and methods is strongly linked with the redesign of the existing platform software. There was a committed roll-out plan, a steering committee and measurement program to support the change. There was a risk that developers and management would focus on technical aspects of the implementation like resource consumption without paying enough attention to piloting and institutionalisation of the new processes. To minimise

Table 9.1. Roll-out and institutionalisation in standard development process

Action:	**Roll out by redesign of existing platform.**
Purpose:	Initial development of work products like interfaces, feature trees, overview functions, etc.
Helpful:	Product line engineering coaches.
Action:	**Series of product line process workshops with middle management.**
Purpose:	Understanding, acceptance and management support.
Helpful:	Management commitment.
Action:	**Embody new process steps in standard development process.**
Purpose:	Visibility of product line engineering integration in process infrastructure.
Helpful:	Management commitment, existing process infrastructure.
Action:	**Training program for product line engineering and architecture.**
Purpose:	Understand product line engineering and internalise new methods.
Helpful:	Use of domain-specific examples.

this risk, special product line engineering-coaches provided initial support for the developers to implement the new processes in a consistent way.

It was important to embody the new process ideas and process steps in the standard development process. One initiative was a series of workshops with the middle management to discuss the new processes and gain their acceptance and support. Product line engineering must be visible in the standard process even if the new process steps are not binding for the whole organisation. The approach was rolled out gradually. A training initiative provided the necessary skills by covering the software architecture and specific elements of the product line approach.

9.3.5 Tool Environment

New tools and data formats were required to support the development and maintenance of the work products and to fully benefit from the information documented in the development process. Here are some examples for required tool support (see also Fig. 9.5):

- Feature modelling
- Architecture documentation
- Interface documentation, interface checks and interface management
- Documenting the linkage between feature model and implementation
- Feature-based product derivation

Due to the lack of commercial tool support for these tasks, Bosch had to specify and develop their own tools. The tool prototypes that were used in the pilot phase were not very user-friendly and were not integrated in the tool chain. In most cases, they required more effort to use than they could save.

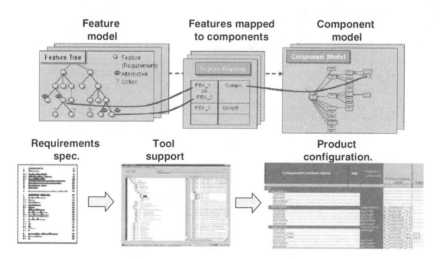

Fig. 9.5. Examples of tool chains

As a result, it was very difficult to motivate the pilot users to use these tools. Based on the experiences with the prototype tools, requirements for the tool environment were specified. The lack of tools leads to a delay of one to two years for the process institutionalisation.

Another tool and data formats aspect concerns the need of sharing software with other business units and with customers. Standardisation on data format level is necessary. This standardisation does addresses not only the code level but also architecture definition and interface description. To address these aspects Bosch participated in standardisation initiatives like AUTOSAR [8].

9.3.6 Organisation

The product line approach not only affects processes and work products, but also has a strong influence on the organisation. One main prerequisite for successful adoption of product line engineering is the assignment of the necessary roles and responsibilities in the line and project organisations.

Consequently, adjustments of the organisation – derived from the software architecture and the new technical development process – are in progress.

These include the following:

- Designation of specific groups for the sub-systems "Core" and "Complex Drivers" (Fig. 9.4).
- Establishing a group responsible for scoping and architecture design.
- A clear separation of organisational units responsible for platform and product development, reflecting the process definition.

9.4 Lessons Learned

This section describes some critical success factors in terms of the management role and the process maturity of an organisation for adopting product line engineering.

9.4.1 Management Role

Changing large organisations is a major challenge for management. The following covers some of the main management success factors in the product line engineering improvement initiative at Bosch.

- Building up product line know-how at Bosch Research.
- Setting up a product line business unit project to investigate and customise product line engineering.
- Roll-out product line engineering into the business unit organisation.

Building Up Product Line Know-How at Bosch Research

In 1995, a Bosch Research department manager adopted the software product line vision for Bosch automotive software. Key success factor in his management role were:

- building up product line know-how
- hiring appropriate software engineers
- piloting small projects within corporate research

Setting Up a Product Line Business Unit Project to Investigate and Customise Product Line Engineering

A department manager for software development at Bosch learned about product line engineering technology in Bosch Research. The following were the important management factors:

- Setting up a project with the task to investigate and customise product line engineering.
- Assigning a project manager with acceptance and standing in the organisation as well as high perseverance. Keeping the team motivated to deepen the product line engineering understanding, while dealing with resistance in the organisation and steering it through a rapidly changing context was a difficult mission.
- Staffing the team with representatives from several development departments (domain experts, software developer, software integrator, process and tool experts) and consultants from Bosch Research.
- Having a powerful promoter in the middle management, who ensured proper funding and who continuously communicated the product line engineering vision to senior management and to the organisation.

Roll-Out Product Line Engineering into Business Unit Organisation

As the project team delivers expected results, management decides to roll out product line engineering in the organisation. That necessitates increased management support. The vice president for system and software development supports product line engineering:

- Product line engineering aspects are embodied in the policy deployment of the software-development departments.
- Capacity is planned and provided to redesign the software according to the requirements resulting from product line engineering.
- A steering committee for the project provides a communication link to other department managers.

At the same time, the project team communicates the ideas and approaches early and continuously to middle managers and key players on the developer's level. This is a major success factor, because of the following reasons:

- In the business culture, consensus on and understanding of new processes is very important for the involved stakeholders.
- Addressing key players on developer's level ensures applicability of methods.

A product line initiative potentially interfaces with every role in an organisation. Therefore, proper and sustained management support can be seen as key in every software product line.

9.4.2 Product and Process Excellence – Product Line Engineering and CMMI

In order to establish an appropriate improvement strategy and to focus the improvement effort, the following aspects have to be considered:

- Market competitiveness
- Product portfolio
- Complexity of products
- Complexity of organisation
- Process maturity

As described in Sect. 9.2, software for engine control units is developed for a highly competitive market in regard to innovation, quality and price with additional requirements for software-sharing between the original equipment manufacturers and suppliers.

For an organisation working in a highly competitive market with a medium or large product portfolio, a strong focus is required on product portfolio management. If the organisation develops complex products within a complex (e.g. distributed) organisation, a strong focus is required on process maturity.

In the case of Bosch, both statements apply. This leads to the demand for a highly mature organisation and the need to set up a clear product management that supports flexible reaction to changing market requirements.

Being aware of these needs, Bosch set up an improvement program consisting of two major steps:

1. CMMI to improve the organisations process maturity.
2. Product line engineering to address software architecture and product portfolio management.

Initially, the improvement strategy chose to put its focus on process excellence (CMMI) over product excellence (SPLE). Since process excellence is the basis for successfully introducing a product line, CMMI was prioritised to be the major process improvement program. The product line engineering activities concentrated on the technical product definition and development issues. Nevertheless, it was necessary to coordinate overlapping improvement activities. In contrast to the CMMI program, it was not intended to cover all practice areas of the Framework for Product Line Practice [38]. Product line engineering was used as a framework and guideline but not as an assessment relevant model. Major milestones of the CMMI improvement activities were the achievement of CMM level 3 in 2002 and CMMI level 3 by the end of 2004. In the product line context, a Product Line Technical Probe (PLTP) was performed in 2001, the software architecture was evaluated using the SEI's Architecture Trade-off Analysis Method (ATAM) in 2002. The most important decisions based on product line engineering were the definition of a second product line in 2003 and the restructuring initiative described in sect. 9.3.1.

The existing process infrastructure based on the CMMI program was an important prerequisite to institutionalise product line engineering. The following were the most important elements:

1. The improvement team for the technical development process. Team leader was a senior manager of the software department and the initiator of the product line project.
2. Definition of process owners (department managers) and process representatives for the new process steps.
3. Documentation of the new process steps in the development handbook of the software and calibration departments, accessible via intranet.
4. Adaptation of existing role definitions and definition of new roles, where necessary.
5. Definition of control boards for product line and architecture issues.

The experience with the two co-existing improvement initiatives over the past three years confirms the decision to put the initial emphasis on CMMI [62], because the product line approach requires a stable, high maturity process organisation to be effective.

9.5 Summary

In the past, the approach of Bosch for developing software for engine control units was based on a very powerful platform development. Product line engineering offered a good framework to further improve product and process excellence and to meet the market requirements regarding quality and costs. Product lines are based on architecture-driven development and therefore help in mastering the increasing product complexity.

The main steps for the adoption of the product line approach for Bosch were scoping, architecture definition and an evolutionary redesign of the existing assets. Scoping is now a part of the product portfolio strategy and is used as a basic input for marketing, platform development and product development. The software architecture supports the important qualities of the engine control domain like encapsulation, software sharing and reuse. This qualifies the architecture as a good basis for standardisation. The product line definition and the architecture were essential inputs for the redesign of the existing software components.

The process organisation (set up in the CMMI program at Bosch), with clear responsibilities for the different steps in the development process, supports the introduction of the new process elements and the systematic and effective development and maintenance of the software assets. Evaluation and adoption of the product line approach were supported by management in each phase. Additionally, early and continuous communication of the concepts was a major success factor for acceptance on middle management and developer level.

Standardising software architecture and supporting systematic software sharing without jeopardising other qualities will remain a challenge over the next years. The lack of (commercial) tools for many activities is a major risk for achieving the intended benefits and final acceptance within the organisation. CMMI-based process improvement and the set-up of a product line complement each other. The product line approach addresses product structure, development and composition. CMMI deals with processes, practices and documentation. Together they have positively contributed to success in a highly competitive market.

DNV Software

with Bjørn Egil Hanssen

Company facts of DNV Software

Organisational size: 100 developers.
Starting Mode: Common support for three production centres.

Experienced improvements:
- Common software foundation, the BRIX™platform.
- Shorter time-to-market, higher product quality and reduced life-cycle costs.
- Stronger alignment across product lines, with respect marketing, sales and development.
- Flexible configuration and integration of solutions in a customer environment, including working processes, organisation and existing systems.

Business: Long-term vision and strategy, involving alignment of production, marketing, sales, product development, processes, platforms and architectures.

Architecture: Second generation BRIX platform.

Process: BRIX platform development process, alignment of application engineering processes.

Organisation: Organisation was changed repeatedly to accommodate changes in the product line and its scope.
Domain and application engineering is done in separate organisations.

10.1 Introduction

DNV is a globally distributed company with a network of 300 offices in 100 countries, and about 5,800 employees. It is among the world's leading providers of services for classification, certification and consulting related to risk, safety and quality. The target industries are shipping, oil and gas, process, rail, automotive and food.

DNV Software is an· independent business unit within DNV providing software products and customised solutions to the same industries, with more than 3,000 customers in 55 countries. One of DNV Software's major customers is DNV itself. As of 2004, DNV Software has about 160 employees, and the development is organised in three product centres and a common support unit as shown in Fig. 10.1.

- *SESAM:* development started in the 1960s addressing the need for strength assessments of large structures in the marine and off-shore industries. The SESAM product line has gone through several technology shifts and major reengineering projects. Today, the newer SESAM products are well aligned on a common platform and architecture developed from 1995 to 2000, while the older ones have a common platform from around 1980.
- *Risk Management Software (RMS)*: started developing products for risk and consequence analysis for the process and off-shore industries in the early 1980s. In 1990, RMS was acquired by DNV. Today, the RMS product line is quite diverse. It is the result of independent product development projects. However, a common software platform for the mathematical models has been established as well as a common software framework for some of the products.
- *Nauticus*: started as a major development project in the early 1990s, initiated by the DNV Maritime business area to support and improve their wide range of services for the marine industry, described in full detail below.

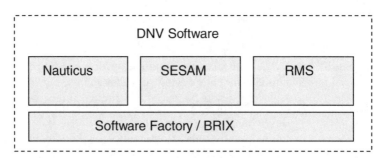

Fig. 10.1. DNV Software's development organisation: three product centres and a common support unit

The purpose of the *Software Factory* unit is to support the three product centres in cost-effective development, maintenance and support of high-quality software. The unit provides a software platform called *BRIX*, development tools and methodology. Software Factory plays a central role in DNV Software with respect to product line engineering.

DNV Software has known two generations of software product line engineering. The first generation was performed at the product-centre level. Development teams within each centre carried out product line engineering to different degrees. The current generation is performed at the DNV Software level. It aims to exploit potential synergies across the product centres, similar to Philips' product population approach [148]. This chapter reports on DNV Software's experiences with both generations of product line engineering. With respect to the first generation, it focuses on the Nauticus product centre.

10.2 Motivation

The main business goals for Nauticus were

- more efficient, streamlined and higher quality services towards the customers
- up-to-date information about vessels and fleet: globally available both internally and to customers throughout the life-cycle of the vessels

This required the establishment of a whole new range of IT services as well as substantial changes to the DNV Maritime organisation and work processes. At the system level the resulting major design criteria were as follows:

- Flexible configuration to meet the organisation's need for evolution.
- Efficient global integration and reuse of both existing and new applications and information across many disciplines.

Supporting the common needs of the Nauticus product line required a substantial effort – close to 40 man-years – to establish BRIX, of a common software platform. The first generation BRIX was based on Microsoft's COM technology [32].

At the end of the 1990s, the major software development units in DNV were organised into one unit called DNV Software. The success of the product line engineering approach as used in Nauticus did not go unnoticed. Great potential for improvement at DNV Software was recognised with respect to the following:

- Reducing life-cycle costs and shorter time to market.
- Creating products of higher quality that are more consistent across product lines.
- Obtaining a higher degree of reuse and reducing duplication of functionality.
- Aligning the product centres and the product lines.

The common software platform approach was perceived as a key factor to
Nauticus' success, and it was desirable to extend the scope of BRIX to all
DNV Software's product centres to realise potential benefits.

In 2000, DNV decided to develop a second generation BRIX platform,
based on Microsoft .NET technology [95], aiming at supporting, aligning and
integrating all three product centres and the corresponding product lines.
These product lines have a high degree of commonality. There is variability
in several dimensions, e.g. disciplines, work processes, deployments and technical infrastructure. The long-term benefit of managing and supporting the
commonality and variability is potentially very high.

Although there is a high degree of similar features in their products, the
product centres differ in many ways: history and culture, technology, development processes and maturity with respect to product line engineering. In
this context, the following are the major challenges:

- Achieving a common platform and technology alignment.
- Succeeding with in-house development for and with reuse.
- Making good decisions, balancing long-term and short-term needs with
  respect to timing, cost, benefit and product life-cycle issues.

10.3 Approach

DNV has known two generations of software product line engineering. Both
will be described in separate sections.

10.3.1 First Generation Product Line Engineering

DNV Maritime set a high-level and long-term vision for Nauticus:

> To establish a common information repository ("product model") con-
> taining or referring all information accumulated for an object, e.g. a
> vessel, throughout its life-cycle. This should enable the transfer of
> information on the object between all involved actors, including feed-
> back of experiences accumulated during the objects life-cycle, for effi-
> cient delivery of high quality services and for continuous learning and
> improvement.

The vision was concretised and illustrated through a series of mock-ups.
These were used to share the vision within the project team, the customer
organisation and the top-level management. The project received full support
from the top-level management.

The Nauticus project started almost from scratch. Some applications existed, but most of the functionality to support the business needs had to
be developed or reengineered. Nauticus avoided the mistake to cement the

as-is customer organisation and working processes, opting for facilitating re-organisation, business process reengineering and business development instead. With respect to this, the architecture team foresaw a strong need for flexible evolution, i.e. variation over time. Other major dimensions of variation were

- *Domains*: from technical engineering applications to administrative information systems.
- *Deployment*: from stand-alone to globally distributed deployment.
- *Networks*: from high-bandwidth LANs to low-bandwidth, unreliable WAN.
- *Actors*: many different actors, e.g. surveyors, managers, ship owners, authorities, etc.

Nauticus development was organised into three sub-projects:

1. *Tools*: focused on delivering end-user tools, which supported the user in carrying out specific tasks.
2. *Common Ship Description (CSD)*: focused on establishing a common domain information model that defined all the data entities for Nauticus.
3. *BRIX*: focused on delivering a common software platform with development tools support, covering the general needs for the whole product line.

The scope of the software platform was in effect determined by the dimensions of variation and a key decision to base the product line on Microsoft technology in general and COM specifically. However, the scope of the product line itself was fairly open to allow future extensions within the constraints of the common platform.

The BRIX software platform put constraints on both the Tools and CSD sub-projects:

- Prescribed software architectures for tools development, with supporting software frameworks and services.
- Common GUI guidelines for tools development.
- Precise semantics and syntax restrictions for information modelling in UML class diagrams, with supporting code generation tools and run-time services for data retrieval and persistence.

The BRIX platform development was driven by the needs of the Tools project and an intuitive understanding of how to support the scope of the product line. Although there was close interaction between the Tools and BRIX sub-projects, BRIX had separate development and release cycles and strict change management of the releases. Hence, the common software platform was managed as a separate internal product and could be considered as a third-party product by the Tools project.

BRIX development was organised as a set of projects addressing various features in the platform. The project iterations resulted in the incremental development of the platform. In the source control system, the development projects worked on separate development branches and integrated back to the main platform branch when a project or iteration was finished. This allowed releases of the platform even during ongoing major developments.

The first generation BRIX platform was tuned for rich client-side functionality and for deployment either in stand-alone or in a global WAN, also including an off-line mode of operation. The platform had several important mechanisms supporting the commonality and variability in the Nauticus product line:

- *Workflow*: it supports the explicit representation of the working processes in an organisation. A process is defined as a composition of isolated tasks. There is an end-user tool supporting the user in performing each task. Often the same task will be done in different processes. Hence, the supporting tools are reused in different process definitions.
- *BRIX Explorer*: it hosts the process instances and tools compliant with the BRIX tool architecture, thus providing a common overall integration, organisation and presentation of different applications. See the example in Fig. 10.2.
- *Common Information Repository and Services* [6]: the database schema and data access code is generated based on the common information model, as described in UML. Combined with generic platform code this provides the tools with a common set of services for accessing shared data. This is an important mechanism for close integration of loosely coupled tools.

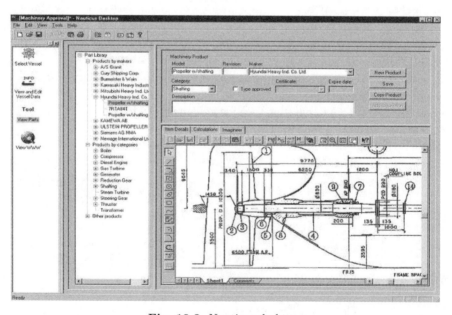

Fig. 10.2. Nauticus desktop

Figure 10.2 shows a screen shot from Nauticus, with work process tasks in the leftmost pane and an associated end-user tool to the right of it for the current task, both hosted in the BRIX Explorer. The end-user tool is composed of several sub-tools by utilising the tool framework's support for nested tools. In this case, at the bottom, a part of a ship design is shown.

In Nauticus a process definition may be considered as a product consisting of tasks and associated tools. That is, a new product may be configured from the common asset base by creating a new process definition. It will typically reuse existing tools and require some new tools to be developed. New tools may be specific for the new product or generally applicable across products in the product line. This results in a high degree of development for and with reuse, growing the base of reusable assets. The workflow concept with plug-in end-user tools supports flexible variation in both space and time.

This flexibility is also supported in the customer organisation, allowing reorganisation and business process reengineering according to improved practice and new business needs. When reengineering the business process, the basic tasks to be carried out and the information needed for task execution often remain the same, but the overall process changes, typically removing administrative tasks. Thus, the domain information model and end-user tools can still be used.

10.3.2 Second Generation Product Line Engineering

When DNV Software was established, the Tools and CSD sub-projects of Nauticus became the Nauticus product centre. The BRIX sub-project became the Software Factory unit, also strengthened with a group focusing on software process improvement.

Although the original Nauticus development was carried out without awareness of product line concepts and principles, the project organisation, processes and organisation of software assets resemble many product line engineering recommended practices.

Business, Organisation and Processes

Before the establishment of DNV Software, there was some collaboration and attempts of alignment between the different software product units. Although some significant integration was carried out, a lack of common management support and commitment limited the results of these efforts.

When DNV Software was established, the new leadership wanted to strengthen the integration and alignment between the product centres to increase the business performance. The following were the two main means to fulfil this objective:

1. A long-term vision and strategy for integration and alignment of the product centres, both with respect to marketing and sales, product development, development processes and software platforms and architectures.

2. Development of the second generation BRIX common software platform, as part of the new strategy, extending the scope from Nauticus to the whole of DNV Software.

Although the first generation BRIX platform was generic and domain independent, it was not adequate as a future common platform for DNV Software for several reasons:

- It was too comprehensive, proprietary and constraining, and did not provide possible migration paths for existing products; it required full reengineering. Also, the platform enforced too many architectural decisions and thereby excluded too many products from using it. Most importantly, it had limited support for server-centric systems.
- Several components in the platform were difficult to use due to insufficient quality, testing and documentation, in addition to the complexity of the Microsoft COM basis technology.
- Microsoft had announced a major technology shift from COM to .NET. That made it unattractive to invest in a COM-based platform.

Despite its limitations and weaknesses, the first generation BRIX was successful. But with the extended scope of the second generation platform, new variability requirements were added:

- *More flexible workflow*: should support both fixed, predefined work processes as well as more dynamic, evolving work processes.
- *More flexible deployment*: across various infrastructures, e.g. stand-alone, smart clients, off-line clients, web-clients, web-services.
- *More flexible operation*: across different trust boundaries, i.e. intranet, extranet and Internet.

The development of the second-generation platform took a revolutionary approach, but the platform supported evolutionary adoption by products developers. Major concepts from the first generation were refined and reimplemented from scratch on the new .NET technology platform, as illustrated in Fig. 10.3. To distinguish the two platform generations, the existing one was renamed BRIX.COM while the new one was named BRIX.NET. When BRIX.NET started, BRIX.COM was used across all of Nauticus and needed to be supported for several years ahead, up to and including 2005.

No changes were made to the line organisation. The BRIX group had about six to ten members at any moment, and a yearly budget for development and maintenance of common software assets that was financed through the product centres. In agreement with the management team, the resources in the BRIX group were reprioritised for development of the new platform. Only support and a minimum of maintenance were carried out for the existing platform.

The scope of the BRIX.NET platform was all of DNV Software's products, even though the product lines are very diverse. The platform was designed to be open and inclusive rather than closed and exclusive. Business benefit was

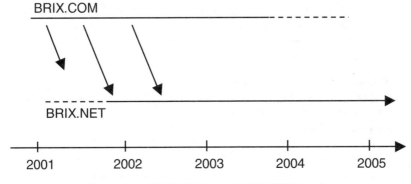

Fig. 10.3. BRIX.COM and BRIX.NET tracks

maximised by utilising the platform on all products to the greatest possible extent.

The following were the main high-level design directions for the new common platform:

- *Non-enforced and under-specified architecture*: it is not feasible to have a common architecture for all products. Some parts of the architecture will not be specified, leaving design decisions to the product development. Other parts of the architecture will be specified, but are not applicable to all products or are in conflict with specific product requirements. Hence to accommodate these products the architecture is non-enforced.
- *Modularised features*: to allow the products to use only those platform features that are relevant, it is important that the platform features are loosely coupled and have a focused area of concern.
- *Open and transparent*: to allow product development to make specific extensions or substitutions, it is important that the platform is in line with the underlying technology and does not add unnecessary layers of abstraction. In this case, the mainstream use of the Microsoft .NET technology was promoted, sometimes just by providing guidelines for how to use the technology instead of providing executable software components. This also makes integration easier at all layers.

There was a need to build competence on the new technology, and the first half year was mostly spent on technology studies and prototypes. After the initial phase, several platform development projects were started:

- *BRIX.NET Modelling and Data Access (MDA) services*: to migrate and enhance the BRIX.COM Common Information Repository and Services layers and the information modelling approach.
- *BRIX.NET Security*: to specify infrastructure requirements and establish a set of services for secure authentication but flexible authorisation of end-users for access to product features.

- *BRIX.NET Workflow*: to establish a new set of workflow services accommodating the existing workflow solutions and future needs. As part of this, a BRIX.NET Explorer was developed, providing client-side hosting similar to the BRIX.COM Explorer.

As a result of these projects, a BRIX.NET-recommended architecture was defined, specifying the logical layers and alternative physical deployments. Several minor projects were also carried out to establish an efficient development environment, including automatic build and test, exception handling, logging, etc.

During the development of the second-generation BRIX there was a stronger awareness of the importance of running platform development projects parallel to and in close co-operation with one or more product development projects. This allowed progress in the long-term direction while providing short- to mid-term business value. Many good ideas for common assets may be suggested, but if there are no product development projects to use and validate an idea, it should be postponed or rejected. Otherwise, a substantial investment will be made with uncertain long-term return. Common assets do not have any business value before they are used in a product that is sold to a customer. As in all software development, it is difficult to develop useful common assets without real requirements and customer involvement.

Architecture

The major components of BRIX.NET, as shown in Fig. 10.4, provide important variation mechanisms. The figure depicts the major BRIX constituents and which layers of the high-level architecture they support.

BRIX.NET MDA is a model-driven data access architecture. It supports the generation of databases and data access layers from information models, Fig. 10.5. It is inspired by OMG MDA [100]. The information models are expressed in UML class diagrams.

BRIX.NET MDA provides the following variation mechanisms to support commonality and variability across a product line:

- *Basic models and view models:* a *basic model* is a model for which there exists a persistent (database) implementation. Information quality and maintenance are key issues for basic models. A *view model* is an application-specific view on information that is derived from one or more basic models.[1] The distinction between basic models and view models allows a product line to share a database model – e.g. the Nauticus Common Ship Description – such that each application can have one or more private (view) models with its own customised view of the data.
- *Role models:* the use of role modelling for information modelling [5] is novel and different from role modelling in general [83, 56]. It is characterised by

---

[1] The relationship between basic and view models is more formally described in [4]

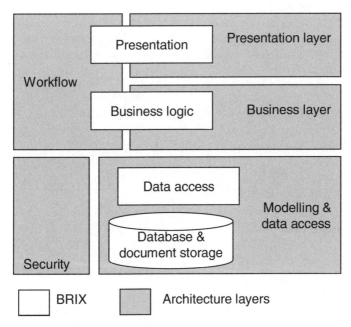

Fig. 10.4. Major BRIX constituents in relationship to the architectural layers

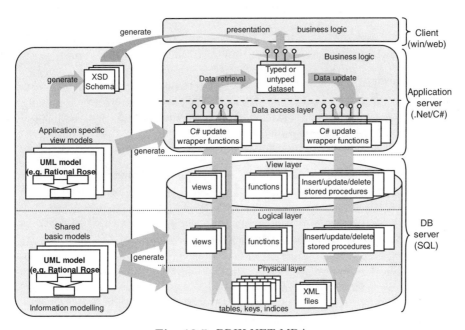

Fig. 10.5. BRIX.NET MDA

being conceptually trivial and easy to implement, but nevertheless useful in a pragmatic model management setting. The essence is that a particular information object can play any number of roles, simultaneously or over time, and each role has a set of properties corresponding to, e.g., a UML class or a database table. An object is linked to its roles via its unique object identifier. Role play and inheritance are similar, but a key distinction is that role play is dynamic while inheritance relationships are static for the objects involved. The use of role models allows development of pure general models with a well-defined area of concern to be shared across a product line. In a specific product, these can be combined with product-specific role models to cover the extra need for information.

- *Model-driven development:* a model-driven approach accommodates variability with respect to generating implementation for different target technology platforms, like Microsoft SQL Server and Oracle. It also supports commonality across the whole product line by using the same conventions and best practices during generation. Variability is served by using different conventions and best practices, especially as these evolve over time.
- *Physical versus logical database layer:* the clear separation between physical and logical layer allows schema changes on tables, views, procedures, indexes, keys, or similar for performance or scalability purposes, while maintaining a stable logical layer as long as the database semantics are unchanged. The physical layer can be optimised differently in different products and installations according to specific needs in product or installation.
- *Logical versus view layer:* Corresponds to basic versus view model at the implementation level.

BRIX.NET Workflow supports flexible and dynamic product configuration according to organisational needs [31]. The configuration is achieved by defining process templates consisting of sub-processes and activities with associated end-user tools. This gives good support for commonality and variability both in product development, configuration and its use in a customer organisation:

- *Breeding and sharing of best practices in a customer organisation:* process templates are shared across an organisation and can be evolved as the organisation learns, allowing commonality and variability over time.
- *Sharing of sub-processes:* the same sub-process can be reused in different super-processes, thus supporting commonality and variability in super-processes.
- *Open super-processes*: a super-process template can be incomplete, i.e. some sub-processes have to be defined after instantiation. This allows variation at process instance level, by either dynamic definition of a sub-process or reuse from existing predefined sub-processes.
- *Binding to end-user tools:* the same tool can be reused in different process templates. Also, the same logical activity in different templates can be associated with different tools, e.g. to allow local variation. Hence, the explicit representation of associations between tools and process activities supports both commonality and variability.

- *Integrating with third-party applications:* process activities may also be associated with third-party applications, allowing product configuration and integration with other applications in the customer's organisation.

The combination of the above variation mechanisms allows variability in both space and time, both across a product line and for a specific customer installation. In simple cases where the necessary end-user tools already exist, a new product can be configured by defining a new process template.

BRIX.NET Security provides a set of services and an infrastructure specification that supports secure authentication of users and flexible authorisation to applications and products, especially when deployed on extranet or Internet. To some degree it also supports licensing through the authorisation mechanism. BRIX.NET Security supports the following commonality and variability, also illustrated in Fig. 10.6. A product contains one or more configurations of services. A service is associated with one or more features. An organisation has a number of users being member of one or more user groups. An organisation buys one or more products and different user groups are authorised to use more or less of the product's service configurations.

- *Sharing of features (services) in different security contexts*: a product contains one or more security configurations of services. This allows sharing of features in different products and security configurations and also products and security configurations to evolve, e.g. introducing a new feature in an existing product as part of an upgrade.
- *Flexible configuration of authorisations*: a user is member of a number of groups, through which he or she is authorised access to a set of features through a number of security configurations.

The configuration of authorisations is also used by Workflow for authorisation of users to carry out different activities.

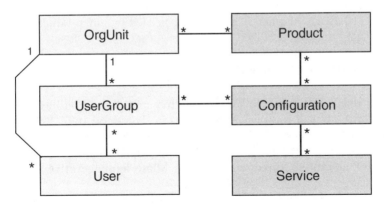

Fig. 10.6. BRIX Security information model

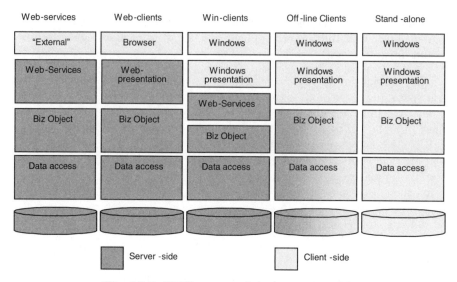

Fig. 10.7. BRIX supported deployment models

The BRIX.NET-prescribed architecture supports commonality and variability with respect to deployment models. At the various layers, components may be reused across different deployments suitable for different infrastructures, as illustrated in Fig. 10.7.

The mainstream use of Microsoft .NET technology in BRIX.NET supports integration on all layers, with both third-party components and external systems. This makes the products more adaptable to variations in their deployment environment, e.g. what other systems exists.

BRIX.NET has no dependencies on BRIX.COM, neither development time nor run-time, but end-user tools based on BRIX.COM may be hosted in BRIX.NET. Hence, products based on BRIX.COM may choose between an evolutionary or revolutionary migration to BRIX.NET. This makes it easy to terminate BRIX.COM when it is no longer needed by any products.

10.4 Results and Impact Evaluation

Nauticus was initiated by DNV Maritime to support their business services. The major roll out of Nauticus applications in the period 1997–1999 has had several direct impact on DNV's Maritime business.[2] The efficiency of services has increased, e.g. approbation time of a mid-ship section has been reduced from three months to three to four days. Many administrative tasks have

---

[2] In addition to the Nauticus system, a new IT infrastructure has been established in DNV, and DNV Maritime has developed its business and organisation. These changes also contributed substantially to the above business achievements

been eliminated and the technical tasks are carried out faster. The increased volume and richness of the services have been handled without increasing the number of staff.

After initial resistance to change, Nauticus users are very satisfied and now consider the system essential to their business. Nauticus is also an integral part of DNV Maritime's marketing profile.

The Nauticus product line is fairly complex, and the approach taken in the first generation was crucial for managing this complexity and supporting the needs for commonality, variability and integration. The approach allowed different development teams to focus on their area of concern. The BRIX team focused on non-functional requirements and common platform support, the CSD team dealt with domain information modelling and the Tools team worked on functional requirements.

All Nauticus development was done using the common platform, resulting in a uniform look-and-feel, uniform code, easier reuse, maintenance and integration. However, maintenance was still expensive due to the complexity of the basis technology combined with varying quality and transparency of the BRIX.COM platform.

The second generation product line engineering was driven by the business needs of the newly established DNV Software unit, while still including the ability to serve DNV Maritime as a key customer.

It was based on the experience with the Nauticus development. The BRIX.NET platform has several important characteristics distinguishing it from the BRIX.COM platform. It has a non-enforced and under-specified architecture, more modularised and orthogonal features, and is open and transparent. The results of these changes are as follows:

- *Faster return on investment*: application developers can utilise what is available in the platform and do the rest on the application level.
- *More inclusive*: easier acceptance and adoption in the SESAM and RMS product centres. Currently, there are major migration activities both in SESAM and in RMS that move existing features to BRIX.NET. For example, SESAM Workflow will be replaced by BRIX.NET Workflow; an RMS product was partly ported to utilise the support for Oracle in BRIX.NET MDA; a higher level domain-specific framework for risk and consequence analysis applications is being developed based on BRIX.NET.

As a side effect, the BRIX platform has also been adopted by application development projects in other parts of DNV.

As discussed in Sect. 10.3.2, BRIX.NET Workflow and BRIX.NET Security provide important variation mechanisms, allowing flexible configuration for a specific customer and reconfiguration during operation. This flexibility of the DNV Software product lines has also become a central marketing concept. "Best Engineering Practice" [48] refers both to DNV's high competence in different industries and to BRIX Workflow's support for breeding best practices.

10.5 Lessons Learned

Key success factors for both the first and the second generation product line engineering have been the establishment of a shared long-term vision, strong management support and leadership and commitment and endurance in the development organisation. Sven Ullring, CEO of DNV from 1985 to 2000, stated that the development and implementation of Nauticus was the achievement he was most proud of during his CEO period.

During both the first and the second generations of product line engineering, platform development has been organised in a separate unit with its own resources and budget. This has been important in order to set and maintain a long-term strategy, and to allow for platform investments exceeding budgets of single product development projects. BRIX is currently financed through the product centres. This is an incentive for the product centres to utilise the platform as far as possible.

From the first to second generation there have been essential changes in the approach to BRIX development. All platform development is now carried out in close co-operation with product development. This validates the platform features against real needs and also gives a more rapid return on investment through use in the products. BRIX resources spend substantial time in product development projects to secure proper adoption of the BRIX platform.

It is important to be realistic about development for reuse and to push development with reuse. The first generation product line engineering in Nauticus was successful both in reuse of the generic BRIX platform and in reuse of domain functionality (tools) between products. However, there was a naïve belief in the reusability of tools just because they could integrate in the same framework. To some degree too much effort was spent on development for reuse without actually achieving reuse. Now, more conscious and clearer decisions are made on when to develop for reuse, considering feature maturity, feature commonality, short- and long-term costs and benefits, time to market and resources available. A feature may well be developed specifically several times and later possibly generalised. Once the investment in a reusable feature has been made, its reuse should be strongly promoted.

Organisations should invest in training courses for major domain assets, like common platforms. To promote the use of the BRIX platform, there are BRIX training courses, for both the first and the second generation. This has been very valuable both to quickly make new developers productive and to reduce the number of support requests to the BRIX team.

When starting the second generation BRIX development, the vision was to provide a common product line architecture for all software development in DNV Software. This vision was not sufficient to meet short- to mid-term needs for integration across the existing product lines. It is not realistic to migrate all existing products to the same implementation platform for the sake of easy integration: it is simply too expensive. Rather, products should evolve on their existing architectures and technologies as long as they are able to serve the needs of their customers cost-effectively. Eventually, they are to be reengineered or migrated to a new architecture. So, other means for integration were needed and the vision was revised:

- To establish a DNV Software product line architecture for all development based on .NET technology.
- To establish a common DNV Software service–oriented architecture for internal integration between product lines and external integration with customers or partners.

A project is currently running to define the DNV Software service–oriented architecture. It mostly deals with the internal standardisation of things like message formats, invocation mechanisms, security control, and also with how to integrate in the BRIX Workflow, which is a central framework. Products will comply by using the prescribed BRIX architecture.

10.6 Outlook

Currently, the product centre organisation has not been able to address the complete potential for alignment of domain assets in all parts of the organisation and there is still too much parallel development. To address this and to achieve better coordination in general, DNV Software was reorganised at the beginning of 2005, as shown in Fig. 10.8. Product centres reorganised to achieve better coordination of marketing and sales activities and alignment of domain functionality.

The Software Factory unit will still be developing BRIX. The Products unit will develop products for mass sale, while the Solutions unit will do

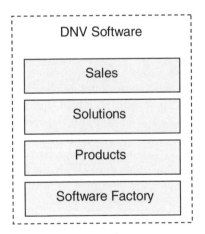

Fig. 10.8. New DNV Software organisation

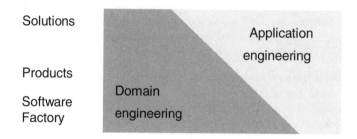

Fig. 10.9. Domain and application engineering effort

custom development, with extensive reuse of software assets from BRIX and Products. The level of domain engineering versus application engineering in the different units is illustrated in Fig. 10.9. Development in the Solutions unit is typically application-specific, more domain engineering in the Products unit, while SoFa/BRIX mostly does domain engineering. This also reflects the time perspective of the development, the Solutions unit look for short-term opportunities, the Products unit has a mid-term focus and Software Factory aims for long-term alignment and integration.

It still remains to be seen how the new organisation will perform. However, product line engineering has been central in DNV Software's product development through two generations, especially from the common platform and technical side, and increasingly also from a marketing and sales perspective. It looks like it is going to stay that way.

market maker Software AG

with Martin Verlage
Thomas Kiesgen

Company facts of market maker Software AG

Organisational size: 25 developers.
Starting Mode: Strategic focus, development from scratch.

Experienced improvements:
- Reduction of time to market: 2–4.
- Break-even: after about five products.
- Reduction of maintenance costs: ~60%.
- Reduced cost of quality (reliability in the field).

Experienced side-effect:
- Increased issue resolution time.

Business: Product line engineering was a key strategic element in addressing a new market segment.

Architecture: A new reference architecture was developed. Assets included open-source and in-house components.

Process: The shift to product line engineering led to a transformation of certain established roles and the addition of new ones.

Organisation: From the start a new organisational unit was set up for product line development.

11.1 Introduction

It was in the year 1999 when a newly formed team at market maker Software AG,[1] Kaiserslautern, Germany, began to develop a software product line for managing and displaying stock market data and financial market news. Starting from a sound basis of domain knowledge in that area, the developers were expected to create a set of new products on a technology-based new market maker. The basic idea was to use web technology as a common infrastructure in all applications for delivering services to customers, as it was the time of the "Internet hype". It soon turned out that the company had to change both the processes and the organisation of software development. More dramatically, the way of thinking about product definition changed. This chapter summarises the changes made to the processes within market maker and the lessons learned over the past five years, when the product line idea was introduced.

11.2 Motivation

market maker is a small-sized company in the south-west of Germany. At the end of 2004, market maker employed about 60 people, from which around 25 developed software for several product lines. The annual revenues continually grew and are now at €5 million per year. market maker's business is domain-centric, meaning that all products and services focus on stock market data including financial news. The job is to collect data from numerous exchanges and contributors, validate and store it, analyse, aggregate, repackage and distribute it. The data is delivered as raw data as well as displayed in client software developed by market maker. Revenues come from software licenses, data subscriptions and service provisions.

New products are based on the experience the company has gained over 15 years of developing software for stock market data analysis. This was especially important in 1999, when markets were boiling and the demand for innovative products was immense. Not knowing exactly what customers – e.g. banks or independent asset managers – would ask for the next month, one thing was clear: the market for web-based products would become too important to be ignored. Thus, future products had to be based on web technology. Although the company had little experience in this field, the decision was made to invest in this area. Right from the start the new products were considered a product line. All products in that product line would share configurable, customisable and tailorable components in order to save development power when creating similar products for different markets and customers. Thus, the "i*ProductLine"[2] was created.

---

[1] From here on, the term 'market maker' is used as a short hand for 'market maker Software AG'

[2] Pronounced "i-star"

In mid-1999, market maker was growing rapidly. Its main software product then was an application which consisted of a set of specialised tools for managing, analysing and displaying stock market data and news. The tools were packaged and sold as modules. However, the software always contained the complete functionality; packages were simply activated by means of a key. The product was written in Borland Delphi and C++. Access to databases containing all relevant data was available on subscription. The main product and the databases embodied 10 years of experience in the application domain. A major release was available at least once a year. A software development team was constantly working on the product.

Due to technological developments and the "Internet hype", market maker decided to enter the Internet market too. As no one knew exactly which products had to be built, the question arose: How to determine future assets? At this time, the idea of employing a product line approach was born. In those early stages, some key decisions were made:

- To use a component-based approach in order to quickly build products from validated blocks and to allow for flexible development.
- To build a new team to cope with new technology demands.
- To finish first projects within twelve months.
- To build products without spending too much time on individual projects and maintenance in order to set people free for new projects.

At that time, the company was in close contact with the Fraunhofer Institute for Experimental Software Engineering (FhG IESE). FhG IESE was then researching a new approach to product line engineering called PuLSE [122, 19]. Co-operation was attractive for both partners: market maker did not have a research department that could tailor an immature approach to the company's specific needs, and FhG IESE was interested in having a validation partner for their novel approach.

Today, the i*ProductLine is instantiated for various markets: information systems for asset managers in banks, market data servers integrated in brokerage systems for online ordering, specialised data display services for metal traders and grains and oilseed traders, content provisioning for financial web portals, data aggregation and delivery to batch processes for risk assessment in financial institutions and image production showing price charts of shares and other securities for websites. Most parts of the product line are implemented in Java 2, with small parts written in C++. Sample product instances[3] are as follows:

- *WIP*: a platform for tailorable public Internet websites offering stock market data and news.

---

[3] In 2004 market maker was acquired by Vereinigte Wirtschaftsdienste GmbH (vwd). This led to a renaming of these products to *vwd web manager, vwd market manager (web), vwd data manager (xml)*, and *vwd portfolio manager (web)* respectively

- *INFO-AGENT*: a web-based information service for bank employees who advise customers, or who need to look up market data.
- *XML-Market*: an XML interface to the data services used by banks for real-time portfolio evaluation, display of data in web services not operated by market maker, and delivery of small pieces of data for special-focus services operated by third parties.
- *Publisher*: a service for extracting raw or evaluated portfolio data which then are stored on a secure web server that only registered users have access to.

Figure 11.1 shows a screenshot of the "INFO-AGENT" product which is used by bank employees for retrieving stock market data in order to inform customers with regard to specific questions about their investments. The field labelled "Kurse" in the top left-hand corner contains information on the current market situation; the same data are displayed in the chart to the right of this area. The box in the top right-hand corner contains news headlines related to the company. In the bottom left-hand corner, a historical chart shows the price development over a period of several months. The field labelled "Stammdaten" contains stock-related data, e.g. the ticker symbol used by the exchange where the stock is traded, or the International Stock Identification Number (ISIN). The bottom right-hand corner shows consensus estimates for that stock, e.g. earnings per share.

The set of data is a unique aggregation for one particular product. Other products may require different data sets, hence variability must be provided by the data management components of the i*ProductLine.

Variability within the INFO-AGENT product relates to several dimensions. For every customer, the following features are configurable:

- *Skin*: appearance of the web pages (colours, fonts, graphical items and the position of data items on the page)
- *Data universe*: customers subscribe to single data packages, access is granted only to these sets.
- *Data quality*: for real-time trade data, customers have to pay license fees to the exchanges. Often this data quality is not required, so the system delivers delayed data, which is less expensive.
- *Functionality*: advanced INFO-AGENT features, e.g. the advanced search function, or price data charting, are available at a higher charge.

These variabilities apply to a very small set of similar products only. Other products differ more fundamentally.

Services, that are provided by the products, are either anonymous or require user authentication to build up sessions during data access. Protocols provided for data access are HTTP, FTP, JDBC and SOAP. Data is delivered in raw ASCII, HTML or PDF format, in binary formats of spreadsheet applications, and in portable networks graphics format. Stock market data streams into the system at rates of several thousand updates per second. Databases

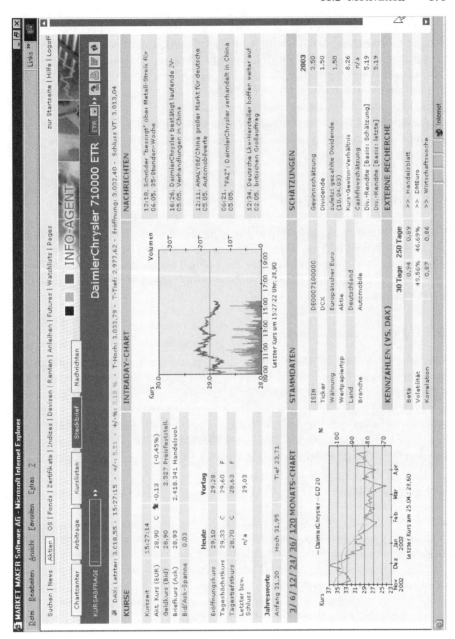

Fig. 11.1. Screenshot of INFO-AGENT, an i*ProductLine product

from more than a dozen content providers are accessed for importing data or deriving more aggregated data by computation. Availability requirements for certain services may exceed 99.9%. These facts should give an overview of the demands on the system.

The reference architecture covers approximately 25 coarse-grain components, like user data management or real-time stock market data processing. Components live in a general-purpose container which is responsible for providing context, instantiating, starting, pausing, stopping and connecting components.

11.3 Adoption Process

When the decision was made that the new products would be part of a product line, some issues turned up, either implicitly or explicitly, which later proved to be important to the success of the product line. This section describes some of them which are also important for understanding changes to the organisation and the processes.

11.3.1 Fast Time to Market

Soon after the start of the project, the first business talks with potential customers began. The developers knew that the first product instance had to be delivered within 12 months after the start of the project. This pressure helped to take decisions when the reference architecture was discussed. Domain engineering is customer-distant by nature, so there was a danger of over-engineering the software and never finishing it. Any product line engineering effort should carefully define criteria for the end of development.

11.3.2 New Team

All i*ProductLine developers were newly hired. They had no history in earlier market maker products, and their attention was not distracted by other projects. Nevertheless, the new development team was integrated very closely into the company so that they could benefit from the domain expertise of their colleagues. Lots of discussions gave developers from other projects the opportunity to review the current status of the development work and to share their experiences regarding special cases. On the other hand, the i*ProductLine developers helped to identify implicit assumptions embodied in the legacy systems, which were used as encapsulated components in the i*ProductLine.

11.3.3 Early Focus on Applications

The primary tasks were to identify requirements by scoping and to define the reference architecture. Emphasis was put on the technological aspects when the spectrum of requirements was clear. Domain engineering was stopped, and a first product instance (the INFO-AGENT application shown in Fig. 11.1 on p. 171) was built which served as a prototype for testing the ideas for the product line. The immediate testing of the reference architecture helped to identify and remove design flaws early.

11.3.4 No Separation of Domain and Application Engineering Teams

In order to avoid the isolation of ideas and to enable feedback from initial product line customers, there was just one team performing both domain engineering and application engineering activities. Domain engineers could observe their components in real life and determine further requirements.

11.3.5 Encapsulation of Legacy Systems

As the company-owned software had matured for more than ten years, it was a booster for the project to define interfaces that encapsulated these components and integrated them into the overall system. This way, the legacy software helped to concentrate on the main issues when developing the product line. Later, some legacy systems were substituted by code written from scratch.

The legacy systems written in Delphi were encapsulated by Java wrappers which communicated with the components' COM interface. The wrappers helped to easily integrate the legacy components into the overall system. No development effort had to be spent on domain issues; nevertheless, some effort went into the technical solution, since Java and Delphi/COM were not as easily integrated as supposed in the beginning.

11.3.6 Simple Architectural Style

Due to the complexity of application servers and high license fees for commercial application servers, the components of an early version resided in a self-developed container. *Inversion of control* was chosen as a main architectural style i.e. the component is controlled by its container and does not maintain its own state. Later, this turned out to reduce maintenance effort. Communication between components is based on Java Remote Method Invocation (RMI) which is used to establish an asynchronous, SEDA-based style[4] to address high-performance requirements. This architectural style allows for high scalability. The whole system can run on several real machines; each machine is allowed to host multiple containers, and each container may carry several components of the same type. The components are instantiated and connected using configuration files.

---

[4] More information on SEDA can be found in Sect. 11.4.2, p. 179

Using Java interfaces consequently helped to adjust components to different contexts. By means of instantiation parameters, components are tailored to show a specific behaviour for a single product instance. Moreover, parameters determine which of a component's interfaces will be used. This helped to design interfaces for special purposes rather than populating a single interface with methods and method variants.

11.3.7 Effective Communication

Defining product instances, caring for their development and pushing them into the market was done by a small group of people. The main task was to share the vision of the new product line and its instances among all employees. Decision makers directly communicated their ideas to the developers and got immediate feedback on the feasibility. Experienced sales people helped to scope the product line and shared their knowledge about the way customers think. The development team was not left alone with decisions concerning the flexibility of components, which compensated for the partial lack of domain knowledge. Differences in the understanding of requirements and software could be determined in regular meetings, and conflicts arose rarely.

11.3.8 Immediate and Reliable Decisions

The vision of the new product line was developed in response to changing market demands and new technologies. All decisions made during the development of the i*ProductLine could be measured against this vision. It was clear which directions were reasonable for the projects and how to prioritise the projects. Everyone in the team knew why a certain decision was taken, and that it was consistent with the vision. Reliable decisions were important to keep the team motivated and focused.

11.3.9 Coaching

The research co-operation with FhG IESE helped to tailor the PuLSE approach and to get coaching during the application of the new knowledge.

11.3.10 Small Investments

The pressure of immediate market introduction helped to drive the projects into a direction where success and potential gains could be analysed early within twelve months. Especially for small companies, it is necessary to prove within a short timeframe whether an investment in a new technology is successful or not.

11.4 Current Process

From a business perspective, the introduction of product line engineering at market maker was quite successful. The i*ProductLine produces a significant share of the company's revenues and helps to increase business. Although it is impossible to measure the effects of the new technology exactly because of the uncontrolled setting, and because data from previous, similar projects is not available, management estimates can provide a rough understanding of the improvements.

11.4.1 Business

Today, setting up a new website for displaying stock market data takes only a couple of days, compared to the weeks it took in the beginning. During scoping and requirements definition, it turned out that layout and design is a crucial factor for customers. The architecture reflects this, and open source packages like Velocity [150] help to quickly define and change the appearance of web pages. According to our estimates, this reduced initial project time and effort by more than 50%.

Understanding product instances as flexible, interacting components helped to win projects market maker never targeted before. Instead of building a product and offering it on the market, individual projects were identified in co-operation with the customers.

The overall cost, not including the cost of learning product line engineering itself, but covering the initial investment in the product line, has paid off. Gains are primarily caused by reduced maintenance costs. Especially, the variety of products would be too expensive to maintain without a product line approach, so that only some would be updated, while others would be left unchanged. When creating a product, the average cost reduction is estimated at some 30%.[5] In general, controlling projects differs because the effort of overall activities, e.g. refactoring in order to keep components structurally clean, has to be assigned to each product instance.

Quality itself, understood as reliability in the field, did not change in comparison to the "traditional" way of development since the developers have always strived to deliver high-quality software. What did change dramatically was the *cost* of quality. Building product instances on a foundation of already tested components saves time and money, which in turn justifies higher efforts in product line engineering for impact analysis, complex design and coding.

11.4.2 Architecture

The latest version of the system contains about 500,000 lines of Java 1.4 code in about 2,000 classes. The architecture of the i*ProductLine is organised in

---

[5] Excluding the first five projects, which were less efficient due to learning and process optimisation

layers, so that a traditional multi-tier system is built. Each layer consists of a number of component instances which reside in a common framework to control and bind them. Variability of the overall system is mainly controlled by instantiation parameters of the components. The instantiation parameters are specified in central configuration files which are passed to the components while creating them. One of the components is the "chicago" component for data processing, which will be described in detail now.

The component processes financial information related to stock market activities. This information is read from a number of data streams from different sources (feeds). Here, we limit our view to the price feed that contains mainly trading information such as bid and ask prices, trade prices, volumes, etc., but also information about securities such as security names and ISINs. The feed arrives as an ASCII-character stream to be read from a socket. Data records in the stream represent a certain type of information (incremental or complete update, delete of a record sent previously, etc.), a unique security identifier (vendor-key) and a number of key-value pairs representing the actual update information. Depending on the record type, only a subset – usually a small subset – of the several hundred defined field keys is present. Secondary information can be derived from the feed, including indicators such as volatility and more complex calculations.

The main task of the chicago component is to store primary and secondary feed information and to make that information available by means of some application programming interface. Data is stored as soon as it arrives.

It is important to distinguish between real-time and delayed stock data, because access to real-time data is in general more expensive. For delayed data, the amount of delay usually depends on the stock exchange that distributes the data. For each instance of the product line, we have to decide whether it should store and provide access to delayed or real-time stock data, or both.

The product line's non-functional requirements are dominated by performance, throughput and scalability. The data volume of the security feed reaches approximately 500 KB – several thousands data records – per second during peak times. Thus, storing the feed data within seconds after arrival is the most important problem to be solved by our architecture. Experience also shows that the feed's volume tends to increase slowly but steadily over time, which underlines the importance of scalability.

There is a broad range of product configurations that are part of the product line. The following list provides some prototypical examples and the way they deal with storing the data feeds in time:

- Backend for Internet based general-purpose financial information systems. Provides real-time and delayed data, uses a PushedCache for better performance.
- Backend for special purpose information systems that also offer derived data. Includes RatioCalculator that calculates security type specific secondary data.

- System to create official stock market reports that document every trade that happened on a specific day. No delay feature necessary.
- Delivering end-of-day data to build historic price databases. No need to store TickData, no delay.
- Providing intra-day snapshots for desktop applications.
- Backend for clients that receive real-time push data. Uses a number of PushedCache instances.

Logical View

Figure 11.2 shows a conceptual overview of the i*ProductLine. Boxes, arrows and cylinders represent components, data flow and data stores respectively. The architecture can be roughly thought of as structured in layers. The lowest layer processes incoming data and provides an abstraction over the multitude of different data feeds. These data feeds encompass both real-time feeds directly connected to a stock exchange and the existing market maker pm[x] system which is encapsulated by a Java wrapper.

The incoming data is handled by a multitude of FeedConnectors. A Feed-Connector ensures quality of service of the incoming data stream. If a disconnect with an existing data source occurs, it is capable of replacing this with a data source with lower priority and to switch back once the higher priority

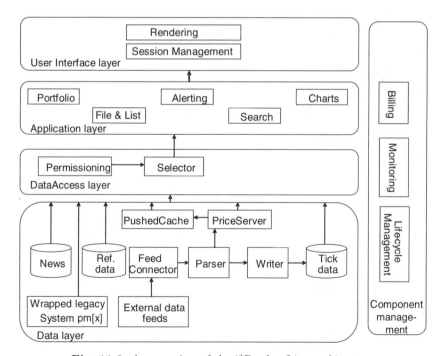

Fig. 11.2. An overview of the i*ProductLine architecture

data source becomes available again. A FeedConnector forwards its incoming data to the Parser component. The resulting information is made persistent by a Writer component.

The interface to the remaining system is formed by the combination of a PushedCache and a PriceServer component. They share the same interface. Depending on the specific configuration, the remaining system can connect to either one without the need for any adaptation. The PushedCache component adds a caching layer on top of the PriceServer component; in case the PushedCache is not able to provide the data, it queries the PriceServer in turn.

The application layer contains the end-user visible presentation services like Charts, Filters and Portfolio definition. The user interface is provided by a web server which uses JavaServer Pages.

The management services include billing and monitoring. The life-cycle management is responsible for launching, starting, stopping, pausing and resuming components.

Hardly any component is present in all product configurations. Several strategies are used to support the sophisticated handling of variability. For example, a lot of update information is exchanged among the various components. This was addressed by developing a single – although complex – UpdateRecord object, which provides a sound approach for exchange information among arbitrary component subsets.

In order to ensure that components are easily plugged in, a set of rules is available together with a software development framework that enforces them. In a previous version, the framework Avalon Phoenix was used, which is expected to die as an open source project. More recent versions use the Spring framework. Both frameworks have the following useful features that improve reusability and testability:

- They define a domain-independent life-cycle model for binary components.
- The life-cycle interfaces, like starting and stopping a component, are defined based on the inversion of control and separation of concerns principles.
- The framework focuses does not put any constraints on a domain-specific solution.

The framework, the defined interfaces and the concrete classes that support them are very mature. During our work on the product line, the team never encountered a situation in which the framework would either have been awkward to use or have been unusable at all.

Product Line Support

The Spring application container is well suited for product line development because of the following reasons:

- It allows for easy definition of product line instances.
- It allows for easy configuration of components.
- It offers very effective and pragmatic means to specify component services and component dependencies in the code. Thus, it is very easy to extract and use that information during the build-process.
- It offers effective and efficient means to provide a low-level management interface based on a per-component model. Thus, it provides the "right" management interface for every instance.
- Spring prevents typecasts so that a component cannot cast a service object it uses to the type of the implementation class. Typecasts rely on assumptions about peer components that go beyond the roles agreed upon and are therefore bound to lead to architectural mismatches.

SEDA-Inspired Multi-Threading Architecture

In order to meet the scalability and performance requirements for the i*Product Line, the team of market maker had to implement a sophisticated multi-threading strategy. Since most of the components perform a lot of I/O and thus tend to spend a lot of time waiting, it was clear from the beginning that every component should run in its own thread(s) of control. Threading was started from scratch as follows:

- A component registers a callback interface "UpdateRecord" at ServiceManager so any other component can send messages to it. In particular, the ThreadManager provides threads and calls them via the ServiceManager.
- Every component depends on a ThreadManager component that provides access to named thread pools, from which the component can obtain threads to run its own services.

Implementing such a design is awkward and error-prone. Every component acting as a distributor of UpdateRecords needs to implement a service that keeps track of the number of components interested in receiving those objects. Furthermore, every component has to implement a mechanism that allows it to buffer incoming data until its own thread is able to process the data.

Once the team developed more and more components, it became clear that a different approach to implementing the processing stages was needed. The Staged Event-Driven Architecture (SEDA, [132]) was evaluated for improving the situation. Core elements of a SEDA are processing units called Stages, which are connected by Queues. Each stage performs the following steps: first, it reads an event (object) from one of its input queues, then it processes the event and finally it enqueues the processing result to an output queue. These steps are performed within a single thread of control and each stage has its own associated thread-pool. Therefore, the queues do not only transport data between stages, but also act as synchronisation points: One thread enqueues an event and another thread in another stage dequeues that event for further processing. In addition to that, the queues act as buffers. Whenever one stage produces events faster than they are consumed by a connected stage, the queue can compensate for this difference temporarily.

The SEDA concept is well suited for product line development because of the following reasons:

- It combines the benefits of SEDA (scalability, throughput) with the benefits of the component framework (ease of instantiation, reuse). Product line instances do not suffer from poor performance due to the overhead introduced by configurability.
- If offers a very powerful means for wiring components together that goes beyond the capabilities of the component framework. This does not complicate the task of deriving product line instances, because configuring the different queues is an integral part of the overall application configuration.

11.4.3 Process

It should not come as a surprise that market maker does not have a fully defined and documented software development process. The team is small, and the project environment changes rapidly. But this does not mean that the development team is not process-aware. The introduction of product line engineering has had an enormous impact on the process. After five years of adapting the process to the needs of everyday project work, we must admit that not every change was foreseen and foreseeable. Post-mortem analysis of the changes showed that most of the process changes fall into a few categories. They are described in this section. Here, we do not cover those process areas where no specific efforts were required for the introduction of product line engineering.

Scoping

This process was not present at market maker before the creation of the i*ProductLine. Instead of extending and maintaining existing products, a company team came together for the first time to forecast the market. So far, new products had rarely been added to the product portfolio. New products were developed only due to demands that were identified by accident. Scoping – or more precisely product portfolio scoping [122] – dramatically changed the company culture. Some of the products identified in 1999 have never been developed, but they helped to clarify requirements for all the others. Scoping performed in a team of experienced people supported a common vision and helped to prioritise products. The most important document, as interviews with the development team revealed, was the genealogy chart [122], which documents the product instances and their relationships in terms of commonalities and differences.

Architecture Assessment

After two years of developing the product line, it turned out that due to project pressure and the fact that various developers were working on central parts of the system there was the danger that the reference architecture might become too complex. In search for instruments to measure the structural quality, the FhG IESE approach "M-System" was chosen and introduced [61]. On the basis of fairly simple measurements to determine the coupling of classes and components, all of the i*ProductLine code was regularly analysed, and the results were discussed at quarterly team meetings where the architecture was assessed and plans for corrections and quality goals expressed by the measures were set. The measures selected (Table 11.1) are not considered the ultimate answer to all questions on structural quality. The major reasons for choosing them were ease of data collection (including availability of a tool), agreement by all persons involved that the measures contributed to the measurement goal and simplicity. Noise had to be accepted due to the human-based interpretation. Defining the measurements more precisely would have resulted in a worse cost/benefit ratio and would have made data collection more difficult.

Table 11.1. Selected metrics for architecture assessment

Name	Definition
CBO	Coupling between object classes. Given a class C, the number of classes coupled through method call or attributes. The classes C and D are coupled to one another, if methods of one class use methods or attributes of the other, or vice versa.
CBO_IL	CBO – Internal Libraries. The same as CBO, but class D is part of an internal library.
CBO_EL	CBO – External Libraries. The same as CBO, but class D is part of an external library.
OMMIC	Import coupling through methods of two classes. A class C is coupled to a class D if C calls a method of D or if C has a method with parameters of type class D.
MPC_EL	Message passing coupling – External libraries. The number of method invocations from C to methods in external libraries.
OCMEC	Export coupling through class-method interaction. The number of times a class C is used as a parameter of a method from another class.
OCAEC	Export coupling through class-attribute interaction. The number of times a class C is used as type of an attribute in another class.
IH-ICP	Inheritance information-flow-based coupling. The number of method calls to inherited methods, weighted by the number of parameters of the invoked method.
NIMP	Number of implemented methods.
NMINH	Number of methods inherited.

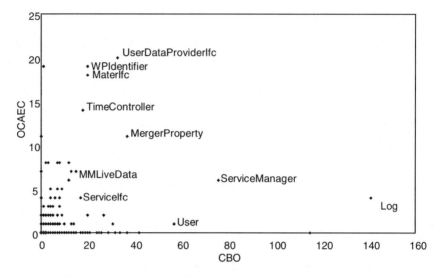

Fig. 11.3. Example of Quantitative Architecture Assessment

Figure 11.3 shows an example of a two-dimensional chart that relates two coupling metrics. One task during architecture assessment was to discuss the outliers in such charts. A basic assumption was made that classes with extreme values are always problematic. However, it turned out that this is not necessarily the case. Sometimes an extreme value reflects the nature and role of the class. The Log class (lower right corner of Fig. 11.3) is an example of such a class. It must be coupled to many classes, as its role is to keep track of what is taking place in these classes during the execution of the application. In other cases, e.g. the User class (lower centre of Fig. 11.3), the developers agree that the coupling to other classes was too high and that it indicates that this class should be analysed more closely.

Domain Design

The product line is continuously evolving. Not all requirements or product instances could be foreseen during scoping and domain analysis, and changes sometimes have a deep impact. Learning about the system itself and newly available third-party components put additional emphasis on steadily caring about the design. Here, refactoring can help to keep the system under control. Sometimes refactoring is triggered by architecture assessment, sometimes major changes force a separate software branch and must be integrated after project deadlines have successfully been passed. Returning to component design afterwards requires management awareness. Developers need time to refactor components without any customer paying for it. Therefore, these efforts are counted as additional costs when talking about the gains of employing a product line. It must be understood that there is not only an initial investment in setting up a product line, but also continuous work in cleaning up the components from ill-structured code. Towards this end, the developers follow standard guidelines.[6]

Domain and Application Unit Testing

The product line code was first tested by the developers as part of their everyday work. Later, acceptance tests were performed. The components and the implementation of the reference architecture (i.e. platform assets) are common to many products. Changing a single component may affect many other products and component behaviour might be changed by accident. On later updates this erroneous code would get productive and cause failures. Costly error removal and annoyed customers would be the consequence. Hence, unintended effects of changes on products must be detected as early as possible. Unit tests written using the JUnit testing framework [77] that check the components' interfaces were added early to detect errors.

Automated Build Process

The component tests are part of an automated process which is invoked every time a developer checks in software to the central repository. The process performs compilation, binding, and calls JUnit. Developers receive feedback about the process state within minutes by e-mail, so that they can react immediately to compilation errors and failed unit tests. This process has been implemented using Cruise Control [41].

Change Management and Issue Management

In contrast to most of the other processes listed here, change management is a highly product- and company-specific task. It depends on the way a company deals with its customers and how much pressure a bug report creates on the development team. We believe that change management and issue management needs to be tailored to a large extent to the existing processes in an organisation. Two major drivers have been identified for changing and improving this process. First, each incoming issue report must be analysed in order to identify the impact on the product line. Small errors may have a huge impact if basic parts of the software need to be changed. Secondly, the time between reporting of an issue and the delivery of a software version that addresses it tends to be longer in product line engineering. This might sound surprising given the fact that time to market declined. Simply speaking, the process of resolving an issue is more complex in product line engineering than in single application development. Issue management was defined as a separate process and is supported by a tool to keep track of issues reported.

---

[6] Examples of such guidelines can be found in [21, 84]

Today, two senior staff members are responsible for screening incoming issues and planning changes.

For every change it must be decided whether time pressure requires to create a separate branch of the software just to satisfy project deadlines or to meet the customer's needs. It is also part of change management to plan for the incorporation of changes to one branch into the main branch, and to delete the old branch.

11.4.4 Organisation

Introducing product line engineering at market maker had an impact not only on software development processes but on the organisation too. Prior to the product line introduction, the development team was organised as a group of people with similar roles. Every developer was responsible for a set of features or classes assigned to him.

Because the product line team was built after development had already begun, parts of the software had already been written while the organisation was still to be formed. Some of the organisational issues had been answered implicitly. For example, the role of the developers of the standard market maker products was left unchanged as these products had already been encapsulated and integrated.

Software product line engineering requires to structure the software development team, regardless of its size. We decided to define a set of roles that were assigned to individual developers. Management did not prescribe how to fulfil responsibilities, but it did carefully control the process.

The prime reason for creating the roles was to be able to split up the development team into two groups: one group was meant to perform domain engineering and the other group application engineering. However, this separation was not implemented completely for the following reasons:

- A team size of five persons is small enough to be managed as a single unit.
- Using and extending components does need domain engineering knowledge, especially in mission critical projects. Here, senior staff must guide junior employees.
- The platform evolves. Not only due to refactoring, but also because of major redesigns that serve to extend it for previously unforeseen use.

The introduced roles, described in detail below, are scoping team, domain expert, architecture manager, component developer, change manager, request dispatcher, issue tracker, build manager and product line manager. A single person assumes more than one role. These roles do not cover all activities within product line engineering, and they were not completely new to the organisation either. However, it is important to note that a separation of responsibilities took place.

Scoping Team

As mentioned above, scoping was one of the key processes introduced. To address the importance of this activity, it is conducted by a team of experienced people. The team does not exist permanently, but is formed each time a major scoping process is to be performed. Team members are from software development (not only of the i*ProductLine but also from other units) management, sales and marketing. The aim is to bring together as much brain power as possible and not to leave important decisions to individuals. The most important reason for this is to share the vision and reach consensus on the development goals.

Domain Expert

Senior software engineers are responsible for development, maintenance and enhancements to the components and the general framework. Severe domain knowledge is necessary in order to shape the components correctly.

Architecture Manager

The design of the overall system is crucial for the success of the product line. To keep a consistent picture of the whole project, a single senior employee was chosen for supervising the main jobs on the reference architecture. One of the tools he uses is architectural assessment with the "M-System" tool.

Component Developer

Less-experienced developers are assigned to application engineering tasks.

Change Manager

After the creation of a first product line version, the change manager is the most important product line engineering role. He guides the process of impact analysis, evaluates change proposals from sales and management, triggers or accepts proposals for refactoring and determines schedules for releases that are shipped to the customer. As market maker is still fairly small, only one person is assigned to change management on a part-time basis. It was a good choice to select the most experienced person, because a lot of implicit and in-depth knowledge about the system is necessary in order to do this job right.

Request Dispatcher

Each issue coming into the development unit needs to be screened. Those classified as minor issues are assigned to developers, whereas all others are assigned to the change manager. On average one or two major issues are documented per month. The request dispatcher needs in-depth knowledge of the system.

Issue Tracker

Each issue reported needs to be watched carefully for its deadline. In addition, communication with the customer needs to be established and maintained. A person was hired for this task, which also includes the preparation of evaluations of the issue database in order to control the process as well as product quality from a statistics point of view. The issue tracker should not be part of the development team in order not to get too deep into the projects.

Build Manager

In order to get an instant build that can be validated against the JUnit tests, the automated build process must be clearly defined and constantly maintained.

Product Line Manager

A strong, visionary person is needed to drive the introduction of product line engineering and to prioritise process and organisational changes during development of the product line. Sound research knowledge as well as pragmatic decisions are needed. The product line manager is responsible for setting overall schedules, sponsoring components and resolving conflicts that cannot be resolved internally.

11.5 Results and Impact Evaluation

The i*ProductLine is a success story of market maker. A variety of seven standard products is derived, and additionally more than two dozens specialised individual solutions are provided to customers with very specific sets of requirements. The goals of the product line have been achieved:

- Time to market is very small, for standard solutions less than a week. We don't have figures of projects former to i*ProductLine, since there were none delivering web-based solutions. Estimates of management are that without the product line project time would be two to four times longer.
- There was no detailed analysis of the cost-benefit ratio of introducing product line engineering. Some figures identified on developer analysis assume that maintenance effort has been reduced by some 60%. According to sound estimates, the time required for maintenance is also reduced by at least 50%.
- More than 70% of the projects performed today are specialised or individualised solutions for a customer. We would not expect to win such projects in case a standard product would not exist.

- Sometimes conflicts between application engineering and domain engineering occurred. For example, an urgent project was brought in by sales during component redesign. For economic reasons, it was important to accept the demand and create a branch in version management. The more urgent the project deadline was, the better it turned out to first create a separate branch and to integrate the changes into the main branch later.
- An unexpected observation was that although initial project time was reduced, resolving issues took longer. This is due to the increased effort needed for impact analysis and time lacks caused by scheduling work in a more complex setting compared to traditional single system development.
- Customers are not interested in whether a product instance stems from a product line and do not want to pay for product line engineering. The company learned from this fact and now offers projects on a fixed price basis instead of getting paid for effort spent.

The results must be interpreted in the context of software development for the i*ProductLine. Even within the company it is questionable whether the same results would have been achieved in another organisational unit, where desktop applications are developed. We see the following circumstances as important for the success:

- The introduction of product line engineering profits from having a small team. Not only small teams can build a product line, we do believe that this team size reduced problems by compensating for missing organisational structure. Turnover of staff was very small, so much of the company's tacit knowledge survived over the years.
- The domain is fairly stable. Stock markets seldom create new products. Product line engineering benefits from stable domains. Here, the power of scoping becomes fully visible as it enables better planning.
- Encapsulation of legacy systems in Java wrappers saved development effort and helped to get started on a stable platform of domain functionality. This was later regarded as one of the top reasons for the success of the whole product line.

11.6 Lessons Learned

Apart from process and organisational changes, there was a number of other important issues addressed or identified during the introduction of product line engineering that were uncovered in the post-mortem analysis. Some of the findings are listed below:

- A simple, yet flexible and stable set of architectural principles (e.g. SEDA, inversion of control, consequent use of interfaces) supported a strategy of divide and conquer for the components. This directly relates to maintenance efforts and the ability to adapt components to changed or extended requirements.

- Prioritisation of work takes place on component level, not on feature level. This enables the development team to work on larger chunks of software changes and to minimise efforts for the integration of modified components.
- The first customer might be dangerous because the system will be designed and developed to his vision.
- The reference architecture is the central piece of software in any project. A strong emphasis was put on this in order to avoid situations where application engineering ignored the domain engineering results (see e.g. [20]).
- Rigid process definition was not needed because of the small team and the developers' competence.
- Developers work in both domain engineering and application engineering, especially in the first customer projects. This enables short feedback cycles and helps developers observe their components in real life, which already caused major changes primarily to component deployment and management in the beginning of the i*ProductLine.
- Automated builds including testing with JUnit turned out to be the key for higher quality and helped avoid defects slipping to later phases. The quality of the work leaving the developer's desk and entering the platform is important.

Introducing product line engineering gave our research partners the opportunity to watch the application of this technology and to receive feedback about the pros and cons. Several interviews, either on specific approaches or on the overall project, were conducted with developers and management. Data was gathered in questionnaires, which helped researchers improve the methods and techniques:

- The use of PuLSE helped to improve the approach, and the experience gained supported applications in other projects [122].
- Testing, especially regression testing, must use information on the commonalities of product instances. Currently, a separate research project focuses on tool support for generic test scripts being instantiated on configuration information of product instances.
- Interviews with developers and managers helped to justify the appropriateness of the product line approach in a small company and influenced the definition of later versions.
- Component extraction as a new approach to reverse engineering was applied in order to retrieve core assets from legacy systems. The application showed the limitations of the approach in the given environment, e.g. missing tool support and consideration of variability.
- A prototype technique to link business goals and architecture elements identified road blocks early and helped to set the focus right.
- Architectural assessment showed that the reference architecture tends to use mechanisms like Java's reflection and late binding. Static code analysis cannot detect such relationships between classes since information on

which class to instantiate resides in configuration files. Dynamic analysis using run-time information is needed [61].

11.7 Summary

This chapter reports about a small company which decided to develop a product line in order to build as many product instances as possible based on their competence in the stock market domain. The i*ProductLine has existed for little more than five years now, and it can be considered as being successful both from a business and from a technology perspective.

More than a dozen products have been developed by a small team that took care of sound engineering principles and modified the processes and the organisation to address certain issues brought up by product line engineering. The processes added or changed emphasise which parts of traditional processes must be considered when applying a product line approach. Major changes had to be made in domain engineering. Especially, adding the process of product line scoping dramatically changed the way market maker acts on the market.

Organisational changes have been implemented in order to identify roles as sets of responsibilities. Usually, individuals were assigned multiple roles. The processes to be performed were not documented in full detail because processes changed due to the learning curve associated with the introduction of a product line. A mapping between processes and roles was performed in order to demonstrate that a complex relationship between roles and processes resulting from product line engineering exists.

Lessons learned were uncovered during the final evaluation of the project as part of research projects that tried to gain a better understanding of the nature of product line engineering in general and the relevant factors in this project in particular. Major lessons concern the impact on time and effort, as well as consequences concerning the relationship with customers.

After four years the introduction of product line engineering was considered finished, although certain processes still need to be optimised and improved. The product line continues to evolve and more years of interesting work around software product line engineering lie ahead.

12

Nokia Mobile Phones

with Claudio Riva
Jianli Xu

Company facts of Nokia Mobile Phones

Organisational size: >1,000 developers.
Starting Mode: Strategic focus, based on existing assets.

Experienced improvements:
- Better understanding of software evolution.
- Better insight in commonality.

Business: Architecture evolution supports changing business needs.

Architecture: Architecture models ease its evolution.

Process: An approach to architecture modelling and documentation.

Organisation: Needs of different stakeholders are taken into account.

12.1 Introduction

Nokia is the world leader in mobile communications. Backed by its experience, innovation, user-friendliness and secure solutions, the company has become the leading supplier of mobile phones and a leading supplier of mobile, fixed and IP networks.

Before 2004, Nokia consisted of two large business groups, Nokia Mobile Phones and Nokia Networks. At that moment, Nokia had over 19,800 people in R&D, which is 39% of the total personnel. The total R&D expenditure in 2003 was €3,760 M, which is 12.8% of the net sales.

Nokia Mobile Phones is the world's largest mobile phone manufacturer. With its comprehensive product portfolio covering all consumer segments and standards, Nokia is a market leader. Its mission is to enable people to connect with one another and to information regardless of time and place. Nokia's technology and applications are designed for human needs and are based on solutions that function seamlessly and effectively together.

The mobile phones group is responsible for a diverse and large portfolio of mobile phones, multimedia devices and mobile services for corporations. In January 2004, the Mobile Phones business group was split into three smaller business groups:

1. *Mobile phones*: for developing mobile phones.
2. *Multimedia*: for developing both voice and non-voice multimedia technologies (e.g. camera, video, mobile TV, games and more)
3. *Enterprise solutions*: for developing corporate-wide mobile solutions and services.

This chapter concentrates of efforts done within the first group, the Nokia Mobile Phones[1] to business.

12.2 Motivation

Nokia has several product lines in development. Although all BAPO aspects are relevant, this chapter focuses on architectural modelling. An important aspect is that product line architectures tend to be very large. This means that the architecture must be represented in multiple views to be comprehensible by its stakeholders. Each of these views describes the system from a different angle, focusing on certain characteristics of the system. This chapter shows how security concerns can be addressed based on architectural diagrams. The case study was conducted with the co-operation of Tampere University of Technology.

A common architectural view describes the decomposition of the system into parts. The whole system is divided into sub-systems which can be further

---

[1] From here on, the term 'Nokia' is used as a short hand for 'Nokia Mobile Phones'

divided into other modules. An important aspect of the architecture is that it has to be understood by many stakeholders. Each stakeholder may need his own view.

The following are some of the relevant questions with regard to decomposition:

- Are the sub-systems only used on the highest level?
- Can a sub-system contain other sub-systems?
- What does each sub-system contain?
- What are the modules?
- Does a module contain actual code or binaries or some conceptual elements?
- How is everything eventually mapped to concrete assets like classes, files and files structures?

12.3 Approach

The software architecture models of a system are meant as a basis to analyse the characteristics of the system before it is implemented. This supports risk management by enabling the examination of quality attributes of the final system. Therefore, the architect needs the ability to express those properties in an easily communicated manner that makes the fulfilment of the wanted characteristics explicit.

Effective communication of architectural properties can be achieved only with concise documentation: when the amount of the architecture documentation increases the benefits of the documentation decreases rapidly. It is very hard to find inconsistencies in a document of more than 500 pages.

Nokia strives to describe architecture in a way that provides concise documents that directly address the wanted characteristics. This effectively allows finding out potential problems of the architecture. In addition, it enables the attachment of various measures to those architectural views in a way that assists evaluating the properties of the architecture.

Nokia aimed to find the correct ways to describe software architecture in the product line context, which allows easy specification of the wanted quality attribute. The approach is presented using security as an example. Nokia has investigated how it is possible to describe product line requirements [2] and how it can connect requirements and the quality attributes to the relevant design choices [116].

Early detection of the actual properties of the architectures potentially lowers cost by reducing the amount of correction effort. Full life-cycle quality enforcing mechanisms promise higher quality systems that do better match the actual needs of customers.

For practical reasons, Nokia has chosen to use existing viewpoints to describe the qualities: these viewpoints are already in use within the company.

Previous results [102] include the use of the already-defined quality meta-models and defined ways to describe quality attributes. These models are applied using the collected practical viewpoints, Fig. 12.1. These viewpoints show the current ways that Nokia uses to describe architectures. The viewpoints are adapted to accommodate the quality characteristics by adding new types to the model and derive existing types with quality annotations.

Using generic views has many benefits. They are easily understood, since a known view is only slightly modified to add quality information. This makes them easy to be used to model many products and variants, since they are not as domain-specific nor do they concentrate only on one quality, which may not be of interest to another product. The generic view is, therefore, ideal to describe trade-offs among quality aspects since all of them can be potentially described in the same architectural view.

On the other hand, quality-specific views concentrate on one quality at a time, which reduces the amount of entities that must be presented, since the view concentrates on the issues that directly address the quality. This allows easy analysis and easier formulation of rules.

Additionally, it is necessary to define measures for each of the viewpoints to actually say whether the selected quality is fulfilled by the concrete architecture specified in the architectural view. The description of the architecture using the quality-annotated viewpoint helps to decide whether the selected solution supports desired quality characteristics.

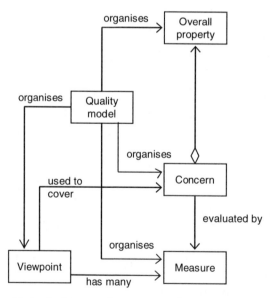

Fig. 12.1. Architectural viewpoints (UML class diagram)

12.3.1 Typing and Quality Characteristics

Typing is in the essence of architecting. Types provide restrictions that are the key for maintaining architectural consistency. When the reference architecture formulates the architectural rules using types, it is easy to maintain these architectural rules during system design. In an ideal case, the architectural rules are maintained by the toolset used by the software architects and developers.

Over time, an effective set of architectural types creates a common language within the project team. Everyone knows what is assumed when an element is declared a server or when a client connects with the server. Having a common language makes communication much easier because the team does not go into the common details of every element, rather they can focus on the differentiating facts. The types and their known properties, therefore, ease exposing potential problems.

Some of the types can be more or less domain independent. The generic terms such as sub-system or layer must be defined so that their definition is clear. Then domain dependent types can be refined from the more generic types. The properties of the generic types are inherited by the domain-specific constructs, but there are constraints how these types can be used in the domain-specific architecture.

The architectural type system must be grounded on reality, on things that can be verified to exist. This process is done to every view. On the lowest level there have to be file folders, actual files, build scripts, DLL's etc.

12.3.2 Traceability

Requirements and features have to be traced to the architecture. Traceability is facilitated by making the connection at the right levels of abstraction. For instance, the refinement of a performance scenario – such as a response time of two seconds for credit card validation – needs to be connected to specific design choices. Through traceability, it is possible to map the requirements to the corresponding architectural elements. This allows justifying the architectural decisions with the requirements and previous design decisions.

Preferably, the design can be traced back to the requirements as well. While refining the system design into its final realisation, we should continuously match the design choices and the corresponding requirements. It is key to make the mapping in a suitable level of abstraction. Both requirements and design decisions are refined throughout the architecting process and the connections should be present at the same level of abstraction.

Consider a very generic quality attribute such as security or performance. This can be mapped to almost any design element. Every line of code has some implication on the performance of the system and coding mistakes may jeopardise the security of the system regardless of where they take place. It is crucial to have the traceability connection in the right level. The refinement of the performance scenario – "response time of two seconds for credit card validation" – can be connected to design choices. This makes it possible to map the requirements to the corresponding architectural elements. Traceability allows justifying the architectural decisions with the requirements and previous design decisions.

Requirements are situated in the problem domain. They are used to describe the needs of customers. During product line engineering, a product line model of requirements can be constructed and selections are made for each new product. Nokia found that it can be helpful to organise the model as a forest, in which the requirements are related to each other in parent – child relationships.

Features are situated in the solution domain. During product line engineering, a product line model of features can be constructed and selections are made to generate the assets of a new product. Information on the requirements of the software product line is needed to create the feature model. The construction of the feature model requires the knowledge on the architecture because that model reflects the variability that exists in the software architecture.

Similarly, the features influence the requirements. A set of rules can be defined to connect the variability in the requirements with the variability of the features. Within Nokia , the rules for mapping requirement variability to the features variability is specified as follows [115]:

1. *Mandatory requirements*: if any requirement in the set of requirements specifying a feature is mandatory then the selection criterion of the feature is *mandatory* itself.
2. *Optional requirements*: if any requirement in the set of requirements specifying a feature is optional and no mandatory requirements exist in that set, then the selection criterion of the feature is *optional* itself.
3. *Obsolete requirements*: if all requirements in the set of requirements specifying a feature are obsolete then the selection criterion of the feature is *obsolete* itself.
4. *Non-reusable requirements*: if all requirements in the set of requirements specifying a feature is non-reusable then the selection criterion of the feature is *obsolete* itself.
5. *Multiple and single adaptor mapping to optional*: if the children of a single or multiple-adaptor requirement each depend upon mutually exclusive features (or set of features each), that are independent of any other requirements, then each of the childs requirements is treated as optional for the selection constraint propagation purposes and thus (by earlier rules) their related features are *optional* too.
6. *Feature composition*: if a requirement R1 has child requirements R1.1 and R1.2, and feature F1 has child features F1.1 and F1.2, and R1.1 specifies F1.1 and R1.2 specifies F1.2, then this can be composed to the simple

relationship R1 specified F1. Rules 1 to 4 then apply to set the selection criterion of F1.

7. *Variable mapping to mandatory*: if a feature is specified or implied by each variable requirement wherever it is in the forest of requirements then its selection constraint value is *mandatory*.

12.3.3 The ART Environment

The ART environment – shown in Fig. 12.2 – covers software architecture design, architecture model analysis and processing, architecture model reconstruction and maintenance, during the entire life-cycle of a software product-line [116, 115]. The architecture description/modelling language is UML, customised with domain-specific architectural profiles. This allows

1. to use UML, which has already been widely used as a program design language, in both architectural and detailed design in Nokia.
2. To use the best available UML CASE tools in architecture modelling – at least the model editing, UML syntax checking and model management functions of those tools.
3. Most importantly, to give UML more precise semantics for architecture modelling by using architectural profiles, so that the profile-based architecture model validation tool can be used to check the architecture design.

The ART environment provides strong and efficient tool support to software architecture design and maintenance in the context of large product-line development. ART has been used intensively in the architecture design and

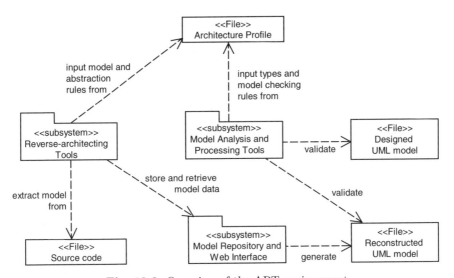

Fig. 12.2. Overview of the ART environment

maintenance task of a main product-line of Nokia mobile terminal products, and has been partly applied in another product line.

The results achieved so far are significant to the further development of the product lines. Nokia has already started the large-scale deployment of the environment in Nokia mobile terminal software development.

The aim is to extend the current ART environment and approach to better support the evolution of software product line architectures.

Figure 12.3 [116] shows how the tools from the ART environment are used to support the evolution of the product-line architecture in a simplified process. ART's model operation tool is extended with a set of model operations that can identify the common parts and changes between UML models of different product releases. The view/model generation tool can merge the newly

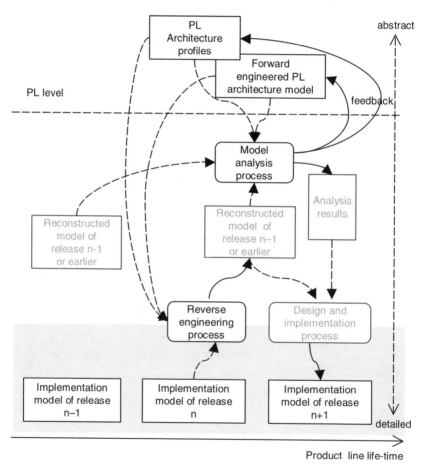

Fig. 12.3. Software product line architecture maintenance process

detected common subset of models to the original software product line model and create the new software product line model.

The ART environment consists of three main toolsets: the architecture model analysis and processing toolset, the reverse-architecting toolset and the model repository and its web interface. The model analysis and processing toolset works with UML architecture models including not only the models created by architects using a UML CASE tool (i.e. IBM Rational ROSE) but also the UML models generated by the reverse-architecting tools. It allows the software architects to create the UML architectural profiles and design models, check models against the profiles, generate views at different abstraction levels and from different viewpoints and finally analyse models and views. The aim of this part is to provide software architects a complete and consistent view of the architecture, and to help them to make the right decisions.

The reverse architecting toolset is used by the software architects to reengineer or recover the architectural model from an implementation. Resulting models share the same concepts and same model structure with the designed architectural model, and can provide the same views at the same abstraction levels as the design model does. Hence, the same architectural profiles can be used to check the recovered models to discover any violations in the implementation.

Comparison of the recovered model with the designed model can also reveal significant architectural changes introduced during implementation. For a fast evolving product line, being able to monitor the changes and keep the evolution under control is extremely important.

The model repository provides an efficient way for managing and retrieving all the architecture model elements. A model repository is necessary when one has to maintain the architectural models of a large number of implementation releases of a product line.

In the ART environment, a relational database is used to store architectural models. A web interface provides easy access to the model repository to software architects located in different sites.

12.4 Example: Security

In this section, we take a closer look at security as a quality aspect, and how it relates to views, traceability and types. Security concerns are represented in multiple views on the architecture. Different aspects of the security are exposed in the distinct architectural views. We use three different viewpoints: problem domain, structural architecture and deployment. Problem domain models are ideal to capture requirements and features, whereas structural and deployment models reflect how the model entities are connected to the properties of those selections.

- Structural architecture shows the mapping between the detailed security requirements and the architectural elements.

- Deployment describes how the architectural elements are in fact connected to actual hardware units.

The architectural viewpoints used within Nokia support an incremental design process. Initially, requirements impose constraints on which kind of design alternatives can be chosen. Next, an architecture style is chosen. This style limits the number of actual architectural mechanisms and tactics. Finally, an actual implementation mechanism is selected in combination with the tactics to complete the approach for the system, in this case the security approach.

We start with a domain model description to create a model of the domain that has all the relevant constructs and that allows to discuss the key requirements of the system. The requirements are preferably phrased in terms in the problem domain model.

Nokia does not model the requirements themselves graphically. Although graphical modelling may be beneficial to make the connections between the requirements and problem domain model constructs very concrete, that is considered to consume too much effort. Instead, the requirements are done using natural text.

The final problem domain model is obtained by combining two different models. The initial problem domain model is combined with the relevant constructs from the generic security model.

The simplified domain model (Fig. 12.4) describes the key concepts of the web store application. It defines the main terms of the web store without any specific focus on the security concern. It is related to the scenario that there is a user that views items. If the user logs in to the application then he becomes a validated user. Such a validated user can act as a buyer who purchases items via a purchase transaction that requires money.

The generic security model (Fig. 12.5) is based on the common criteria. For each concern, like security, a generic model can be created. This model defines the main terms and concepts that can be used to describe what security means.

The basic domain model is not really tied to the security concerns. It rather defines quite generic concepts of any web store. Naturally, any real domain

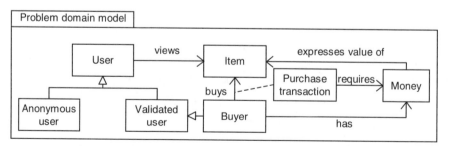

Fig. 12.4. A simplified problem domain model (web store)

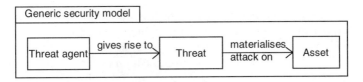

Fig. 12.5. A generic security domain model

model would be more extensive and have thoroughly defined constraints. The generic security model, on the other hand, has no information on the web stores. It can be applied to many occasions where security is a concern. Independently, these two models provide only limited value. Combining the models brings out the true value of the approach.

Figure 12.6 presents the combined model. It shows the generic security model, adapted to the current context. The threat agent is defined to be a type of a user. The money is an asset where the threat focuses on.[2]

The structural architecture is clearly part of the solution domain. It shows how the system is divided into components and how these components are connected together. Additionally, it describes the security-specific constructs in the same diagrams as the architecture. The main types of security constructs are different security mechanisms and zones. However, present day application development cannot rely on truly safe zones. Even behind firewalls, various techniques need to be used to secure local computers. Clearly, multiple tiers of countermeasures provide better security than only one boundary layer relying on one specific technique. In any case, security zones still play a role

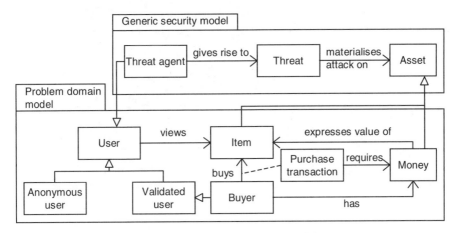

Fig. 12.6. The combined model

---

[2] This model is a simplified version of the complete, real world model. One could easily discover other types of threat agents besides the actual user. For this example, the new combined model provides enough information

in architecting secure systems. Different zones allow rationalising on security levels and techniques, since the threats vary along the zone.

It is very natural to use different methods for boundary crossing interaction, e.g. across public Internet, than for communication that takes place inside a boundary like the intranet. Therefore, typically, the security zones align with the deployment of the system, but the concern is still driven by the security problem not by the architecture. The security zones should be selected and scoped based on the threat that this area is exposed to. Aligning the security zones with other similar overlapping areas reduces the number of types. This makes the architectural type-language more expressive and allows for easily expressing important concepts.

We consider the same web store example in the structural architecture model. The architecture (Fig. 12.7) is composed of three main components:

1. *Presentation* describes items to users. It can be used by both valid and anonymous users. This means that no account validation can be required for these users. Therefore, we declare this component as part of the public Internet security zone.
2. *Account validator* is responsible to allow users to register into the service and validate them as registered users that can make purchases. The account validator thus uses the security tactic access control.
3. *Purchase manager* is responsible for allowing the validated user to make a purchase transaction. This component guarantees that the user will eventually get the item that he or she purchased and that the money is eventually charged from the user's credit card (using the external interface).

The external interface from the purchase manager is specified by the credit card authorisation organisation and uses encryption when connecting over the

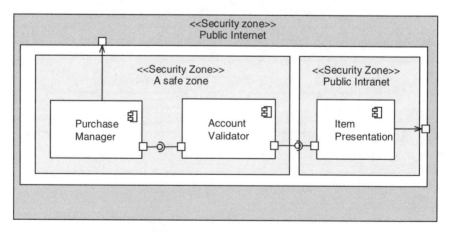

Fig. 12.7. Structural security architecture

public Internet. The definition of these three components and security zones allow easy specification of architectural rules. For our system we formulate a generic security rule: use an encrypted connection (Secure Socket Layer, SSL) when transmitting confidential information over security zone public Internet.

The deployment architecture describes how the components are mapped to the actual hardware. The generic constructs are the nodes, assets that are deployed into the nodes and communication links between them. In this view, the security concern is represented by security zones overlapping some nodes and communication links, threats on generic constructs and security mechanisms that are used as countermeasures to the threats.

The deployment view defines constraints on the allocation of software entities to processing nodes. On the abstract level, this means to specify constraints on the deployment. In fact, at the concrete level it is the actual mapping of the software element to the processor. Nodes represent either hardware devices or software execution environments. Nodes are nested and assets are deployed on the nodes.

Figure 12.8 shows a very simplified picture of the deployment architecture of the web store. All components are deployed as their own .jar files. The *Item presentation* component is actually deployed at the client machine where it allows a special, customised entrance to the web store. This means that this component is part of the high-risk environment, here represented as threat environment. Since the component is deployed at the client machine, it is

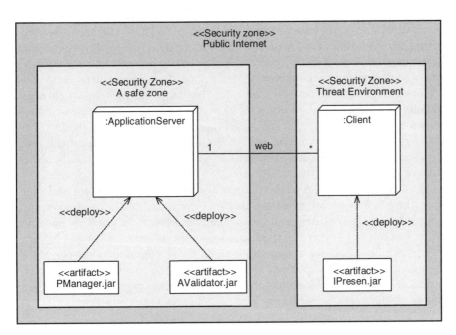

Fig. 12.8. Deployment security architecture

vulnerable to reverse engineering, communication sniffing and other hacking approaches. Nokia decided that no major countermeasure is to be used here. The component only takes care of the presentation and allows SSL connections to take place, but otherwise it does not contain any information that would make it a valuable asset to attack the web store.

The server side is deployed in a safe domain. Both the *Account validator* and *Purchase manager* components reside in this zone. The main countermeasures are physical ones. The computer running the web store is placed in a safe location, in a locked server room. Additional security could be obtained by having the two components running in different machines. Getting the root password into one system would not jeopardise the whole web store. Even then the ability to get root access to the *Account validator* allows the hacker to soon get access to purchase transactions on the expense of other user's credit. For this reason, it is decided to keep it simple and only run intrusion detection software in the server machine with automated scripts to close the connection (and set of the alarm) if intrusion takes place.

The communication between the server and the client takes place through public Internet where non-closure information is a clear security concern. The countermeasure is to use encryption.

12.5 Lessons Learned

The motivation of the case study is to develop and test the tools for supporting the evolution of software product line architecture. Software product line engineering is an iterative process. The software product line architecture evolves to deal with new requirements introduced by new products. Nokia has developed the UML model operation tool that can help to induce new commonality from individual product architecture models. This helps to derive the new product line architecture model based on the new commonality. The extended UML model operation tool of the ART environment has been used to identify the commonality of several selected products of a mobile phone software product line.

As with any method, a more concrete method that really solves and evaluates the concrete architecture thoroughly is preferred by its users. However, such a method always carries a lot of domain knowledge. This makes adapting such a method outside of its application domain difficult. A careful balance must be achieved between the usefulness and the domain independence of the approach. In the approach, there is no formal way to prove that the requirements are satisfied by the architecture. Rather, Nokia explicitly relies on the abilities of the particular software architect to make the connection.

12.6 Outlook

The architecture models of several different products in a mobile phone software product line are compared using the UML model set operations of the model operation tool. Table 12.1 and Table 12.2 show the result data of the set operations on the models of two pairs of products. Table 12.2 also gives the detailed analysis data about the changes of dependencies from product model B to model C.

Table 12.1. Data from comparing the architecture model of product A and B

	B	A	A int B	B - A	A - B
			common	B specific	A specific
Package	231	197	195	34	2
Class	786	1,169	668	120	501
Dependency	9,892	9,141	7,191	2,701	1,950

Table 12.2. Data from comparing the architecture models of product B and C

	C	B	B int C	C - B	B - C
			common	C specific	B specific
Package	235	231	219	16	12
Class	816	786	752	64	34
Dependency	10,246	9,892	9,019	1,227	873

The same set of operations can be performed again on the two common subset models to obtain the commonality of the four selected products. This final common model subset is the candidate to be merged to the software product line architecture model. The merge is not a simple union operation on two models, the common model subset is carefully analysed against the new requirements of the software product line and new variation points. Through these steps, the irrelevant model element in the common model subset are filtered out and the rest can then be merged into the software product line model. The current tool support helps in gathering the initial input model data for the analysis of new software product line level commonalities. Especially when there are large models of many different products, tool support is necessary.

13

Nokia Networks

with Osmo Vikman

Company facts of Nokia Networks

Organisational size: > 1,000 developers.
Starting Mode: Strategic focus, based on existing assets.

Experienced improvements:
- Improved management of very complex systems.
- Improved visibility and reuse of available assets.

Business: A shift from in-house development to partnering and
                  finally to an extended enterprise.

Architecture: Evaluation framework.

Process: Asset management.
                  Multi-partner, multi-project, multi-site develop-
                  ment.

Organisation: Separation in domain and application engineering.
                  Data warehouse within a complex development
                  organisation.

13.1 Introduction

For a general introduction to Nokia, refer to Chap. 12. This chapter deals with Nokia Networks[1] that provides network infrastructure, communications and networks service platforms, as well as professional services to operators and service providers. It focuses on the GSM family of radio technologies.

At the end of 2005, Nokia had more than 150 mobile network customers in more than 60 countries, its systems serving in excess of 400,000,000 subscribers.

13.2 Motivation

A major topic of interest for Nokia is asset management in a complex organisation. This involves both process and organisation aspects. Complexity has grown over the years and Nokia is facing even more complexity in the development of their network elements.

In the early 1990s, almost all of Nokia's research and development was done in-house. There were only a few sub-contractors, which were typically working on Nokia premises, and some third parties provided functionality or accessories to Nokia products. That was the situation when Nokia decided to concentrate fully on the telecommunications business.

During the latter part of the 1990s, the telecommunications industry grew at a very rapid pace. It became impossible for telecommunications systems vendors to develop everything in-house, unless they were willing to hire thousands of new developers each year. Instead, they increasingly used sub-contractors and off-the-shelf components in their product development, even outsourcing part of their mature product development to partners (cf. Fig. 13.1). This shift from do-it-yourself to partnering made the need for sub-contract, supplier and vendor management competences greater than that for more traditional software, hardware and mechanical design skills.

Nokia's present business environment consists of a number of independent business units and product lines. Each of them develops its own products and has its own product and platform roadmaps, business objectives and priorities. The network systems are based on such individual products, platforms and components. Some are delivered by development teams of in-house business units, others come from sub-contractors or third-party suppliers. It takes a lot of cross-organisational co-ordination to develop systems in such an environment.

Nokia's development style can be characterised as product population engineering. System development is organised in in-house systems integration programs. First, the system-level capabilities are specified. Next, commitments of the involved parties for delivery of product releases are solicited. Program

---

[1] From here on, the term "Nokia" is used as a short hand for "Nokia Networks"

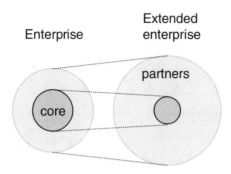

Fig. 13.1. Organisational evolution

management teams are responsible for co-ordinating product or platform development work, and for maintaining the system view throughout system development. All the actual development resources are owned and controlled by the business units, sub-contractors and third-party suppliers.

Even with the new matrix organisation in place, the organisational complexity is immense. Dozens of concurrent development programs demand deliverables from technology platforms in a multi-site, multi-project and multi-partner development environment.

Asset reuse within a business unit is relatively simple if the original developers are available for implementing consecutive variants. Reuse between different business units or between different technology platforms is much harder. Even though the technology platforms organisation provides the primary asset reuse capability, cross-organisational reuse is still rare.

There are several layers in the system development organisation (Fig. 13.2):

- *Product lines* are run by business units. They produce systems that are delivered to the customers.
- The product lines use software, hardware or electromechanical *platforms*. The platforms can be Nokia proprietary, commercial off-the-shelf or developed with partners in a consortium.
- A platform consists of numerous software, hardware and electromechanical *components*. Components are developed in-house, by sub-contracts or bought as commercial off-the-shelf products from third-party vendors.
- In turn, the components use *materials and technologies*.

At the top layer, a system must be delivered to customers. The customer and end-user requirements must be allocated top-down, spanning all lower layers. These requirements must be managed in a matrix with the layer-specific requirements. The in-house and external development resources are distributed geographically within the extended enterprise. Each layer has its own specific requirements based on technology, legislation, regulations, standards, compatibility, interoperability and other forces.

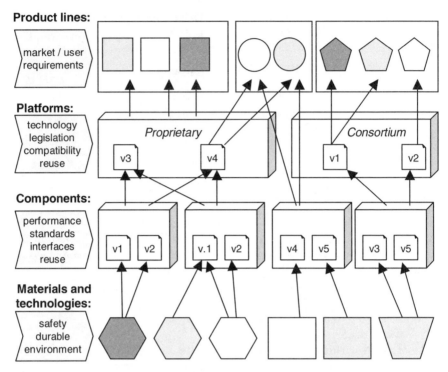

Fig. 13.2. Layers of product population engineering

Specific systems are described as a set of features. Their implementation is allocated top-down over all development layers. Features are the top-level sales items. They have been sold to the system's customers. It is therefore necessary to keep track of the features throughout system development to be able to verify that the system lives up to its promises.

Feedback on field failures from the existing customer base is needed to keep the system and product asset base current throughout its life-cycle. The correlation of these failures with the software product line assets should be analysed and the results fed back to in-house development groups and external suppliers.

There are three primary processes:

1. *Product creation* spans from stakeholder need identification up to the release of product designs to the delivery process.
2. *Delivery* contains manufacturing, supply chain management and distribution of products.
3. *Care* deals with the needs of the existing customer base. It provides a feedback channel for potential problem reports from customers and end-users through field service centres.

Typically, asset development is done in a transient project organisation, with projects disappearing after delivery, leaving the assets ownerless. The projects provide dedicated development resources (software, hardware, electromechanical and others) to numerous parallel development programs. The organisations for delivery and after sales are separate from those for asset creation. Asset developers are often not available when problem reports for an installed system start flowing in from the field service centres. This asymmetry makes it hard to connect customer feedback to specific assets.

13.3 Approach

Systems engineering aims to maintain the system view through all phases of the system life-cycle (Fig. 13.3)[2]:

1. *Concept:* systems are defined as sets of (additional) features.
2. *Development:* software, hardware, electro-mechanics and services are designed for developing the capability for the system.

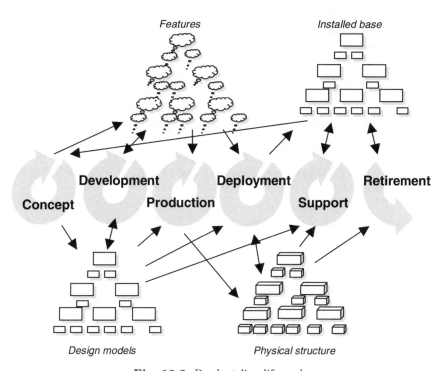

Fig. 13.3. Product line life-cycle

---

[2] These are the phases as described in the ISO/IEC 15288 System Life-cycle Processes standard [70]

3. *Production:* physical product structures are created for manufacturing or acquisition of the constituent parts of the system, and the systems are produced.
4. *Deployment:* systems are sold, delivered, installed and configured.
5. *Support:* systems in the field are actively maintained and serviced.
6. *Retirement:* systems are replaced, customers are informed. After retirement, systems are no longer maintained or supported.

System engineering starts with the top-level system concept and a set of common system features and proceeds to refine and allocate the requirements onto the various parties involved in the process. Throughout subsequent phases, commitments get increasingly more detailed. Finally, they reach the level where the effort to produce a deliverable is not split any further. Typically, a system iteratively evolves over the first four stages. When its assets become obsolete, there is a need for a technology refresh to extend the life of the system. If that is not feasible, it reaches the retirement phase.

Using an existing asset base is less risky than starting a software product line from scratch. However, proper processes, methods and tools are needed to assist in the recovery and integration of their assets. Long-term maintenance of the software product line asset base supports the need for faster, better and cheaper development of new products.

System properties above the component level have to be controlled and managed during design, test, use and maintenance to be able to create and guarantee the desired system properties. Therefore, the dependencies between the customers and suppliers of the various assets must be managed. This is addressed by a good asset management system. It provides a means of storing, retrieving and managing assets throughout the life-cycle of interdependent software product lines.

The primary focus of asset management in system development lies in ensuring the integrity of a feature set across all parts of a system. Asset management for product lines reaches beyond the scope of a single system. Accumulating and managing a reuse repository may then span a whole company plus its external sub-contractors and third-party suppliers. This adds a new dimension of complexity.

The main challenge of asset management for mobile networks is to keep track of the backward compatibility of the assets at all layers and all phases of the life-cycle, with business processes producing deliverables incrementally.

At least four types of assets need to be configured to be useable in a subsequent step in a system development cycle:

- *System requirements* at each layer are configured for design.
- *Design items* at each layer are configured for production.
- *Sales items* describe a system and are configured for installation and commissioning.
- *System features* describe the upgrade of the installed base of a system and are configured for the new capability.

Such configurations call for configuration management of assets. Configuration management is commonly used in the product creation process, but it does not extend to the delivery and care processes. Currently available commercial tools are not useful because their scope of use is aimed at design and implementation assets, and relationships are not well managed.

Nokia's change management system is based on a commitment traceability repository. It provides means for evaluating the effects of a change request before it is submitted to the change management process. What-if scenarios may be simulated at any level of a system structure and at any phase in the system development process. The change management system is accessible to all involved parties at any level of the system product structure.

Currently, a prototype data warehouse application is used to record the development assets and their dependencies for all development programs in the business units (Fig. 13.4). It was originally built for global product creation reporting purposes. The data warehouse collects once every day asset-related data from all product, platform and component development programs or projects (Fig. 13.5). It acts as an organisational recorder for all product creation–related activities. An asset management prototype extracts and analyses asset-specific data from the data warehouse. The maintenance group can use this information to traverse the system, platform and component development V-models in the reverse direction in case of a field problem report. This way, the problem report can be correlated with the correct system asset.

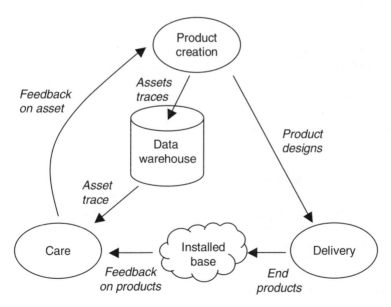

Fig. 13.4. Closing the feedback loop between asset development and end-users with a data warehouse

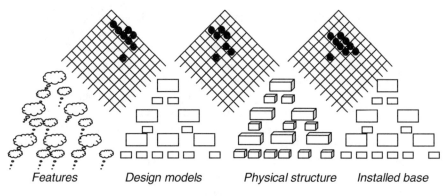

Features   *Design models*   *Physical structure*   *Installed base*

Fig. 13.5. Asset transformation

In order to enable feedback to the development processes, each asset has a unique identifier, determined at creation time. This helps to identify any relevant asset-related data sources. An end-to-end information model spans all data sources to enable asset tracking over the whole life-cycle. Development programs share their product line assets through a systems engineering assets repository. New assets are mostly created by those programs that solve new problems or take advantage of new opportunities. In contrast, evolutionary development programs, e.g. those programs that develop the next release of a stable system, may take existing assets from the repository and apply them in their software product lines.

The commitment traceability mechanism was originally proposed as a basis for a decision support system for end-to-end feature management. It was then refined and extended to cover both the pre- and post-development phases of a system. The simulation model contains the requirements screening, roadmapping and release management processes. It is also used to integrate requirements management and resource and schedule management tools as data sources for the commitment traceability repository.

13.4 Lessons Learned

Asset life-cycle management is still in its infancy. Most of the software product line research has concentrated on the front-end and middle-part of the life-cycle: scoping, architecting, domain engineering and management within a development organisation.

A systems engineering asset repository is harder to define and implement than an implementation technology–specific repository. Systems engineering assets are more abstract items than technology assets, and they are more difficult to identify, define and describe. Current asset-reuse practices focus on implementation technology–specific assets rather than reusable systems engineering assets. A complete systems engineering repository is not available today.

Nokia's data warehouse provides a view on the parallel and distributed creation of assets and their dependencies across organisational boundaries. Currently, there is a large number of isolated asset-related applications and tools spread across the life-cycle of a software product line. A harmonisation program deals with this by creating an end-to-end product information model. This will unify data management for the various disciplines like requirements management, architecting and system design. In the delivery and care processes, more uniform solutions already exist, e.g. Enterprise Resource Planning and Product Life-cycle Management systems.

A project-oriented development organisation is a big obstacle for long-term product line asset management. Individual projects are reluctant to reuse existing assets if there is no easy way of validating and adapting them to their contexts. Company-wide reuse schemes are hard to implement and deploy if there is no buy-in from the business units. But proving the benefits of asset reuse is a chicken-and-egg problem: reuse is supposed to provide faster, better and cheaper results for projects, and project managers will only be convinced when concrete evidence from past projects is available.

There is a conflict of interest in the priorities of the business and technology development. System development has a relatively short development cycle compared to platform and component development. Business units typically aim at six to twelve months development cycles,[3] while development of a major new release of a technology platform may take several years, especially for hardware platforms. In the past, new technologies drove the development of platforms, and products used whatever technology was provided by them. Now, the tide is slowly turning and business wants to drive technology development on their terms. This conflict must be reconciled in order to guarantee the schedules of parallel programs competing for development resources. A common asset management model would help in identifying the dependencies between asset creation and consumption and thus in deciding on the best use of development resources.

The evolution of an organisation from self-sufficient do-it-yourself towards a collaborating enterprise requires collaborative development, recovery and integration processes, as well as methods and tools to support product line engineering across geographical, organisational and cultural boundaries. The organisation should be network-centric, not project-centric. Asset management gets more difficult when a company trades dedicated in-house development resources for the capability to orchestrate suppliers. Asset life-cycle management then changes from managing one's own assets into monitoring the availability of external innovations and technologies, and identifying and evaluating appropriate suppliers.

---

[3] With the exception of completely new software product lines

13.5 Outlook

The transformation of assets from one stage of a development cycle to the next is complex. It is currently impossible to trace these transformations through all stages of the system life-cycle from concept to retirement.

Current technologies are replaced by new, more affordable and efficient technologies at an ever-increasing pace. In particular, critical technologies that have been incorporated into software product lines must be monitored constantly for obsolescence. Reference architectures should accommodate technology replacement. There must be a technology-refreshment plan for the whole life-cycle of such technology assets, including permanent research and road-mapping processes.

Asset management through all the life-cycle phases of a system is still a long-term vision. Organisational entities typically have ownership of assets for the duration of a single life-cycle phase only. Afterwards, they pass the responsibility to the next silo. The continuity of asset management suffers from this. Assets are often left ownerless when they are handed over from system development to the delivery process, which has to deal with assets of many development projects.

Replacing the prescriptive project-centric approach by a proactive and flexible network-centric approach would improve the collaboration among parties within the extended enterprise. That would enable effective allocation and de-allocation of resources in the various phases of an asset life-cycle.

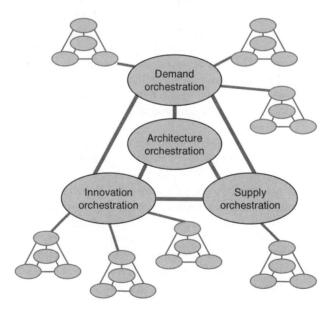

Fig. 13.6. Extended enterprise with orchestration capabilities

The next step is to create extended enterprise-wide orchestration capabilities for innovation, demand and supply based on system and platform architecture orchestration (Fig. 13.6). In practice, this means that the primary competence of such an organisation is system integration. It should not matter where and by whom the constituent parts of a system are designed and implemented. The architecture-centric orchestration capability would transcend business domain boundaries, because that capability would be valid in any domain.

14

Philips Consumer Electronics Software for Televisions

with Rob van Ommering

Company facts of Philips TV Software

Organisational size: 250 developers.

Starting Mode: New architecture, reverse engineered code.

Experienced improvements:
- A single software product line for all of Philips' mid-range and high-end television products.
- Able to produce the variability desired by marketing.
- Variability no longer a key problem for architect.
- Software development no longer on the critical path of product development.
- Still no need for a new software architecture after six years, while previous architectures lasted less than five years.

Business: To support the required variability, while maintaining a high quality-level and enabling combi-products in the future.

Architecture: A compositional rather than a decompositional approach is taken. The Koala component model and architecture description language is tuned towards use in resource-constrained systems.

Process: A change from a project organisation to a products and assets organisation.

Organisation: A product-oriented organisation was changed into a single development organisation that hosts asset and product teams.

14.1 Introduction

Philips Consumer Electronics, a division of Royal Philips [103], is one of the largest consumer electronics companies in the world. It has an annual turnover of €10 billion and a sustainable profit of 5%, which is considered quite well in this domain. Philips Consumer Electronics has 16,000 employees and is present in all regions of the world.

Televisions are responsible for one-third of the turnover of Philips Consumer Electronics.[1] Though a quite traditional product, they are an important factor in shaping the brand image that will allow all Philips divisions to create and enter new markets in lifestyle, healthcare and technology. Philips has a market share of 10% in televisions, roughly equal in size to its main competitors.

In this chap. we study the software product line that was set-up to create the software for televisions. The technology for this product line was created in 1996, the product line itself was initiated in 1998, and the product line has been in actual use since 2000. The approach is extensively documented in [148].

14.2 Motivation

Televisions were one of the first consumer products to contain embedded software and hardware. This started with an 8-bit micro controller and 1 KB of memory in 1978, and since then both hardware and software have grown following Moore's Law quite closely [29]. Fig. 14.1 shows the size of software in high-end televisions as a function of time.

The most important reason for this growth is the continuing integration and miniaturisation of hardware, with an accompanying decrease in costs. This allows to implement more and more of the functionality in software:

- A large part of the control shifted from hardware to software, for instance setting the tuner, detecting stereo sound and blanking the screen during zapping.
- Software made it possible to create fancy user interfaces, starting with character-based On Screen Displays, followed by character-based menus, then 2D graphical menus and now moving to 3D graphical menus.
- Data processing in a TV (Teletext) was done in hardware at first, but is now mostly done in software; only the basic capturing of data is still done in hardware. Other examples of data processing are closed captioning[2] and electronic program guides.

---

[1] From here on, the term "Philips" is used as a short hand for "Philips Consumer Electronics"

[2] Closed captioning means displaying a transcript of the audio part of a television program

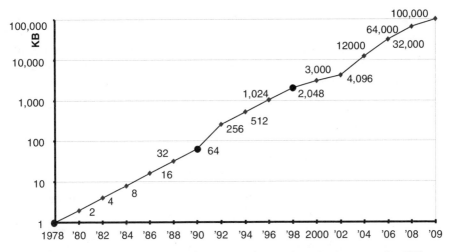

Fig. 14.1. Growth of software (code+data) in high-end televisions (in KB)

- Sound processing – decoding, featuring and rendering – has shifted to software quite a few years ago already, and image processing has recently shifted to be implemented mostly in software.
- Modern digital standards such as MPEG-4 make processing in software obligatory.

While this trend may alleviate the design of hardware to some extent, it certainly makes the design of software more complex. Managing this complexity is one of the challenges that we are still facing: a television is roughly as complex as a personal computer ten years ago.

The second challenge stems from the need for the company to bring out its products globally. While the global market was very diversified at first, around 1996 the common parts of the functionality in a TV grew larger than the region-specific parts, making a product line approach feasible. But profiting from this phenomenon and reflecting this commonality and variability in software is a non-trivial task, as many companies have experienced.

The third challenge was the upcoming convergence of products. Prototypical example of a convergence product around 1996 was a TV with built-in VCR, which allowed features such as a one-button "record what you see". The first such product consisted of two separate hardware and software systems that were very loosely integrated. To become more cost-effective, the two software architectures had to be integrated to run on a single CPU and in a single memory. More convergence products were expected, such as a TV with built-in DVD. A significant part of the problem was that TV and VCR (later DVD) software was developed in different divisions, each with their own profit and loss responsibility.

These three challenges combine to the following problem statement. The complexity of software is growing, and the number of product types increases, while the lead-time must decrease and the quality of the software must be maintained (consumers do not expect products to crash regularly). Philips took a number of actions to achieve this:

- *Urgent*: achieve "reuse in space", leading to an almost classical product line approach.
- *Medium-term*: achieve "reuse in time": making sure that products with new features can be produced every year.
- *Long-term*: solve the convergence problem.

Reuse in space involves properly managing the diversity of complex software in a product line. Obviously this involves more than maintaining a simple list of variability parameters: there will be hundreds of such parameters so at least some form of hierarchy is needed, and also the structure of the software will depend on variability.

Reuse in time requires evolution rules that dictate how parts of the software may be changed without breaking other parts of the software. This may seem a simple "backward compatibility issue", but there are many subtleties involved that make this very difficult in practice, as anyone will understand who has upgraded his operating system to a newer version and found his favourite applications not working anymore. This issue includes a proper anticipation of changes in hardware and coping with this in software.

But even if we manage to reuse 100% of our software over time, that will not solve all problems. Because in a world following Moore's Law, that would only delay our problems by two years.[3] The more fundamental solution is to obtain software from elsewhere. Not by outsourcing it – as that solves the people problem but not the cost – but by getting it from vendors who leverage their development costs over multiple customers.[4] For a consumer electronics company, part of the software can be obtained from the hardware supplier (the semiconductors company), and part can be obtained from independent software vendors.

The convergence problem is the hardest to solve, as it also involves crossing organisational boundaries within a company. The technical solution is to use composition instead of decomposition. To address the organisational issues, the existing situation of loosely coupled product teams was changed into a single development organisation, with asset- and product-oriented teams.

---

[3] Imagine a new product coming out every two years, where the size of the software has doubled. Even with perfect reuse, half of the software will be new. This implies that one still needs a team that grows exponentially in time, only two years shifted in time

[4] Thus establishing reuse over company borders

14.3 Approach

Before we delve into the technical details of the product line approach, we will first describe how the product line was actually set up.

In 1996, software architects in the Philips TV department foresaw severe problems in managing variability and asked Philips Research for a solution. By that time, there was already a long-standing co-operation between the TV department and Research in managing the ever-growing complexity of software, which had resulted in the software architecture that was used then.

Philips Research responded by comparing different software component models and creating Koala from the most suitable elements of these to solve complexity and variability issues in resource-constrained systems. This component model was transferred then, but using it to create the next generation software architecture turned out to be difficult while also maintaining the current architecture: key people could not be freed to work on the new architecture without endangering the current set of products.

Therefore, Philips Research was asked to set-up the next generation architecture and to fill this by reengineering the existing code. Interestingly, the resulting software architecture outlived the original hardware architecture for many years!

Research spent one year in setting up the architecture (1998), and then one year to build a lead product with this architecture together with the TV department (1999). The choice of the lead product proved to be critical: a product was chosen with high visibility and low risk. The lead product actually failed for non-technical reasons, but the second lead product was successful (in 2000), and within two years the software architecture and accompanying approach was used in the full range of Philips" TV products.

In the first two years (1998–1999), most of the developers of the TV department were still maintaining the old architecture to bring out the majority of products (and thus generate income). After that, developers gradually moved from the old loosely coupled product teams into a new single development organization.

Choice of the team also proved to be a critical success factor. The initial architecture team consisted of three architects, one experienced in software, one in business aspects and one in the domain. Five high-quality developers were soon added, experienced either in the domain or in software engineering (or both). An experienced project leader was added too.

As important as the team itself were the champions in the product division, monitoring and defending the new approach. The direct owner of the research work was the development manager of the TV department. The research was sponsored by the software director and monitored by the software process manager of Philips.

14.4 Business Aspects

The television market is an established market: it does not grow much, but it is very important for a company such as Philips to maintain market share, as this provides 10% of the Philips turn-over (30% of Philips Consumer Electronics). Also, it provides an important brand image for Philips to sell a variety of other products.

This market shares some typical characteristics with other consumer markets. Features initially introduced in high-end TVs soon become commodities, i.e. they are not positively discriminating anymore but they are *must-haves*: they negatively discriminate a product that lacks them. To maintain market share, development should be focused on adding new features, rather than on reimplementing old features.

The television market is a global market with quite some regional variability and a large range of prices. While individual products last over ten years, waves of new technologies tempt customers to buy new products sooner: black and white to colour, Teletext, sound and image quality, 100 Hz, 16:9, flat displays, picture browsing and connectivity are examples. The pace of introduction of new products onto the market increases from yearly to half-yearly or even shorter. Competition increases since PC and display technology make it possible for other companies, such as Hewlett-Packard and Dell, to enter the TV arena.

The short-term challenge for software development is to stay away from the critical path, to support as much variability as marketing requires and to maintain the quality level required for consumer products. The long-term challenge is to enable convergence in the form of combi-products and to compete with the PC industry that is trying to capture the living room.

14.5 Architecture

Many researchers in the field of software product lines believe in an a priori analysis of commonalities and differences of products in the portfolio, followed by the creation of a single reference architecture with explicit variation points.[5] While this may work for a small product line of TVs, we were in doubt whether it would work for the whole range of TVs that Philips produces, and we were sure that it would not allow us to create combi-products, if only because it is very difficult to agree on a common software architecture between different product departments.

We therefore opted for a *compositional* rather than a *decomposition* approach, partly inspired by the way that this was already possible in hardware. We designed the Koala component model, inspired by existing models such as Microsoft COM and Darwin [89], but tuned towards use in resource-constrained systems.

---

[5] See [11] for a discussion

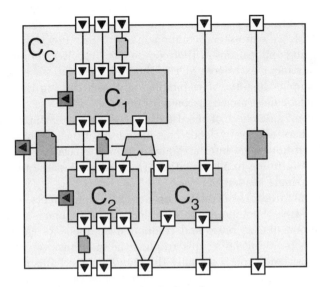

Fig. 14.2. An example Koala software component

Figure 14.2 shows an example component in Koala that illustrates many of the features of the model. First of all, a component is a unit of design not only of reuse, but also of implementation. In plain words, this means that a component has a description of the interfaces at its borders so that it can be used in various contexts, but it also has a specific implementation that cannot be separated from the component: a component is a specification and an implementation.

Koala components are implemented in C. The document-shaped objects in Fig. 14.2 represent C files. The squares with embedded triangles represent functional interfaces, with the triangle pointing into the direction of function call. A component not only specifies the interfaces that it *provides* to its environment, but also the interfaces that it *requires* from its environment: all communication with the environment is routed through interfaces. Configurations of components where the required interface of one component is provided by another one again form components. Thus, the component model is hierarchical.

In the file system, a component is a directory with a set of (C) source files and a file containing a Koala component description. There is no makefile for the component: the makefile is automatically generated from the component description. Put differently, the component description takes the place of the makefile in traditional development.

Interfaces are defined, syntactically and semantically, in separate files and in a separate language – the Interface Description Language (IDL) part of Koala. This allows us to reuse interface definitions to create multiple implementations of a functionality (remember that each implementation is a separate component). Also, by using an interface model similar to that of Microsoft COM, we can extend components with new functionality without breaking existing applications of that component. The Koala interface mechanism does not incur extra cost at run-time, as most interface bindings are resolved at compile-time. Interface binding only results in run-time code if the binding cannot be determined at compile-time.

An important side effect of the use of an IDL to specify interfaces is that interfaces are kept relatively clean. This includes a proper separation of type definitions from functional interfaces and a proper separation of a functional interface from an inline implementation. In classical C, these two facets are combined in a single header file.

Because configurations of components are again components, a product is a decomposition tree of components. Note that a product line is a composition *graph* of components, as basic and compound components can be used in multiple products. Maintaining this graph is the main task of the architect.

The composition graph is actually the high-level mechanism to deal with variability: different products may have different sub-systems sharing (a subset of) the same components. Diversity parameters[6] provide a low-level variability mechanism to parameterise code. These diversity parameters are organised into the so-called *diversity interfaces*, which are treated as ordinary required interfaces. Switches allow to implement structural diversity in the configuration of sub-components as an internal variability of the compound component (steered by diversity parameters), thus forming the bridge between the "high-level" and the "low-level" variability mechanism.

Packages group components and interfaces into private entities for use within a team only, and public entities for use by other teams. Packages are hierarchical: sub-packages allow a team to internally structure complex packages, while super-packages allow to model dependencies between packages in a hierarchical way.

The television software is divided into three layers – all made by Philips initially – with standard APIs between them (Fig. 14.3). This architecture had a clear intention: on the longer term, the operating system (OS) part

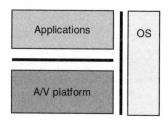

Fig. 14.3. Basic division of television software in three layers

---

[6] 'Diversity parameter' is the Koala terminology for a 'configuration' - or 'variability' - parameter

would be obtained from independent software vendors, while the audio/video (A/V) platform would be obtained from the hardware supplier, leaving only the applications to be developed by the television department.

The use of an architectural description language (Koala) enables enforcement of certain rules, such as allowed usage relations between packages and easy checking of other rules, such as multi-threaded use of interfaces. The ADL has a textual and a graphical syntax: the textual syntax is used in the product generation, while the graphical syntax is used in design discussions. Approximately 10% of the code is written in Koala; the rest is in C. The Koala compiler generates C code and header files from the Koala descriptions. The graphical component diagrams are made either by hand with Visio, or by using a tool that automatically generates a diagram from textual descriptions.

14.6 Process

We have described some of the technical aspects of the software product line approach in the previous sect., and they are indeed important success factors. But a development department cannot switch to a product line approach by incorporating technology only. The development process and organisation has to be changed as well. We found the most important change to be the move from a project organisation to a products and assets organisation. Previously, there was one large team per product, doing a complete waterfall life-cycle for that product. In the new way of working, medium-sized asset teams have an iterative development process, and small product teams integrate assets.

Of course, work is still organised in projects, but there are now two kinds of projects: long-running projects to develop and evolve assets and relatively short-running projects to build products. Figure 14.4 shows the relation between these types. There are various models for organising asset and product development, but we found the most workable to be an $m{:}n$ relation between sub-system and product development: sub-systems working for m products, and products integrating n sub-systems. This relationshop between products and sub-systems is defined by the architecture. Other models have a platform integration step in between, but this adds an extra delay between implementing a new feature and utilising it in a product.

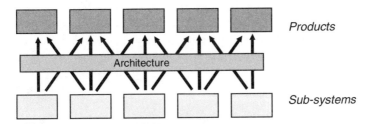

Fig. 14.4. The relation between sub-system and product development

The way software is documented also has to change. A traditional, project-oriented software development organisation typically creates requirements, global design and detailed design document, describing what is going to be made. Our product line documentation includes component and interface data sheets, describing what has been made, with additional architectural sub-system design notes, forming a living description of the evolving architecture.

Configuration management is traditionally implemented as one big archive for all software for all products, creating complexity and performance problems, or as separate archives for small sets of products, with opportunistic reuse only between the different archives. We found it convenient to have a configuration management system per asset team and per product team, and have weak links between these archives, exchanging formal releases of the software only. This scales relatively easily to larger organisations.

We are also in favour of an open development environment[7] where everyone can see every bit of software. We achieve this by publishing all releases on the intranet. Of course, there are parts of the software for which this is not possible, e.g. due to licensing reasons.

Testing also has to be adapted. Traditionally, products are created incrementally, with continuous system testing ensuring that new features work and do not break existing features. But if sub-systems are to be used in multiple products, they have to be tested in isolation and this also holds for components within sub-systems. However, testing sub-systems in isolation is a non-trivial issue: many problems become apparent only after integration with other sub-systems. This is why we create pseudo products at an early stage: products that are not to be released on the market, but that serve as early integration test for (new versions of) the sub-systems.

Managing requirements for a product line is a challenge by itself: instead of separate requirement documents per product, one would like to optimally profit from commonality between products, but at the same time keep individual documents readable. We also found that improperly structured requirements documents, where the product line aspects were not taken into account usually result in improper design structures. While this can be solved at the design level, the harm is still done at the requirements level.

As a final remark on the consequences that a product line approach has on the development process, the fact that sub-systems are used in multiple products implies a road-mapping activity that plans and agrees on deliveries between asset teams and product teams. In our organisation, a release matrix is used to maintain a view on releases as functions of time.[8]

---

[7] That is, open within the company. This is sometimes called Inner Source
[8] See [138] for another discussion on this topic

14.7 Organisation

Business needs must be translated into an architecture, and the architecture shapes the development process. To execute this process effectively, the development organisation must be adapted as well.

In Philips, software development was traditionally organised in product teams responsible for the development of a particular product or a small set of such products. We changed this in a number of steps into a single development organisation that hosts asset teams and product teams.

The asset teams are in principle funded from a single source, derived from the sum of contributions of the product teams. This is possible because there is a single development manager heading all developments. Although in theory asset teams work for multiple products, we have seen cases where product teams requested specific sources from asset teams to work on their product. While there is nothing wrong with asset teams being very aware of the specific products that use their sub-system, we generally object to "people shopping".

The balance between generic and specific development is delicate. In principle, asset developers have the long-term applicability of their assets as goal, while product developers have the successful release of their product onto the market as immediate goal. But long-term assets have no value if short-term products fail to be on the market in time. We have seen various models to successfully build products in our organisation, including asset developers joining product teams for short periods of time, and asset archives being split into product specific branches. This may be appropriate in certain cases, but there must also be a force pushing towards product independence and long-term value of assets. At the end of the day, the only way that we managed to achieve this is to make it the personal responsibility of the asset teams, and reserving sufficient resources for asset development.

Another complicating factor is distributed development. TV development sites were traditionally distributed around the world, with many locations in the USA and in Europe. Development sites have also been opened in India and in the Far East. We found it important to align the architecture, the project structure and the organisation. In plain words, a sub-system is developed by a single (asset) team located at a single site. We initially had four cases where this alignment was not optimal – i.e. distributed teams were working on a single sub-system – and in all cases the result was severe communication and integration problems. Others report similar experiences [153].

14.8 Results

While in 1996 variability ranked high on the list of issues of the software architects, variability has completely disappeared from that list since the introduction of Koala and the accompanying product line architecture and approach. The team is now able to create the diversity of products required by marketing, and to produce these different variants on time.

An interesting side effect is that architects who joined the team in 2002 or later have not experienced variability problems themselves and sometimes fail to see the added value of a solution like Koala. Since it always costs a certain amount of effort to maintain a proprietary solution, some want to remove it altogether. This shows how a success factor can become a failure factor later. Replacing a proprietary solution with a solution obtained elsewhere is a different issue, and should be done as soon as such a solution is available, and the cost of conversion is not too high.

Although the initial lead product failed for non-technical reasons, the second product succeeded. After that, there was a quick ramp-up and, within two years, all of Philips" mid-range and high-end televisions were produced with this approach.

Another indication of success is the fact that so far there has been no need to develop a new architecture. Previous architectures lasted at most five years. Of course, with software size still growing according to Moore's Law, setting up a new architecture from scratch is almost unaffordable.

14.9 Lessons Learned

The most important lesson that we learned is that all facets of BAPO must be addressed otherwise the introduction of a software product line approach will fail.[9] There must be a business drive to create a product line, there must be a proper software architecture and component technology, the development process must be adapted and the organisation must be made to fit.

It took us three years to become successful, and even longer if you measure elapsed time. We sincerely doubt whether the introduction of a product line approach in this context could have been done any faster, given the amount of change that was needed in architecture, technology, process and organisation. But keeping such an activity alive for three years without intermediate results is very difficult, and has failed in some other parts of Philips. A technique that can be introduced incrementally would therefore be highly welcomed. But we also have experiences that changing an architecture incrementally is a process that may be too slow to obtain significant results within a few years.

A successful product line organisation requires a very delicate balance between application and domain engineering. The introduction of a similar approach failed in another part of Philips. After setting up the structure, the organisation could potentially produce many products, but fell in a genericity trap and did not succeed in creating even a single product. As a result, the organisation changed back to a structure that successfully produced a single product but the potential for creating a product line was mostly removed.

One of the failure factors of a product line organisation is to have too many dependencies among deliverables. If a change in sub-system A has to

---

[9] In fact, the case described here was one of the inputs in the creation of the BAPO approach

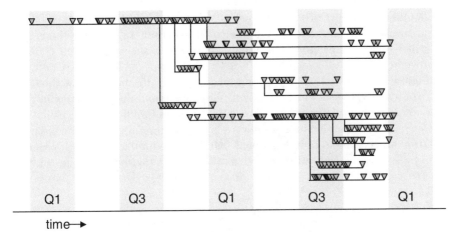

Fig. 14.5. Actual branching of sub-systems

be integrated into sub-system B before B can be released to C, then the time between fixing a problem or implementing a new feature can become too long. The *m:n* delivery model as described above is better, but requires strict evolution rules and still some form of pre-integration.

The configuration management strategy is another critical factor. Many configuration management systems claim that they can manage variability, but they can do this only at the level of files, and they can only handle compile-time variability. It is better to solve variability in the architecture, and use a traditional configuration management system for version management and for temporary branches to safeguard a product that is to be released from changes to sub-systems made on behalf of other products. This scheme worked fine for us initially, but then temporary branches were kept alive increasingly longer, resulting in many parallel branches to be maintained. Figure 14.5 shows an example of this. Each vertical band represents a quarter of a year, the horizontal lines represent different branches of development, and the triangles represent (intermediate) releases. The longest living line is the main line of

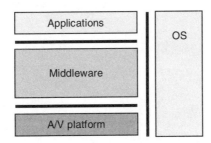

Fig. 14.6. The top-level architecture as it evolves

development, the rest are side branches. We measured the amount of effort spent on side branches and found this to be less than 15% [149]. Therefore, we still regard our product line approach as being successful, even though improvements are still possible.

Figure 14.3 showed our initial top-level architecture, based upon the idea that the three parts would be implemented by three different parties in due time. This is in fact currently happening, with one addition: between A/V platform and applications a middleware layer is emerging, with software provided by an ecosystem of independent software vendors, which again reduces costs by leveraging the software over more products, as shown in Fig. 14.6.

Philips Medical Systems

with Gerard Schouten

Company facts of Philips Medical Systems

Organisational size: >1,000 developers.
Starting Mode: Strategic focus, based on existing assets.

Experienced improvements:
- Two to four times effort reduction.
- Reduction to less than 50% time to market for reused functionality.
- Product defect density to 50% of original rate for reused functionality.
- Ease of feature propagation from one product to others.
- Common look-and-feel: Vequion.
- Better product planning and use of roadmaps.

Business: Alignment of planning, licence model to pay platform effort.

Architecture: Based on shared components, interfaces and semantics in several layers. Hierarchical product line model.
Process: Any product line amplifications for CMMI level 3. Multi-partner, multi-project, multi-site development.
Organisation: Separation of domain and application engineering organisations. Improved collaboration.

15.1 Introduction

Philips Medical Systems[1] produces imaging equipment that is used to support medical diagnoses and interventions. Some systems are capable of image acquisition. Examples are X-ray, Magnetic Resonance Imaging (MRI), Computer Tomography (CT) and Ultrasound. Typically, such a product will scan the patient in one way or another and produce images to be viewed immediately. Other products deal with image interchange, archiving and recovery for later viewing, and image processing and annotation. Fig. 15.1 shows several situations of this equipment in use.

The company is distributed all over the world, with product development in several countries. Product groups (divisions) are responsible for specific market segments. Typically, several (marketed) product lines are available in each product group. Although the product lines differ a lot, there are also possibilities for software reuse. All products deal with storing, retrieving and exchanging medical images, and many product lines support image-processing and viewing.

15.2 Motivation

In 1997, an initiative was started to produce the common software for all the product lines as an imaging platform to be used across Philips. During the introduction, several acquisitions have taken place increasing the portfolio to come to a complete range of imaging products for hospitals. There is a strong drive from the board of management to increase the synergy between the newly acquired and the original groups, and to reduce the total development costs. The imaging platform is a means to support this. The platform must be usable for all product groups.

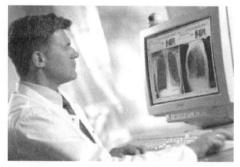

Fig. 15.1. Examples of medical imaging systems: X-ray equipment and a viewing workstation

---

[1] From here on, the term 'Philips' is used as a short hand for 'Philips Medical Systems'

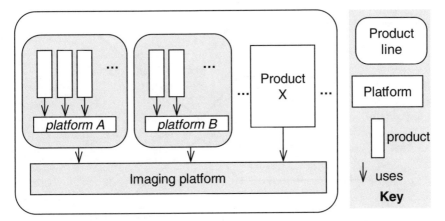

Fig. 15.2. Hierarchical product line at Philips

This chapter reports the main findings of the development and the introduction of this imaging platform. The initial ideas of producing the platform emerged in 1997, when the first meetings of architects of several development groups were set up. In 1998, a start was made with the design of the reference architecture, and the production of the first software components. In 2001 the first version of the platform was released, and used by the first product lines. After that, the number of product lines that uses the platform has increased rapidly. The platform has grown to cover many core medical software components.

The imaging platform and the product groups using it form a hierarchical software product line+(cf. Fig. 15.2) Each product group uses its own platform variants and configurations in their own product lines. The imaging platform supports several software product lines, and it must support a broad scope of variability requirements. This set-up induces interaction and interdependency between the development processes of the imaging platform and the product groups. The resulting overhead is paid back by the reduction of duplicated developments of similar software.

15.3 Approach

15.3.1 Adoption Approach

We will discuss three phases of the adoption of software product line engineering at Philips: conception, birth and growth, depicted in Fig. 15.3.

Conception

There are many well-known reasons to start with software product line development. Typical examples are to efficiently use the development effort and

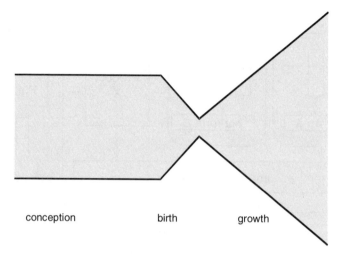

conception   birth   growth

Fig. 15.3. Evolution of the scope of the platform, curve by Rob van Ommering

reduce lead-time, to improve quality, to exploit similarity among products and to increase similarity. Most of these reasons apply to Philips. An important way to improve development efficiency is to centralise the development of common functionality of different products. A software product line engineering approach reduces the development effort by reducing the amount of duplication of coding and other development activities. In addition, it helps to reduce the time to market, which was originally several years to about one year. Of course, the quality level of the products is maintained, or even increased.

The development efficiency increases through a shared, Philips-wide architecture, with standard interfaces and reusable components. An important goal is to increase the similarity among products. This impacts both the marketing – showing the customer a large variety of similar products with a characteristic look-and-feel – and system creation possibilities, through the configuration of several products together. It also enables the so-called multi-modality applications. For instance, viewing magnetic resonance imaging pictures on X-ray equipment.

Since Philips' products are used within hospitals, they are subject to high quality standards. A common platform must support strict dependability concerns and should be of high quality if it is to be used as the basis for medical products. The confidence in the platform grows with the installed base of products successfully using it.

Shared architecture meetings were organised to initiate software product line thinking, and to get commitment of the involved parties. Architects from several development groups discussed the options and problems of moving towards a shared platform. One development group was making workstations for viewing, storing and exchanging medical images. This group was the most natural candidate to become the platform supplier. Two other product development groups produced X-ray and MRI products. These groups were seen as the first potential customers of the platform.

In the mean time, business commitment for initiating the reuse program for system product lines was obtained. This was facilitated by a visit of Martin Griss, co-author of *Software Reuse* [71]. Management and senior architects decided to proceed with managed reuse. The department heads appointed a platform development manager.

Domain engineering was performed in an ad hoc way. The architects were all very well acquainted with the domain of medical imaging. The discussions lead to a handful of crucial architecture decisions about the set-up of a component-based, layered architecture. Shared interfaces and a shared information model based on DICOM [46] to distribute medical images were defined. The platform was built upon commercial basic software, its core being based upon the existing software in the workstations product group. It was planned to package this software into components with well-managed interfaces, and to include it in the product lines of all three involved product groups.

Birth

The first middleware components, interfaces and data models were implemented soon after the architects network was set up, management commitment was obtained and the initial reference architecture was determined. These components incorporated the kernel functionality of the platform. Development was organised as a formal release project, involving a lot of prototyping. The architects in the network assessed the first component implementations jointly before they were released. The involved product groups incorporated them in their product lines in the next product releases. The architect's network was kept alive and was used to obtain conformance and agreements over the different product group borders.

Project management for creating the platform was set up incrementally, based upon and using the resources of the product creation projects that already existed in the organisation. In a similar way the support organisation was set up.

As changes in the imaging platform can have company-wide effects, change-control boards were established before the release of the first components. Since an evolutionary approach was envisioned, future adaptations were inevitable and carefully planned for. The change-control boards had to decide when and how to introduce changes, balancing long-term and short-term objectives. Separate change-control boards were set up for architecture, components, interfaces and information models. A program steering committee, consisting of managers from different product groups, was responsible for the overall planning of the program.

Growing

Growing the platform was done in several directions simultaneously. The architecture evolved to include more domain-specific functionality. Other development groups became involved, both as users and as members of the architect's network and software community. Existing functionality within other products was migrated to the platform. In addition, third-party software was selected to be included in the platform as well.

A pragmatic approach was used for growing the platform. Domain-specific parts were developed in-house, taking full advantage of the expertise of the product groups. Non-domain-specific commodity software was bought on the market. Initially, the platform was designed not to be too generic (see Fig. 15.3) During conception it covered mainly the needs of the three involved product groups and the envisioned few next users. When constructing the initial software components and interfaces (birth), the scope was further reduced to cover only a part of the needs of the directly involved product groups. After the initial release of the platform, the scope was enlarged again to support the needs of a growing number of product groups. Presently, more than ten product groups use the platform.

Growing the architecture and functionality of the platform implied that many interfaces and components were included. Often this functionality existed already, but in many cases improvements and new features were incorporated. Care was taken that during the evolution of the platform it always consists of living[2] components and interfaces. After first component or interface release there is always a working version available, which can be used by anyone who needs it. No component is released if it cannot be used with the other components in the platform. The data models are always growing through the inclusion of requirements for new functionality. The data models, too, are alive: for each model element, there are components using it. The notion of living components, interfaces and data models has proven to be crucial to build, verify, validate and test software upon a basis of already existing and tested software.

To involve a growing number of product groups, there is a continuous activity to update the roadmap and to plan the platform activities. This is the only way to reach optimal benefit for the increasing group of platform users. Each product group has its own roadmaps, which involve planning when and what to use of the platform. No one is forced to use the complete platform: every group is able to decide the pace of the evolutionary introduction of the platform within its own development. Still, a product group needs good reasons to redevelop functionality that is already available in the platform.

Presently, Philips aims for full-scale adoption and increasing maturity of the platform. The platform content has to cover the needs of all product groups, but to stay focused on generic functionality at the same time. Through

---

[2] "Living" means that the component or interface is well tested and ready to be used

active support of the professional software community and an accompanying maintenance and support organisation, the imaging platform is becoming mature and stays healthy. It can and must be used by all product groups.

15.3.2 Current Development Approach

Business

At the start, it was known that reuse is not a free lunch but needs time and investments. Part of the invested effort was spent by people that were originally assigned to existing products. Increasingly, people who have been working in release projects were moved towards platform component projects. Their expertise and their software moved with them. The imaging platform is growing towards a self-supporting activity within Philips, as investments of previous years have become profitable.

The business model of the platform development does not aim to maximise profit for the platform group. A model that is profitable for the product groups works better. In practice, this means that these product groups together fund the software development of the platform components. They get the platform software much cheaper than if they would have developed it themselves, although the platform software is often more generic than what they need.

The product groups focus on creating the software that makes their products competitive. Although financial calculations were not made in advance explicitly, it was clear that the growth in the number of software engineers across the company was becoming too expensive in the long-term. It was clear that there would never be enough people in the organisation to produce all required software in the product groups themselves. Software development had to be shared, and even outsourced.

The platform development model reduced this pressure significantly. The platform components are built and maintained with about 1.6 times the number of people necessary for a single product group to develop the software itself at the same time. Since there are several product groups using the platform, each of them has to pay only a small part of this 1.6 factor. Payment is done on a yearly basis and dependent on the part of the platform that is used by the product groups. The funding model has evolved over the years. Philips funded the platform development centrally at the conception phase. Presently, all participating divisions pay for it on a yearly basis.

In Fig. 15.4 the business consequences of platform development are depicted. If no platform development is done, the software engineering cost grow linearly over time see, the *No Reuse* line. Different product groups, e.g. PG_a, PG_b and PG_c, using the platform will follow a *Reuse* curve, which involves initially more effort, but over time drops under the *No Reuse* line. Dependent on what is used from the platform the product groups will follow different

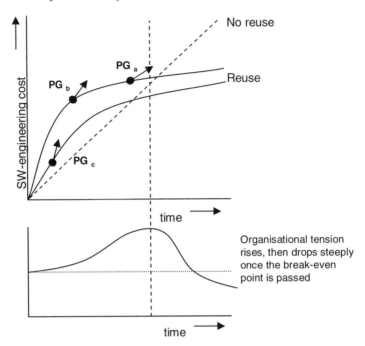

Fig. 15.4. Business consequences of the platform development

curves. The time and pace of the introduction of the platform in a department group determines the position that the particular group has on the curve.

In almost all groups, the tension in the organisation against using the platform is growing until the positive effects of reuse begin to show. Initially, a lot of effort is invested, while the payback is still invisible. Developers and project managers focus on the negative points. The time needed to introduce the platform is seen as evidence for it being counter-productive, and people want to abandon platform use. Management has to be strong to actively support the platform use in that time. After the break-even the tensions drops very fast, and the willingness of using the platform increases equally fast. Because different product groups are at the break-even point at different moments in time, the growing tension is a continuous attention point of the platform development management. Part of the tension can be reduced by delivering those parts of the platform that are important for the groups with the highest level of tension, thus helping them to reach their break-even point sooner.

Architecture

The architectural requirements for the imaging platform are as follows:

- *Facilitation of evolutionary migration*: the only way to perform the transition to a widespread use of the platform was to start with a small basis and extend it in an evolutionary way. The product groups should stay in business during the transition, and revolutionary approaches were not deemed feasible. The architecture and components should be based upon existing software in the products, and then transformed into platform components on a piece-by-piece basis. This leads to a component-based architecture.

- *Technology independence*: technology is changing and the platform should be based upon commercial, changing, software. The product groups have their own pace in adopting new technology. Therefore, the platform should be designed as independent as possible from this third-party software, and at any time be able to cope with certain differences in technology. To solve this issue, patterns such as bridges, adapters and converters were introduced.

- *Suitable for a range of low-end and high-end systems*: the product lines of the product groups were covering low- and high-end products. Therefore, the architecture has to support this, and allow for different implementations – with different quality attributes – of the same functionality.

- *Minimal dependency among components*: the components should be as orthogonal as possible from each other. This simplifies the transition as product groups can initially select only the platform functionality that they really need.

- *High degree of flexibility*: the components should be based upon existing software. This eases their introduction in the different product lines, since it can gradually replace existing software. Moreover, it facilitates the introduction of components, and consequently avoids bottlenecks during development, since most functionalities are already available.

The resulting architecture is open and extensible (Fig. 15.5). The platform consists mainly of components and interfaces in the lower three levels in Fig. 15.5. It consists of common software and software used by several development groups. The *System components* layer mostly comprises of third-party commodity software. They are chosen to provide the basic services. *Middleware components* is the core of the platform and consists of medical middleware that is used by all product groups. Most parts of the *Business-specific components* layer do not belong to the platform. Their functionality is too specific and is only used by one or a few product groups. Should this change, provisions are made that commonality may be extracted from such components, which then may become part of the platform.

The reference architecture is defined by components, connectors and their respective semantics. Components are the reusable units of the architecture, to be selected, configured and used by the platform users. Configuring deals with 'tuning' the behaviour of a component via initialisation and other parameters. Besides straightforward component selection, this is another important variation mechanism, suitable for dealing with varying quality requirements such as performance.

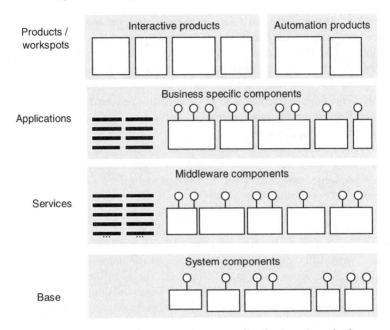

Fig. 15.5. Philips reference architecture for the imaging platform

The connectors are the interfaces which are much more stable than the components. Through these interfaces all users connect components to the platform. Interfaces are conceived as contracts between a server and a client. Seen from the viewpoint of the client, the server provides interfaces that offer functionality. However, in order to access that functionality, it is required that the client implements an attach interface.[3] Interfaces are well managed by change-control boards and this guides the evolution of the architecture.

The semantics of the platform are captured in information models, which improves the stability of the interfaces [147]. The information models are used to interchange data over the interfaces. Therefore, the data semantics are not reflected in the interfaces. The interfaces were designed to deal with generic data access functions only. In particular, data access is abstracted in a uniform way, independent of whether it resides on the network, a database, a file or other media.

Process

Development of the imaging platform can be seen as a large domain engineering effort. Commonalities with respect to image handling across the different modalities are resolved in this platform. Application engineering is the deployment of the platform in the various product groups in order to create

---

[3] This model of provided and required interfaces is further worked out in [75]

the complete systems. In this case, domain and application engineering are strictly separated in different organisational units.

The generic component suite of the imaging platform is developed in an evolutionary way. As a rule of thumb, a regular heartbeat leads to two new version releases per year. The second is fully forward-and-backward compatible with the first one, but this is not necessarily the case for earlier versions.

A mature development process has helped to establish the software product line. It has proven valuable that the organisation that is responsible for the imaging platform has a predictable, repeatable and quantifiable process. The platform group is on CMMI level 3, whereas most of the product groups are on CMMI level 2 (some are on level 1, some on level 3). Following are detailed explanations of some important aspects of key process areas of the imaging platform organisation.

Requirements Management

All requirements for the imaging platform are gathered in a database. This can be in the format of use cases, problem reports, or change requests of the various product groups. At any time, their status is visible to all the product groups within Philips. For each new release, the platform and product groups discuss which requirements are in and which are out of scope. The results of this discussion are reflected by appropriate status changes in the database.

Project Management

Managing projects is done in accordance with regular CMMI level 3 practices. That is, projects are phased and progress is monitored according to well-established procedures and metrics. Furthermore, there is a lot of emphasis on managing risks. Product risks for one or more product groups that are related to safety or security are identified and carefully tracked. Mitigation measures are actively tracked.[4] Specific quality-assurance aspects and measures are included in the project plan. The quality-assurance department of the platform group regularly verifies compliance with internal processes. The product groups are entitled to execute audits on the platform projects.

Supplier Management

Outsourcing of platform development is centralised at the platform development group. Because a single architecture is used, software obtained via outsourcing can be used within the whole product line. To reduce the number of outsourcing-related contacts, the platform development group manages the outsourcing of software that is used by many platform users. Up-to-date architecture knowledge is always available at the organisation that does the outsourced work.

---

[4] In many countries, the approval of legal authorities is required to sell medical devices. These agencies need in-depth insight into all kinds of risk-regulation measures that are taken

Configuration Management

Identifying the right components to share over the product line is one of the most challenging activities in development. Before the users and developers decide what functionality should be included in the platform, it has to be decided which products are going to use it. Planning of future use has to be taken into account as well. Next, the relationship of these assets with configuration items has to be established accurately. This may be an *n:m* mapping.

The verification of completeness and correctness of components requires a framework in which the components execute. Part of the verification requires integrating components in the receiving products. For example, the performance of image-processing components may be different in X-ray equipment than it is for magnetic resonance imaging. This requires special organisational measurements from both the platform and product groups.[5]

In addition, software configuration management concerns the control of the evolution of complex systems. Most Philips products are developed at different sites. This requires that versions of software sources are available at different locations in the world. Furthermore, product releases are developed in parallel projects. At any certain point in time, the same software sources must be ready for configuration according to various requirements for the different product releases. Configuration management systems must support software merging to handle various development streams for multiple sites and multiple projects.

It is even more important to manage the development streams from a product line perspective in order to reduce the number of software merges and software testing. The software architecture deals with this by introducing relatively independent component suites that can be reused as packages by the different development groups. The independence is partially established by using only a few very generic interfaces for communication between the different suites. Of course, each suite enables configuration to make it adaptable to the different users' desires.

Change Control

Change control asks for special attention due to the large range of stakeholders. Change-control boards are organised to discuss change requests and decide on improvements for the coming releases. The versioning strategy of shared components must be in line with the release strategies of the various product lines of the business. Change control requires attention during the whole lifecycle of the product, including the maintenance phase after (internal) delivery of components.

---

[5] More information on dealing with reuse for different groups of users can be found in [72]

Organisation

Many factors contribute to the success of the organisation. An important aspect is stability. Throughout the development of the platform, no major disruptions have occurred in investment, or in the scope of the platform. There were only minor changes in staffing and management. Everyone involved is aware of the activity and its goals. Moreover, product line development originated as a bottom-up activity, and this is still an important driver. To improve their knowledge of the products. the platform developers are placed as closely as possible to the product groups.

The platform development group originally was a separate team within a special product group. This caused tension because people working on the platform were also partially involved in product development. Both tasks demanded time and attention. Eventually, the platform group turned into a separate department in the product group. The remaining parts of the product group became a platform user too, although still within the same organisation. This procedure increased and lengthened the tension curve within that specific product group. Presently, the platform group has its own organisation and a central responsibility for all Philips development groups. An important reason for this is to ensure that all product groups have the same relationship with the platform group.

Over the years, several companies were acquired by Philips. As a result, new and unexpected product groups became platform users. The new groups were treated in a similar way as the other product groups. Their architects became involved in the architect's network and the platform planning and roadmaps were adapted to their needs. At the same time, their own roadmaps were altered to introduce the platform software in evolutionary ways.

At the start, there were very few facilities for cross-division communication. In fact, e-mail was the main tool. Early on, an intranet website was established for publishing and distributing relevant architecture and requirement documents. This site is still used and continuously improved. Co-operation presently occurs over country borders on a day-to-day basis. Teleconferencing facilities are important to enhance communication. Face-to-face meetings are held on a regular basis, even if major travelling is required.

15.4 Results and Impact Evaluation

There is a business model in place to be able to fund the domain engineering unit. Product groups pay a license fee for platform use. It is a useful model, but it needs further improvement to tune the internal customer relationship. The business enforces the use of the platform by all application engineering groups. Technical roadmaps for domain and application engineering are in place, although they are still not completely aligned.

A marketed product line is in place under the name 'Vequion'. It refers to a set of products that are interoperable and that apply the same user interface. Using the platform makes it easy to be Vequion compatible. In fact, the Vequion products are those that use the platform.

There is a single product line architecture available, which is supported by a platform, interfaces and data models. It is used to different degrees by the product groups. Each group specialises the architecture and platform for its own use.

The requirements of the domain and application engineering groups are moving together to be treated as a single set of product requirements.

The domain engineering group is at the time of writing this chapter at CMMI level 3. The other departments are also moving towards this level. The practices are tuned towards use in a product line engineering context. Currently, mainly technical assets are shared between groups. Only a few best practices are shared.

After some intermediate stages, where platform development was part of a product group, there is now a clear organisational separation between application and domain engineering. Many teams deal with product-line aspects over department borders. These teams meet often, both face-to-face and via teleconferencing. Feedback is mainly obtained through change-control boards that are set up for separate issues. The integration is not always ideal, which increases tension. A few departments still do a lot of independent development, leading to duplicated effort.

15.5 Lessons Learned

Co-operation was established such that definitions were made jointly, but implementations were done separately. From experience, it was known that having a single group to define and implement a platform would not work in the decentralised Philips organisation.

Strict interface definition and change control was essential for the Philips reuse program, in which various parties develop software components for one overall software framework. As planned, the interfaces were very stable, thanks to the separation of the information models (semantics) from the interfaces (connectors). The information models changed frequently, but since they can be developed rather independent of the remainder of the software – and especially the interfaces – the effect of each change remains local.

Reuse adoption has to be anchored in processes. The organisation has to support the involved people, who need time to learn how to understand and, more importantly, trust each other well.

Evolutionary growth must be planned and guided carefully. A good initial architecture is crucial for this. This helps new architects to quickly understand the choices, which eases the adoption of these choices.

The platform and its architecture significantly increase the number of possible products that can be assembled. There is a reference architecture, implemented in a shared imaging platform, whose parts are configured in previous unexpected and unforeseen ways.

A risk of using components across multiple product lines is that the functionality of the component may be too generic for specific use. The product line has to extend the component for its own specific use. There is a mismatch between the *assumed* and the *actual* value of a component. This especially holds when the component does not cover the complete product requirements. In this case, the actual value is a lot lower than the assumed value. Philips has learned this lesson. It was expected that a product group could easily deliver the required functionality, based on a reusable and tested component. In practice, it occurs that a product group has to extend the reusable component significantly, without having the flexibility to change the component code. The Inner Source development model reduces these situations. It is meant to support the adoption of improvements to the platform done by product groups. This leads to sub-optimal solutions. Sometimes, workarounds reveal hidden bugs in the component or cause unexpected system behaviour.

15.6 Outlook

Philips uses a pragmatic, bottom-up approach to produce a platform that is used by a growing number of software product groups within Philips. It was started in a well-understood domain that was central to the company. It has grown towards a large collection of common software in medical imaging and viewing. Adoption of the platform was planned by selecting the right common software first. Management support increased the platform use from the very beginning.

The platform did not come for free. Many investments were necessary, both in resources and in learning how to co-operate. However, people learned to trust each other over department and country borders. At any given moment, there is a lot of tension in the organisation, rising from the conflict between short-term product delivery and long-term investment. As soon as the tension reduces in one part of the organisation, it rises elsewhere. This tension is dealt with through stable and sustained management support for software product line engineering.

The initiative started small and gradually involved more people and product groups. From the very beginning, *real* projects were involved as users of the (incomplete) platform, and architects from all product groups were responsible for the reference architecture. This reinforced the commitment of the product groups. Development of the software community at a company level is an essential element to promote reuse in the long-term.

By now, it has been shown that development effort can indeed be shared and costs can be reduced. The economics of scale act through the fact that many distinct product groups use the software. This has increased the market of the platform product group.

The business model still needs improvement. The requests of all product groups need to be satisfied in an objective and fair manner. Feedback between platform users and providers must be improved. A model based on open source development, dubbed Inner Source, may improve this.

The scope of the product line has to expand to serve the needs of all product groups. In addition, more domain-specific shared functionality at a higher-abstraction level must be incorporated in the platform.

Philips cannot perform without the existing product line and its platform. There are simply not enough people available to develop similar software in parallel projects. However, the overall satisfaction is not optimal. Partially, this is due to the tension in the organisation that rises near the break-even point (Fig. 15.4). At such moments, developing on your own still seems to be cost-effective, and result in better products. But given time, the break-even point is reached, and eventually each product group accepts and even embraces product line engineering as a way forward.

Siemens Medical Solutions

with Andreas Reuys
Klaus Pohl
Josef Weingärtner

Company facts of Siemens Medical Solutions

Organisational size: 100 developers.
Starting Mode: Bottom-up.

Experienced improvements:
— Reuse level: ~50%.
— Reduction of development cycle time: ~25%.
— Reduction of cost of quality: ~57%.

Business: The adoption of product line engineering concepts was focused on effort reductions.

Architecture: The architecture is based on a client–server architecture. Only a high-level architecture description was developed for the reference architecture.

Process: The V-model was extended to support product line engineering for testing.

Organisation: The shift had an impact on the organisation, as role descriptions had to be extended.

16.1 Introduction

Siemens Medical Solutions is one of the largest companies providing hospital applications. The portfolio of products covers nearly everything from X-Ray tubes, over Magnetic Resonance Imaging (MRI) and Computed Tomography (CT) scanners to complete infrastructure support in hardware and software for hospitals and all other medical practitioners.

The department Health Services Image Management[1] specialises in software for image distribution and image post-processing. The supported physician is the radiologist. The task of the radiologist starts with patient registration and ends after several activities with reporting and archiving of the images in the report repository (see Fig. 16.1). This workflow is standardised in the "Integrating the Healthcare Enterprise initiative" [69].

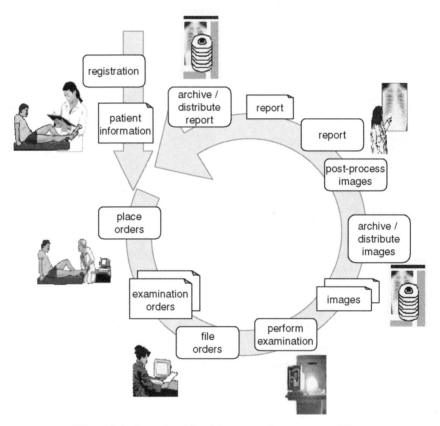

Fig. 16.1. Integrated healthcare environment workflow

---

[1] From here on, the term 'Siemens' is used as a short hand for 'Siemens Medical Solutions Health Services-Image Management'

The experiences described below stem from the development of the SIENET COSMOS product line of a picture archiving and communication systems. The SIENET COSMOS product line is developed with around 100 developers, including requirements engineering, programmers, testers and other stakeholders. Its development is distributed over several countries. SIENET COSMOS is one of the three running product lines, the other two being SIENET SKY and SIENET Magic.

The University of Duisburg-Essen co-operated in the introduction of product line engineering, in particular on the subject of requirements engineering and product line engineering, which are specialisations of the Software Systems Engineering group. This group had an ongoing co-operation with Siemens starting 1999, and thus had insights in the Siemens, internal processes.

This chapter deals with the introduction of product line engineering in the testing process at Siemens.

16.2 Motivation

The main objective of the introduction of product line engineering at Siemens was to reduce development effort. Due to the very high quality-assurance costs in the medical domain, the focus was on the reduction of testing effort [112].

16.3 Approach

16.3.1 Adoption Process

The predecessor of the SIENET COSMOS product line consisted of two rather similar applications. While planning to improve these applications and add a third, the decision was made to develop all three applications with the same assets, because large parts of the functionality were common to all products and it was expected that components were usable in each of them. Besides components, requirements, architecture and test cases were also expected to be reusable.

The decision to develop these applications with product line engineering was not driven by management. The management did support the technicians' intentions to come to a more efficient development by reusing assets, but even though they knew about product line engineering, they decided not to establish formal domain and application engineering processes. The following were the reasons for this decision:

- Budgets and resources were already planned.
- There was a tight schedule.
- Management was not sure whether successes that were achieved elsewhere could be repeated in the context of this specific project.

Management associated the introduction of domain and application engineering with separate teams, additional training and start-up overhead that could not be dealt with in the original plan and schedule. Thus, the project managers decided that only the inevitable activities from product line engineering were adapted to the company's needs. In essence, this was modelling of variability, which included

- defining commonalities and differences in requirements and architecture
- associating variants to the planned applications
- specifying common and application-specific components.

A challenge was that development of the product line was distributed over the world. There were no technicians familiar with product line engineering in the already-staffed project. Therefore, it was intended to concentrate these product-line-specific activities at a single location, more precisely at the project headquarters in Erlangen, Germany. The facilitator had only to support the introduction of variability at this location and that led to easier communication and better support of the adoption process.

The considered part of product line introduction, a case study in testing software product lines, was conducted between March 2002 and September 2003. Eleven meetings were held during that period, each of which had lasted between two days and a whole week. The final meetings were used to measure data and to document the case study.

The case study deals with the introduction of ScenTED (Scenario-based TEst case Derivation). ScenTED is a method for testing software product lines, developed at the University of Duisburg-Essen.[2] The method builds on two basic ideas: scenario-based refinement from use cases to test cases and the preservation of variability. Variability is defined during requirements engineering and is maintained throughout domain engineering until testing. Details of the ScenTED method can be found in [78] and [113].

16.3.2 Current Process

This section explains the effects of product line engineering on Siemens. The effects are discussed along the four dimensions of the BAPO framework. Based on the nature of the case study the focus is on the process dimension.

Business

Based on the developers' intention it was planned to reduce effort and time for the applications within the considered SIENET COSMOS product line. In fact, it resulted in a reduction in development cycle time to about 75%. These development cycles are only roughly comparable, because there were different sets of requirements to be implemented, different stakeholders, tools, etc.

---

[2] This method is described in more detail in [114]

The reduction in development cycles on a long time-scale bears the hope of accelerating the incorporation of customer wishes. Medical solutions are still very monolithic applications and require a very high quality as human lives depend on them. Therefore, customer requirements cannot be incorporated immediately, but must be postponed to the next development cycle. The reduction of the development cycle thus enables a faster response to customer desires.

Architecture

Siemens uses two views on the architecture. The high-level view contains the interactions of the servers and the clients. The low-level view bears all details of component interactions. It was not intended to create a reference architecture due to the limited amount of planned applications. Therefore, only application architectures were created.

Figure 16.2 shows one view on a very generic architecture of the client and its interface to the archive server. The client is depicted with its main components and labelled as SoftCopyReader (SCR-COSMOS). The server and its clients communicate via the HTTP protocol or the new high-speed protocol IMACCESS.

The client contains the user interface (Viewer), the Control element and the specific functionalities depicted by the boxes labelled Ext1–Ext3. Specific functionality is implemented within post-processing applications. The applications implement the common functionalities of the product line, the variant functionalities and even external functionality from the *Syngo* library, which provides dedicated radiology support. Syngo functionalities may be added to any COSMOS client.

Depending on the application, a specific control component, a user interface, functionality and communication protocols are selected and bound. This binding is defined in the detailed design of the clients' architecture. However,

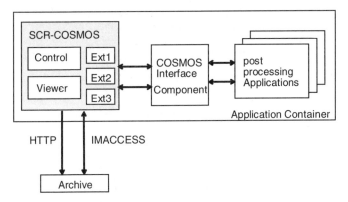

Fig. 16.2. Generic client architecture

some applications allow the binding of functionalities during run-time as they contain a run-time interface to the syngo library.

Process

Siemens develops and tests based on the V-Model cf. (Fig. 16.3). Once the unit test is passed, three test phases are performed: component test, system integration test and system test. The component test supports validation of the components' specific requirements. After that the system integration test verifies the interfaces and interactions among the components. The system test validates the requirements that have not been tested so far and validates the clinical workflow scenarios. The system test also realises the product line application test.

The system specification and architecture are described by structured text documents. Additionally, these documents are supplemented with exemplary scenarios, e.g. the system specification with use cases and system architecture with the standardised clinical scenarios. Fig. 16.3 depicts the development documents in the left part of the V-model. The right part shows the different test phases used by Siemens.

ScenTED consists of three activities to perform the system test. The approach was introduced to Siemens and adapted to their system test to validate three applications of the SIENET COSMOS product line. The following are the three main activities of ScenTED:

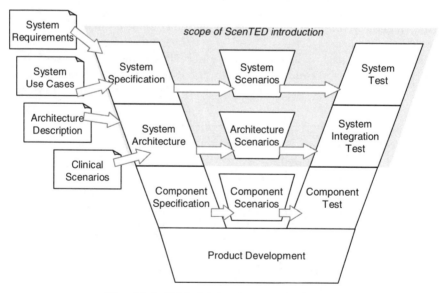

Fig. 16.3. V-Model development at Siemens

Use Case Name:	**Create Report**
Goal:	Create a patient report for the referring physician.
Description:	The radiologist opens the patient record and the patient's images to create the report for the referring physician. Thereby she has all images available. She creates the report by dictating it to a secretary or tape.
Precondition:	The new images are available on the server and the radiologist has been notified.
Postcondition:	The patient record has been marked as "report dictated".
Result:	A printed report has been created.
Variation Points:	1.1 In case of product A or B the radiologist may open the images via invocation X. 1.2 All products may open the images via invocation Y. 2. For product A the images may be opened and processed in other applications.
Scenarios:	...

Fig. 16.4. Domain use case Create Report

1. Creation of activity diagrams representing the control flow of use cases.
2. Derivation of domain system test case scenarios.
3. Derivation of application system test cases.

Each activity is illustrated with a simplified example.

Creation of Activity Diagrams Representing the Control Flow of a Use Case

The radiologist's goal is to create a report of a patient. The use case consists of the attributes that are known from single system development (cf. Fig. 16.4). The attribute *variation points* stresses the product line context, whereas the variability within the use case is specified in that attribute.

Siemens creates UML activity diagrams in addition to the use cases during requirements analysis. The activity diagrams specify selected scenarios. These activity diagrams are extended by the testers based on the use case description and exception scenarios. The activity diagrams are extended with variability during the introduction of ScenTED [113].

The activity diagrams are modelled in IBM RationalRose. Fig. 16.5 shows such an activity diagram. The stereotypes specify the applications that can perform an activity. A stereotype is defined for each possible combination of applications. In Fig. 16.5, the stereotypes <<*Product A*>> and

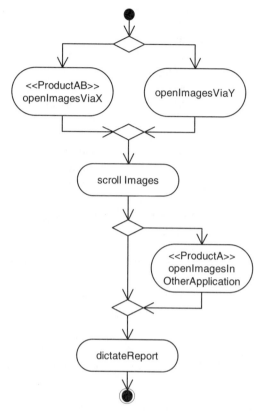

Fig. 16.5. Activity diagram for use case Create Report

<<*Product AB*>> specify the variants and their corresponding applications. Activities without a stereotype are applicable in every application. Variants are called *optional* if they can be performed optionally in addition to the common flow of events. An example is *openImagesInOtherApplication*.

Derivation of Domain Test Case Scenarios

Domain test case scenarios for the system test are derived from the activity diagrams using an adapted branch coverage criterion.[3] The results of the derivation from the activity diagram shown above are two domain test case scenarios (Figs. 16.6 and 16.7). The scenario DT_02 is applicable on all products. The scenario DT_01 can be applied only on the products A and B, the optional activity can be performed only in product A.

---

[3] Details concerning the derivation are beyond the scope of this chapter, but can be found in the description of the ScenTED technique [79, 78]

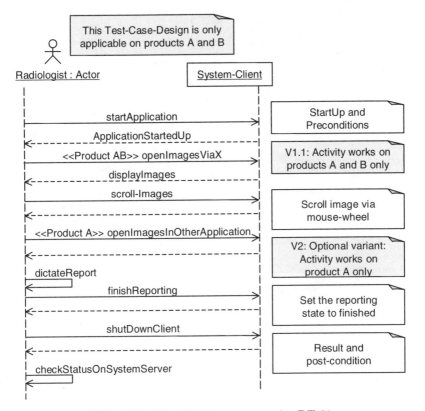

Fig. 16.6. Domain test case scenarios DT_01

Domain test case scenarios are extended with information about test input, acceptance criteria regarding the output for each step, additional steps to ensure the pre-condition and additional steps to verify the post-condition and the result. The documentation of these test case scenarios is also recorded in IBM RationalRose.

Test case scenario DT_01 is explained as an example. The domain test case scenario starts with steps to ensure the pre-conditions mentioned in the use case. These are annotated with the remark *StartUp and Pre-conditions*. They are followed by the core scenario steps of the test case scenario. These steps are detailed, e.g. the step *scrollImages* is extended by the information that the scrolling shall be done with a mouse-wheel. The test case scenario ends with steps that verify the post-condition. These steps are marked with notes, again. Domain test case scenarios contain variability, as shown in Figs. 16.6 and 16.7. The optional activity (*openImagesInOtherApplication*) is still part of test case scenario DT_01. Limitations regarding the applications are depicted as darkly coloured notes (V2 is only applicable on Product A). Thereby it is made explicit that the activity *openImageInOtherApplication* is only

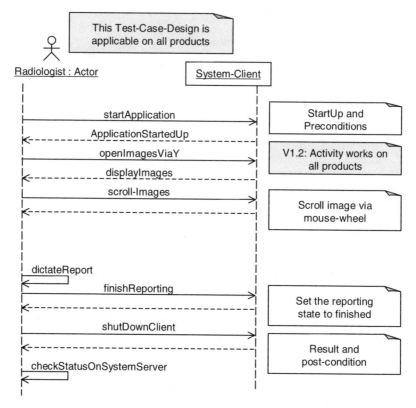

Fig. 16.7. Domain test case scenarios DT_02

applicable in test cases for the application A. The test engineers for application B may use this test case scenario, but will skip this activity. As the considered applications do not contain any run-time variability, all variations can be described in this way.

Derivation of Application Test Case Scenarios

Figure 16.8 shows the test case scenario for application B, derived from the domain test case scenario DT_01. The application test cases are administrated in the tool Mercury TestDirector. The comments for the pre- and post-conditions within the domain and the scenarios have been reused in the *Comment* field in the tool. The scenario ends with the steps to verify the result and post-conditions.

The variability that was included in the domain test case scenario has been bound in the application test case scenario. Binding consisted of the deletion of optional steps that were impossible within the application at hand. As a result, the step *openImageInOtherApplication* has not been taken over to the

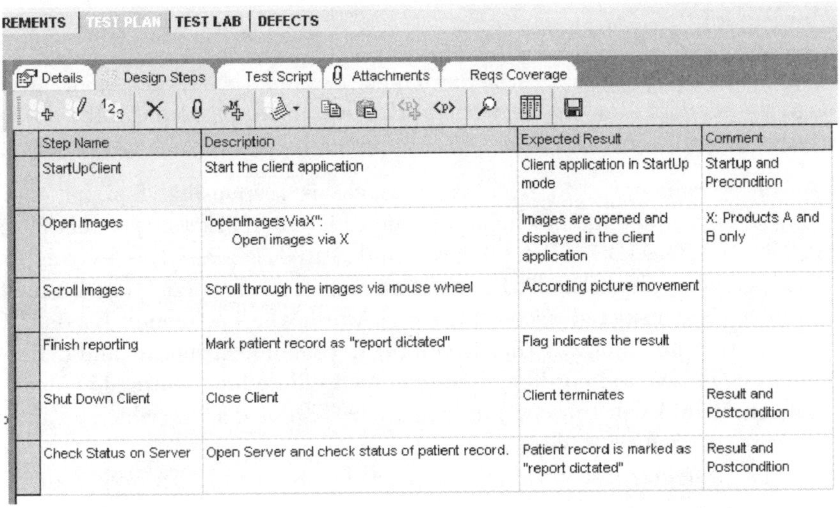

REMENTS | TEST PLAN | TEST LAB | DEFECTS

Step Name	Description	Expected Result	Comment
StartUpClient	Start the client application	Client application in StartUp mode	Startup and Precondition
Open Images	"openImagesViaX": Open images via X	Images are opened and displayed in the client application	X: Products A and B only
Scroll Images	Scroll through the images via mouse wheel	According picture movement	
Finish reporting	Mark patient record as "report dictated"	Flag indicates the result	
Shut Down Client	Close Client	Client terminates	Result and Postcondition
Check Status on Server	Open Server and check status of patient record.	Patient record is marked as "report dictated"	Result and Postcondition

Fig. 16.8. Application test case scenario for application B

application test case scenario, as shown in Fig. 16.8, because the activity is not possible for application B.

It must be recorded which test case scenarios apply to which application. This way the reusable test case scenarios are traced and copied within the next application. Table 16.1 shows this for the considered use case and the applications A, B and C. The domain test case scenario DT_01 includes a variant that preserves the application of the scenario on all applications: "*OpenImagesViaX*". This optional variant is not valid for application C. Table 16.1 can be used to identify the test case scenarios that are applicable for a specific application. The domain test case scenario DT_02 is used to test common functionality. Therefore it is used in all three considered applications. These test case scenarios are reused via an easy copy-and-paste operation directly within another application. The test case DT_01 includes variability. It can directly be used in application A and with adaptation in application B, because the variant V2 is not part of application B. As variant V1.1 *openImagesViaX* is not part of application C, it is not applicable there.

Table 16.1. Application test case scenarios of the three applications

Application	Origin of the application test case scenario
A	DT_01, DT_02
B	DT_01 without V2, DT_02
C	DT_02

Organisation

Activities and responsibilities have changed within the development, even though no product line engineering process was introduced partially. There are responsibilities for

- *Business manager*: the business manager is responsible for the planning and product management for the different marketed product lines (SIENET COSMOS, SIENET SKY and SIENET Magic) as well as for the specific applications within each marketed product line. The business manager is considered a co-ordinator towards the customers. He defines the product line in a way that it will be an economical success and defines the sales contacts accordingly. He has to decide which features are more important and will thus be implemented. He also decides which markets he wants to deliver to with highest priority.
- *Product manage*: the product manager is responsible for requirements engineering of the product line as a whole as well as for the individual applications. Variants are specified as mentioned in the specification. In communication with the business manager, the variants and common functionalities for the next release are planned.
- *Research and development engineer*: based on the common requirements and variants the high-level architecture is defined. The variants are refined in modules within the low-level architecture. The coding of common and variant components starts once the low-level architecture exists.
- *Test engineer*: the test process is adapted as described in the process dimension of the framework. The test process validates the description of the variability and creates reusable test cases for the different applications.
- *Technical services engineer*: there are a lot of technical services that are provided for all applications and through all development stages, e.g. change reporting and management as well as traceability. All of these have changed slightly in order to take variability into account. The process descriptions as well as the tool usage had to be changed and the correct usage was verified by the facilitator.
- *Product development manager*: as overall project leader, he or she is responsible for the development activities of all derived applications. He or she sets priorities to the different applications. The sub-project managers report to him or her.
- *Sub-project manager*: a sub-project manager is responsible for a single derived application. He or she has to schedule his own application and has to consider the interfaces with the other sub-project managers.

These roles are put into practice using a matrix organisation (cf. Fig. 16.9).

Central to the organisation is the assignment of competences and authorities. The extension is visible only in the additional role of the product development manager. The extensions of responsibilities in development roles are invisible in this picture.

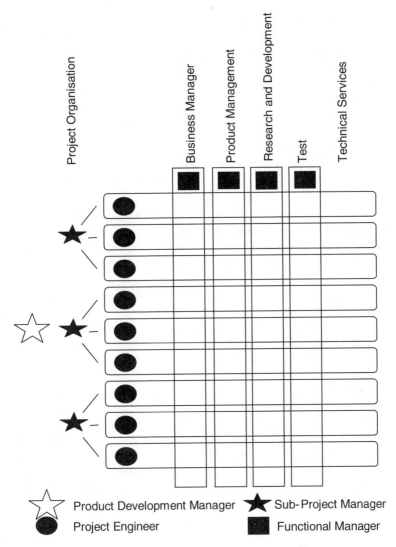

Fig. 16.9. Matrix organisation structure at Siemens

16.4 Results and Impact Evaluation

The ScenTED approach to product line testing was evaluated regarding two aspects: the resulting degree of reuse of test case scenarios and the test engineers' subjective judgement of usefulness. To this end, the degree of reuse was measured after completing the test phase and a questionnaire was given to test engineers.

The evaluation of used test case scenarios during application engineering has shown that 27 test case scenarios developed during domain engineering were reused in 63 scenarios in application engineering. This implies that 36 scenarios were saved comparing to single system development. This corresponds to an economisation of 57% for the considered part of the system.

The test engineers' opinions regarding traceability were determined with a questionnaire on the support of ScenTED during the creation of application test case scenarios with reuse. Statistical analysis of the results has shown that the test engineers agree that ScenTED supports traceability to enable reuse.[4]

16.5 Lessons Learned

Several other observations were made during the introduction of ScenTED.

First, early validation of variability is required. It has been observed that requirements have to be validated and verified between a customer and a developer [105]. A similar observation can be made regarding variability. The textual descriptions used at Siemens led to different interpretations by different stakeholders, such as product management, software architects, programmers and test engineers. Explicit modelling of variability led to more discussions and finally to a shared view among all stakeholders.

A second observation is that test engineers prefer application-related variability models. Methods and techniques must always be adapted to specific organisations and projects, as both come along with specific goals and properties. The modelling of variability in UML using activity and sequence diagrams has been adapted from earlier work [78, 112]. There, a distinction is made between variation points, variants and assignments of variants to applications. Here, application assignments were made directly at the variation points instead of variants for adapted modelling (cf. Fig. 16.5). This way, common and application-specific functionality alike can be modelled and the concept of variability is easier to grasp for the involved stakeholders. Application capabilities are directly modelled and there is no need to learn how to model application-independent variants. This approach is much more intuitive for people without a software product line background. An important prerequisite for the adaptation is that all applications are well known, because this type of modelling does not scale up to many applications.

As a final observation, the organisation of test cases in a use case and an application hierarchy was important. The testing of different applications on a common basis requires structured support within the used tools, especially the testing tool. Each application has a specific folder within the test tool. Below this folder another set of folders was created: one for each incorporated use case. Within each use case all test case scenarios relating to this use case are organised. The test cases differ in the covered paths and data. This folder organisation realises traceability to enable structured reuse. Whenever

---

[4] Detailed results regarding this evaluation can be found in [112]

a new application has to test the use case *createReport*, one can open another application, open the folder for that use case and take the test cases over to the new application.

16.6 Summary

The experience described here focuses on the requirements and test level. Here, variability was explicitly modelled in requirements and in test cases. The modelling of variability in requirements helps to discuss the intended differences among the planned applications within product management and to communicate the commonalities to latter development stages. Modelling variability in test case scenarios helped to perform a structured reuse of test cases.

The reuse gained from ScenTED was up to 57% compared to the application of single system testing techniques. The development of three applications with the same assets led to an estimated reduction of development time to about 75% compared to single system development. Although not in the focus of the case study, it was observed that an early validation of requirements took place and a repeatable process of test case derivation was conducted within the project.

These results caused Siemens to adopt this process in their test process description. The approach is used by the contributing department and propagated within their site.

An obvious shortcoming is that the evaluated ScenTED technique lacks integrated tool support. Although the relevant models can be created and used in commercial tools like RationalRose or TestDirector, creating the activity diagrams, deriving domain test case scenarios and determining application test case scenarios still have to be performed manually.

Telvent

with Jesús Bermejo
   Pablo Trinidad
   David Benavides
   Antonio Ruiz-Cortés

Company facts of Telvent

Organisational size: >1,000 developers.
Starting Mode: A configurable product for many clients with changing requirements.

Experienced improvements:
- Server platform extended to other markets.
- Introduction of run-time variability.
- Improved reference process framework.
- Centralised roadmaps for platforms.
- Market platform in a different domain.

Business: Alignment of strategy and architecture.

Architecture: Use of dynamic abstract factory pattern in the platform.

Process: Improved framework.

Organisation: Separation of domain and application engineering organisations.

17.1 Introduction

Telvent is specialised in solutions in four specific industrial sectors: energy, traffic, transport and environment. Its main clients are in the Americas, Spain and China. With over forty years of experience in industrial supervisory control and business process management systems, Telvent executes projects and provides technical services in the field of mission-critical, real-time control and information management. Telvent provides outsourcing and consulting services, and employs a technology-neutral philosophy. The company manages IT and telecommunications infrastructure for an extensive international client base.

17.2 Motivation

The development of software for control, supervision and management falls within the category of complex system engineering. This type of software deals with strong non-functional requirements such as time responsiveness to accomplish real-time requirements for the control of complex systems, customisability to cover different cultural contexts and national standards, and maintainability. Often, critical systems are controlled, and upgrades must be performed rapidly.

Software product line engineering can be used to manage variants for common issues in the field of control software such as multiple communication protocols over the same channel, communications redundancy, extensive control at the remote terminal unit locations, remote configuration changes, data transfer to and from databases and fault tolerance in the context of a distributed architecture with support for a growing number of communication infrastructures. Many systems use predominantly long-distance communication, although short- distance communication may also be present.

This chapter summarises some aspects of software product line engineering at Telvent for one of its core business domains. It focuses on the conception phase of a product line targeting only a single product for which the requirements were expected to change widely. The experience shows how software product line engineering was successfully applied as a technique to enable the product to adapt to evolving requirements.

The customer asked for a real-time television software framework as part of the product. They wanted software that could capture a television signal from a card plugged into a PC and show the result on screen after applying some filtering and transformations. They did not really know which kind of filtering and transformations the framework had to support in the future. However, it was to be expected that after starting the development of the framework, the customer would want more functionality with similar or improved performance.

Late changes in requirements generally involve reduction of functionality and the loss of quality and time. In the situation at hand, many new requirements were expected to appear, and the architecture would have to be able to support them. Support for change had to be part of the software architecture.

Here, classical requirements analysis would leave a lot of black holes that would need to be solved before designing a flexible platform. Instead, software product line engineering was used to create a platform that supports the needed variability. Software product line development usually starts with domain analysis, where the main features of the platform are detected. In this case, the problem domain was thoroughly studied to define a product that would fit not only the (future) requirements of this first customer, but also the requirements of other companies in the same market with little effort.

To achieve this, the commonalities were analysed among the potential products that the different customers may request in the near future (cf. Fig. 17.1). The first customer wanted to compose television signals, bitmaps, videos and other images and apply all kinds of effects to them. The results of an analysis of existing commercial products in the real-time television market lead to additional requirements. Starting from this information, the common requirements of the platform were determined:

- The software should draw a final image as a result.
- Several sources of images or layers compose the final image, e.g. television signal capture, bitmaps, stored video, video streaming, text and 3D images.
- The layers overlap following a configurable order.
- Effects or transformations may be applied to one or more layers, e.g. black and white, and transparency effects.

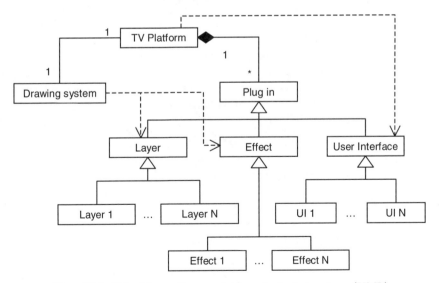

Fig. 17.1. Television software platform logical structure (UML)

- A user interface has to be provided to control layers and effects.
- It must work 24 hours, seven days a week. If used for television retransmission it must never stop working.

In short, the platform draws a sequence of layers, and optionally applies any of a range of filters to them. The platform has to support any kind of layers, effects and user interface. Updates should be supported, but the execution cannot not be stopped for maintenance.

The domain engineering team had to develop two major functional components:

1. *Drawing system*: in charge of drawing layers and effects in the television output.
2. *Plug-ins system*: because it was intended to be a 24/7 system, new versions and updating must be automatically installed at run-time without stopping the system. Layers, effects and user interfaces are considered plug-ins that easily connect to the drawing system.

The application engineering team was responsible for developing plug-ins for specific customers. These plug-ins could be promoted to the platform if more customers would demand them. In this case, the domain engineering would take over their maintenance.

17.3 Approach

The process for software product line engineering described in [106] was used. The following main sub-processes were distinguished:

- *Domain engineering* deals with core-asset development, where common features are developed.
- *Application engineering* deals with product development, where products are developed from common and specific features.
- *Co-ordination* deals with overall product line management, where synchronisation between the other two activities is arranged.

This is the basis to improve the development process and to support the needed variability. An important task is to decide which are the core-assets and which are the customer's product-specific features.

This section explains how the organisation was structured to deal with the business needs. Next, we explain how the domain engineering team dealt with the architecture. Especially, we consider the design of the plug-in system that may be used in other contexts. Its origin is an existing design pattern to automatically support the run-time connection of new plug-ins or components, i.e. layers, effects and user interfaces.

17.3.1 Organisation and Business

Following the process structure, development was separated in domain and application engineering groups. The domain engineering group was responsible for the platform development and the quality of the systems. The software product line infrastructure has to provide solutions not only for existing systems, but also for future systems. It has to deal with the rapidly evolving technological market nowadays. The domain architecture has to fulfil the derived business strategy requirements.

Domain engineering uses an architecture-centric approach driven by the business strategy. The technical solution is shaped according to long-term strategic and business objectives. Interfaces for software variants are tightly aligned with business variants. It is important to analyse them from both business and software perspectives. This keeps the strategy and planned evolution for the whole product line consistent with one another.

17.3.2 Using the Abstract Factory Pattern

The implementation of the product line depends on the Abstract Factory design pattern [59]. It can fulfil many common requirements of the plug-in system and provides fast development of systems in the product line.

Abstract Factory provides an interface for creating families of objects without knowing their concrete classes. Abstract Factory can be applied when a system has to be independent of how its products are created, composed and represented. This fits the requirements of the television framework, where layers, effects and user interfaces should be created independently of their concrete functionality, which varies from customer to customer. The design structure of this pattern can be seen in Fig. 17.2.

The participant classes in this pattern and their functionality are as follows:

- *Abstract Product* declares the interface for a type of product object. In this case, layers, effects and user interfaces will be abstract products.
- *Abstract Factory* declares an interface for the operations that create abstract products.
- *Concrete Product* implements the abstract product interface to define a concrete product that is created using a concrete factory. Examples of concrete products are a bitmap layer and a black and white effect.
- *Concrete Factory* implements the interface of the abstract factory. Each customer will require a set of layers, effects and user interfaces, and will have its own concrete factory implementation.
- *Client* uses the interfaces of abstract factory and product, but does not know about concrete implementations. A customer-dependent concrete factory will be instantiated beforehand.

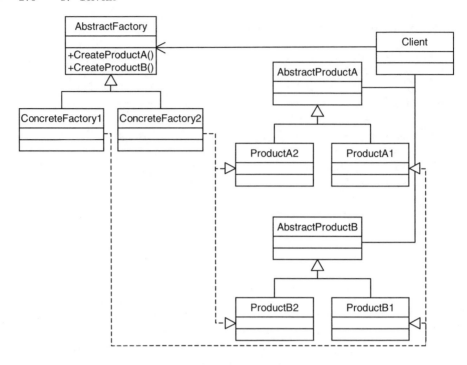

Fig. 17.2. Abstract Factory pattern (UML)

In the television framework, layers, effects and user interfaces are the abstract products to be created. The abstract factory is in charge of creating their implementations as Concrete Products. Each customer-specific product has a specific concrete factory (Fig. 17.3).

17.3.3 Introducing the Dynamic Abstract Factory Pattern

The Abstract Factory pattern has two limitations when it is used to implement variability:

1. Some concrete products are not pre-defined and should integrate into the application at run-time. Abstract Factory can only create concrete products if they are identified *a priori*.
2. A customer may solicit more than one instance of an abstract product. For instance, a customer may need a television capture layer and a bitmap layer at the same time. Abstract Factory allows only one concrete implementation per interface.

Considering these limitations some new features were added to the Abstract Factory pattern, thus creating a new pattern coined *Dynamic Abstract*

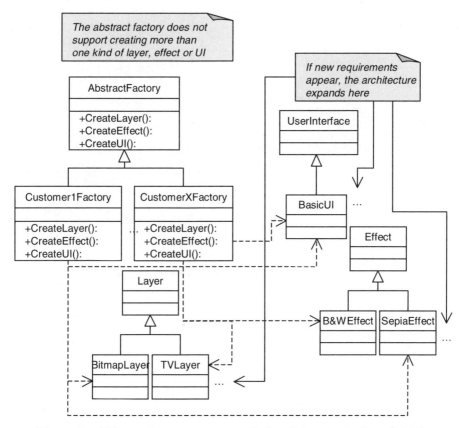

Fig. 17.3. Abstract Factory pattern applied to Telvent's platform (UML)

Factory. The new pattern is considered dynamic because it can change the relations between concrete factories and concrete products at run-time.

Dynamic Abstract Factory allows a concrete factory to create more than one instance of a concrete product. To this end, the methods that create concrete products, e.g. *CreateLayer*, were extended to receive a parameter that indicates which layer to create from all the available ones.

Furthermore, concrete factories were adapted to support new concrete products that were added at run-time. *Register* and *UnRegister* operations were added to Abstract Factory for each abstract product, e.g. *RegisterLayer* and *UnRegisterLayer*. These functions associate an identifier with a concrete product. This identifier is used when creating new instances of a concrete product.

For each customer, a set of layers, effects and user interfaces is available, and many others may be installed and used at run-time. Each customer hasa

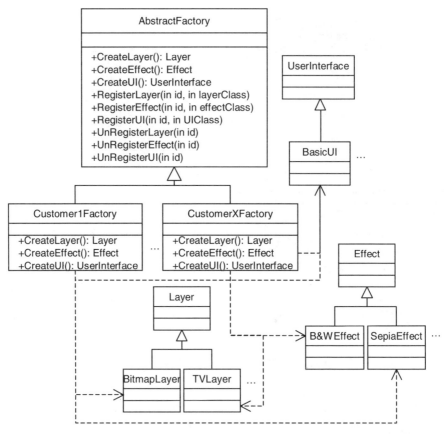

Fig. 17.4. Dynamic Abstract Factory pattern applied to Telvent's platform (UML)

concrete factory that initially registers the available concrete products. A UML model of the Dynamic Abstract Factory pattern is shown in Fig. 17.4.

17.3.4 Reusing the Dynamic Abstract Factory Pattern

To make the Dynamic Abstract Factory implementation reusable in other platforms where different abstract products are considered, some more adaptations were necessary. The *register* and *unregister* type of methods in Fig. 17.3 are not reusable because they are linked to a concrete context through their names. Instead of creating new methods for each new problem domain, a domain-independent method that supports the creation of any concrete product is better reusable. Consequently, a generic abstract factory was defined that creates only one kind of abstract product. The generic dynamic abstract

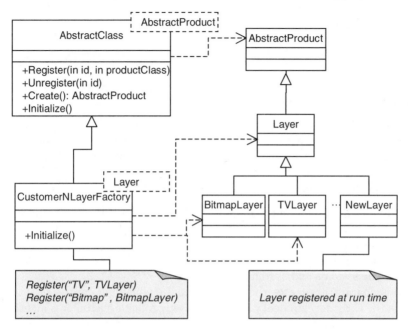

Fig. 17.5. Dynamic Abstract Factory pattern implementation using parameterised classes (UML)

factory designed was based on parameterised classes.[1] A UML model, representing this, is shown in Fig. 17.5. Applying this generic pattern to the television framework yields three concrete factories for layers, effects and user interfaces.

For each customer, the *Initialise* method is adapted and a set of concrete factories created. Support for integrating new concrete products comes from using the register method at run-time. But introducing new products means introducing new code. The insertion of code in a running process is not a trivial task. Depending on the language and environment, the dynamic loading of code can be achieved in different ways. In the television framework, dynamic libraries were used to plug and register new classes into a concrete factory at run-time. Each library contained one or more concrete products. When loading a library, the new concrete product is registered at a concrete factory. When unplugging that library, the concrete product is unregistered again.

The Dynamic Abstract Factory pattern is not linked to a concrete operating system or programming language. The solution is specified at design level, and can be applied using any programming language that allows the dynamic loading of code, for example Java or C#.

---

[1] A parameterised class is a class where one or more types are defined during instantiation. In C++, they are also known as *templates*

17.4 Lessons Learned

Software product line engineering can be applied in domains that are changing fast. In the case presented here, a television framework was set up as a software product line from the very start, when only a single customer was identified. This helped to solve three challenges:

1. The requirements of the initial customer were known to change over time.
2. The product was expected to be interesting to other customers in the same market as well, but development could not be delayed until those customers were identified.
3. The product should be applicable in similar, but different domains as well.

Carefully analysing and managing variability helped to develop an architecture that could deal with future changes in requirements and that was suitable for a broad range of customers.

In this case, software product line engineering proved to be a good way to align business goals and system architecture.

This chapter illustrates that product line engineering can be of interest even in the early development phases, when only a single customer is identified. A product line was set up to deal with the fact that the customer had unclear requirements that were expected to change in the future.

Part III

Conclusions

18

Analysis

In this chapter, we summarise the main findings of part II. We start by summarising the general results. Next, we go into detail for each of the Business, Architecture, Process and Organisation dimensions.

Whenever possible, we present evaluations based on the experience descriptions. Most experiences do not provide enough information to enable a complete Family Evaluation Framework assessment. However, based on the descriptions, we may get an idea of the issues that the companies deal with. This gives a rough indication of the FEF levels of the different companies. Since not every chapter in part II describes all the BAPO aspects, not all of them are evaluated for each dimension. The evaluations are not (and cannot be) formal or complete; we only indicate which evidences lead to our conclusions. Moreover, it should be noted that a *higher* score is not necessarily a *better* score. The optimal score depends very much on the specific situation that a company is in and the goals that it wants to reach.

We end the chapter with a summary based on the lessons learned in part II.

18.1 Motivation

Several motivations were used to initiate product line engineering within the organisations. We discuss them separately in the following sections.

18.1.1 Complexity

There are two kinds of *complexity* that must be dealt with: complexity of the systems themselves and complexity of the complete portfolio. The complexity of the systems increases because the stakeholders require more functionality and quality. The complexity of the portfolio increases because more customer groups need to be addressed. After successfully implementing functionality in one system, it is required to be integrated in other systems too. The complexity is further increased by uncertainty about the exact features that systems need to have. It is never completely clear what the customer wants next. Decisions on resolving these issues must be made quickly. AKVAsmart, for example, mentions the need to introduce late changes and the improvement of product configuration.

A product line approach addresses the management of both kinds of complexity. Variability management supports the reduction of the complexity in the portfolio. The complexity of single products is reduced by managed reuse, which increases the similarity between different systems. Success in reducing the complexity of systems is mentioned in several experiences. In at least one case – AKVAsmart – the code size for the portfolio was reduced because a lot of duplicated code was removed. This was an additional factor in the reduction of the complexity of the portfolio.

Nokia Mobile Phones concentrated on the improvement of design documentation to deal with complexity. Improving documentation is only valuable if its results last long enough. In general, this does not hold for single product documentation, but it does so for a product line. Nokia Networks explains the importance of a design data warehouse, where every development group may get the development data it needs in an effective way. Several experiences mention that dealing with requirements in an effective and efficient way is an open issue that needs to be dealt with. The set of requirements itself is already complex, and good solutions are still lacking.

18.1.2 Variability and Commonality

Variability management is the main reason for introducing product line engineering in several cases. These companies have to produce diverse systems that address many customer groups. Even though single systems do not need to be complex, the variability within the portfolio must be managed.

Several experiences mention an increase in the number of different systems that are actually produced by the product line, showing that they have successfully mastered variability management. market maker's product line enabled a very fast increase in the number of systems produced. For Philips Consumer Electronics, variability was not an issue any more once its product line was deployed.

Several experiences, among them Philips Medical Systems, deal with the need to improve the commonality among products. This is done not only from a complexity management point of view, but also as a marketing issue. The customer wants the same look-and-feel in all products to make it easier to move from one product – or product generation – to another. In addition, Philips Medical Systems mentions the need to increase the synergy among newly acquired and existing development groups. The experiences of AKVAsmart show that commonality and ease of integration were indeed obtained.

18.1.3 Efficiency and Costs

Efficiency improvement and cost reduction are a motivation for most companies. This leads to a shorter time to market, faster innovation, increased productivity and the reduction of life-cycle costs. Significant efficiency improvements and cost reduction are obtained in several experiences. Bosch mentions the success of its product line in a competitive market. Siemens reduced its testing costs. Sometimes, the development product line directly supports a marketed product line, e.g. Philips Medical Systems' Vequion. AKVAsmart increased its efficiency, enabling the fast adaptation of products to different situations, although the impact is not as large as they had expected. Market maker achieved a large reduction of maintenance effort. Setting up the product line reduced the overall efficiency, but after the development of three or more products the efficiency increase was clear. Several experiences mention the use of well-aligned roadmaps for planning domain and application development. DNV reports the reduction of administrative tasks and speed improvements for technical tasks. Some experience results mention improvements of time to market by factors of two or more.

18.1.4 Reuse and Architecture

Often, companies experience a need to improve the architecture to support reuse for both present and future products. One choice is to start a product line architecture. A usual approach is to develop the reference architecture concurrently with the production of the first systems in the product line. Starting from scratch is often too costly, so there is a need to incorporate legacy systems within the product line: already existing products are used as a source of reuse. An exception is the DNV case, where the Nauticus architecture was developed practically from scratch.

Most architectures are based on a platform, supporting the requirements of present and future products. Often there are several similar products that are combined in the product line to improve the benefit of reuse. The development of a common, variable platform is often considered as the basis for introducing the product line in the organisation. Plug-in mechanisms and the definition of the right interfaces seem to be crucial.

18.1.5 Quality

Quality improvement is another reason for starting a product line. It involves better processes and a higher level of trust in a platform once it is used in many products. Both Siemens and Bosch report an improvement of quality. Philips Medical Systems illustrates the improvement of the quality by the fast reduction of the defect density rate.

18.2 Business

In almost all cases, management supported the product line development. Successful pilot projects win the attention of higher management and help to introduce product line engineering further in the organisation.

In order to enable the transition to a product line, several experiences mention the necessity to have strong management support to make the move towards product lines. This is made particularly explicit by the Siemens case study that mentions that it was impossible to start a full-fledged product line because of a lack of management support. In many cases where management support is available, the product line is introduced in an evolutionary way, involving a business strategy, introduction of a reference architecture and adaptations to the organisation. Philips Medical Systems mentions the conception, birth and growth phases and stresses the importance of management commitment to deal with the tension that builds up before break-even has been reached.

Product management uses knowledge of the product line when planning and making roadmaps. This involves planning for the platform and for the products. The time to market often decreased, sometimes with a factor of two or more. Certain companies, e.g. market maker, found that a thorough understanding of the product line was crucial for the marketing department to win commission for products that were originally not envisioned to be part of the portfolio.

Business variants are aligned to product variants to increase the business value of the product line. Philips Medical Systems introduced the Vequion brand to market the products built within its product line. In certain cases, e.g. Bosch, it was decided by product management that it is better to have not a single product line development for all products, but separate ones for different market segments.

Most experiences do not mention how software product line engineering influences the budget and investment decisions. market maker merely mentions that the investment pays off. Philips Medical Systems has a model to compare platform development costs with product development costs. This is used to let the product groups pay for the platform in a way that holds financial benefits for all.

Many experiences include the product line in the companies' long-term visions. Telvent mentions that the long-term vision of the product line also provides solutions for future products.

In certain cases, business aspects were the motivation to initiate the product line development. Often, this is related to the need for more software for more variants. market maker mentions changes in the market – i.e. the internet hype – as a motivation. Philips Consumer Electronics expected a need for cheap, hybrid products that could not be supported by their existing architecture and way of working.

18.2.1 FEF Evaluations

No experiences mention measuring the business aspects of software product line engineering. This indicates that none of them is at level 4, measured or higher.

Some case studies suggest that the companies are near business dimension level 3, *managed*. DNV has a long-term vision and strategy. Its management supports the long-term vision of the business use of the platform. market maker has strong management involvement, and includes the product line in its long-term vision. It uses a strategy of small investments. Philips Medical Systems has clear management awareness, and the product line is an important ingredient in its strategy. Similarly, this applies to the Philips Consumer Electronics case, where business goals are leading in the product line development.

Two companies seem to be near level 2, *aware*. The management of AK-VAsmart supports product line development and uses it in the planning of new products. It is, however, not clear whether it is used strategically. Telvent is also at this level since it does not indicate that the product line is used strategically either.

Siemens does have management awareness, but because product line engineering is only partially introduced, it cannot be evaluated higher than level 1, *project-based*.

There is insufficient information in the Nokia cases to do a reasonable assessment for the business dimension.

18.3 Architecture

In most cases, the product line uses a component-oriented architecture. Configuration mechanisms range from plug-in mechanisms (e.g. AKVAsmart) to proprietary tool support (Philips Consumer Electronics). These mechanisms help to support asset reuse within the products. Reusable components are integrated into the framework, or designed as default plug-ins. The application developers select available reusable components for configuring, and add product-specific components.

In general, the reference architecture provides a basis for standardisation within the company. Standardisation is used to increase the reuse level of the domain assets. Application architects have more or less freedom to add to and adapt the reference architecture. The DNV case mentions a model-driven approach that leaves little freedom for the application architecture. Philips Consumer Electronics provides a single architecture that is supported by tools that enforce architectural rules. Siemens chooses explicitly not to have a reference architecture because of the limited amount of applications involved. In the Nokia Mobile Phones case, only the reuse of solutions for quality requirements is mentioned.

Variability management is reported mainly in the support of configuring components. market maker mentions third-party tool support for this, and Philips Consumer Electronics uses its proprietary Koala tools. Telvent created the Dynamic Abstract Factory pattern to this end. DNV has an explicitly defined list of mechanisms for variability management.

In most cases, the architecture was developed in an evolutionary way, concentrating on small parts of the system first, typically the lower layers. Later, the architecture was extended to include higher layers. In many cases (e.g. AKVAsmart), the reference architecture was initially applied in a few products only and extended to more products in a stepwise fashion. The scope of the architecture at each step was usually restricted to the requirements of the relevant applications. Telvent took an opposite approach: it intentionally started with a platform that was much richer than what was required by their initial – and, at the time, their only – customer. Having a platform with the right variability helped them to win other customers with similar requirements later.

The Philips Medical Systems case discusses the planned integration of existing assets in the growing architecture. DNV did not integrate legacy assets in the architecture. market maker used wrapped legacy components to give its product line development a boost initially, replacing them later with fresh code. Certain cases, e.g. Bosch, mention the development of a completely new architecture for their product lines.

18.3.1 FEF Evaluations

Because of its extensive tool support, Philips Consumer Electronics may be at level 5, *configuring*.

Two companies that can be evaluated to be near level 4, *variant products*, are DNV and market maker. DNV provides a far-reaching architecture involving variant products. It uses an explicitly defined set of variation mechanisms to build products. market maker seems to be at this level too. The reference architecture is used strictly, and variation is clearly managed.

Several companies seem to be near level 3, *software platform*. AKVAsmart has a layered plug-in architecture. Applications are configured through the addition of independent plug-ins. A large part of the software is application-specific. Philips Medical Systems' software platform is used by many different application architectures. The Telvent case reports on a single variability aspect of the architecture. It suggests a defined architecture where the applications obey the architecture rules.

Because of the limited information, certain companies cannot be evaluated above level 2, *standardised infrastructure*. The Nokia Mobile Phones case only covers a part of the architecture dimension: the quality of the requirements documentation and of the architecture itself. This does involve variability management at this level, but the information is too restricted to do a good evaluation. Siemens decided not to have a reference architecture.

The Nokia Networks case lacks information to assign a level in the architecture dimension.

18.4 Process

In most cases, there are separate domain and application engineering life-cycles. These life-cycles are usually performed at CMMI level 3 or 2. Usually, domain engineering is at a higher level than application engineering. In the Bosch case, process improvement went hand in hand with the introduction of product line engineering. Being a small company, market maker chose not to make an explicit distinction between domain and application engineering in the beginning. Once more developers are working on the product line, a separation into two teams will be made. The Nokia Networks case mentions its experiences with asset management at the domain level, which remains an unsolved problem. The Siemens case discusses the testing process. A central part of its organisation performs the domain testing activities.

The separation between domain and application engineering is usually established by having separate units for each of them. Some companies mention changes in the roles that requirements, testing and asset management play in the development process. These activities have consequences over whole product line development. With respect to single system engineering, these tasks have to be better organised.

Several experiences mention the availability of specific groups that collaborate over department borders, involving both domain and application engineering. For example, Philips Medical Systems has a shared configuration management system.

18.4.1 Evaluations

A few cases mention the reached CMMI level of the involved departments, but this result does not include the amplifications for product line engineering.

Several descriptions suggest that the companies act near level 3, *defined*. Nokia Networks has well-defined processes, including domain and application engineering roles. As a hierarchy of product lines is active, application engineering at one level is actually domain engineering for the next level up. The asset management and architecture evaluations activities are the primary focus of this case study. Both Philips cases have clear domain and application engineering processes, and collaboration is well-defined. Although market maker did not separate between domain and application engineering teams initially, the domain and application engineering activities were separated very early on and the company had defined tasks for them. Later also the separation of teams was introduced.

Nokia Mobile Phones describes activities and relationships for domain and application architectures. If other activities are performed in similar ways and the right CMMI level is reached, it may be assumed that Nokia Mobile Phones is at level 3 too.

Most other companies are at level 2, *managed*. DNV has separate domain and application engineering processes. Siemens has a well-defined test process involving both domain and application tests. The description suggests that other activities of domain engineering are also defined. In addition, the matrix organisation suggests collaborations between domain and application engineering. Telvent mentions the separation of domain and application engineering and co-ordination. It is not clear to which extent it is used.

AKVAsmart does not mention its processes and cannot be evaluated for this dimension.

18.5 Organisation

In many experiences, roles and responsibilities were defined and assigned for doing different product line engineering tasks. At least, domain and application engineering roles were distinguished for traditional engineering tasks. The Philips and Bosch cases mention the availability of asset-related responsibilities, for collaboration between domain and application engineering. market maker gives a list of nine differently defined roles.

In most cases, the product line roles and responsibilities are distributed over domain and application engineering units within the organisation. Within market maker this was restricted to the distribution over teams working in the same unit. Philips Medical Systems and Nokia Networks mention a hierarchical organisation with product lines at different levels, where application engineering for one level can be seen as domain engineering for the next level. Philips Consumer Electronics mentions an organisation with many product teams and (domain) asset teams. Siemens has a matrix organisation, where several domain-related roles are placed in the functional dimension.

Several experiences mention collaboration between cross-departmental groups. Examples are asset-related teams and change-control boards, for example at Bosch. Philips Medical Systems reports the *Inner Source* way of collaborating. This is the use of open-source development practices for distributed collaboration within a company.

18.5.1 FEF Evaluations

market maker can be assigned near level 5, *domain-oriented*. There is no separation between domain and application engineering teams, and domain engineering seems to be leading in the organisation structure. In fact, many domain engineering roles are used. In addition, there is an effective communication available for product line issues.

Philips Consumer Electronics seems to be near level 4, *synchronised*, since it has an integrated organisation with a lot of collaboration between product and asset teams.

Several other organisations act at level 3, *weakly defined*. Nokia Networks has a hierarchy of product lines both internal and external to the company. There seems to be awareness of the product line in the organisation, and there is a clear separation of domain and application engineering. Philips Medical Systems also has a clear separation between domain and application activities, involving cross-departmental teams.

Three cases suggest a level 2, *reuse*. DNV has a separate domain engineering organisation called Nauticus. The remainder of the organisation is not changed, but makes use of the platform provided to them. Siemens applies a matrix organisation of functions and projects. Domain engineering is one of the projects. Finally, Telvent has separated domain and application organisations but no cross-functional teams are mentioned.

There is not enough data for Nokia mobile phones and AKVAsmart to do an evaluation.

18.6 Summary

18.6.1 How to Do It

Several case studies mention the importance of management involvement and a long-term vision in the introduction of product line engineering. Some cases make clear that all four BAPO dimensions must be addressed.

An evolutionary approach to platform development seems to be crucial for success. Initially, the platform is designed for a small set of products with limited functionality. Then it grows to support more products and functions. The introduction of the platform in new products should also be planned in an evolutionary way. An exception is Telvent: that company started building a platform that exceeded the demands of its first customer. The success came because the company had a pretty good idea of the required variability in advance.

The Bosch experience shows that process improvement can go together well with the introduction of product line engineering.

The market maker case mentions the importance to organise the work around the development of components and not based on user features. It also stresses that one should be careful not to design the first product too much according to the requirements of the first customer.

The Philips Medical Systems case shows the importance of setting up cross-departmental teams very early in the introduction process to get commitment on shared assets. Together with a strict change control process, this keeps the platform and architecture fit for all stakeholders.

Siemens shows that a partial implementation of software product line engineering can be worthwhile too. They succeeded in reducing their test effort by structurally reusing their test-related assets.

18.6.2 Guidelines

All BAPO dimensions, Business, Architecture, Organisation and Process, should be addressed to enable a sustainable software product line activity. This can be achieved only through strong management support. As a consequence, the organisation should be at level 2 or higher in the business dimension. In addition, evaluation and planning are important ingredients for managing product line development. The Families Evaluation Framework can be used to gain insight in the present status of a company or unit. Product line engineering adoption becomes much more systematic if an appropriate evaluation of the current situation and the particular benefits that are planned to achieve are made.

Align product line variants with business needs. This improves the possibilities to perform internal planning, as well as the knowledge of the product line by the marketing department and customers. Branding a marketed product line may also improve this awareness.

Several experiences emphasise the importance of a single, well-designed architecture for the complete product line. This reference architecture must be stable for a long time. It is the technical basis to develop the product line and is a powerful internal communication tool. It provides technical standards within the organisation. The technical staff understands the architecture and what it means for variability and reuse. The architecture is usually built based on experiences in previous products. It may involve legacy assets that have proven themselves, often extracted from existing systems.

On the other hand, process competence does not seem to be as important as it is sometimes considered. Most companies perform at CMMI level 2 or 3. This means that basic process intelligence is available in the company. An important point is the clear separation between domain and application processes. In addition, it is necessary to have activities to sustain the collaboration and feedback between domain and application engineering.

With respect to the organisation, we see the importance of roles for domain and application engineering. Additional roles can be necessary for supporting collaboration, especially in large, distributed organisations. Virtual organisation structure leads to collaborative groups over organisation borders. This is important to keep the same vision throughout the organisation. It is not always necessary to have a complete distribution of the separate roles in the organisation structure. Especially for smaller companies, a single person may take several roles. As a consequence, part of the organisation structure is only virtual.

18.6.3 Benefits

When done well, software product line engineering pays off. Shorter lead-times, lower costs, reduction of maintenance and increased flexibility are some of the reported business benefits. Several companies found that the staff involved in their product lines was more stable than in other parts of the organisation. This may be a sign of a high level of job satisfaction for the people involved.

The experiences mention the increase of efficiency obtained through the introduction of the product lines. In particular, the development time for the products is reduced to different degrees.

AKVAsmart achieved a large reduction in code size, due to the removal of duplicated code, which helps to reduce maintenance costs.

18.6.4 Concerns

The lack of good tool support is a general concern. It hinders the introduction of product line development. Another issue is that the introduction of a product line affects many parts of the organisation and may lead to reduced attention for equally important concerns of the organisation. Reuse remains difficult.

A balance must be found between developing *for* and *with* reuse. It usually takes a long time to create a reusable platform with enough functionality. Several experiences mention wrapping legacy components of existing systems as a way to speed up platform development.

market maker mentions problems in separating application and domain engineering work. As application engineering is more short-term focused it tends to pull harder at the necessary resources, leaving the domain engineering activities empty handed. Other companies show that a clear separation between domain and application organisation reduces this problem. A secondary structure dealing with functional issues is necessary to have the right level of collaboration with the product line organisation. This may not be applicable to small companies, such as market maker.

Several experiences stress the fact that requirements and testing in a product line development is still an issue that needs more improvement. Nokia Networks mention the fact that, in their complex situation, asset management needs a lot of improvement. Especially when the organisation is structured around products, a lot of assets become ownerless sooner or later.

Negative points, or at least disappointments, of product line development are also mentioned. AKVAsmart found that the reduction of the development time was not as substantial as was anticipated. Several other experiences show that the introduction of a product line takes a lot of time and effort. The patience required before the benefits can be reaped may lead to tension within the organisation. At such points, management support is indispensiable.

18.6.5 Evaluations

No formal evaluation can be made for any dimension or any company. The nature of the experience descriptions does not allow that.

In the Business dimension, the highest level that was reached is level 3, *managed*. This level applies to most cases. If a product line is considered, it will influence the business strategy eventually. In the architecture dimension, we find evaluation results that cover all levels except 1. One company has reached level 5, two reached level 4. The high level for the architecture suggests that architecture is the first subject that is considered in doing product line engineering. In the process dimension, the highest level reached is level 3. Most companies obtain this level. This is in line with the fact that most companies do not act at higher CMMI levels as well. At least there is a clear separation between domain and application activities, and also the importance of collaboration is reflected in this level. Finally, for the organisation dimension, there are companies acting at all levels, except level 1. Levels 4 and 5 are only assigned to a single company. Most companies act at level 3.

By summarising the levels in all dimensions, we see that most evaluations for any dimension are at level 3. This suggests that at this level the most important ingredients for doing product line engineering are available. Many case studies mention problems. Solving those may lead to shifts in their FEF scores.

19

Starting with Software Product Line Engineering

An important question that will come up when one is interested in introducing product lines (or any major change) in an organisation is, what now? How does one start to do software product line engineering?

Unfortunately, there is no simple answer to this question, because there is no right or wrong way of doing product line engineering. It depends completely on the given situation. The question cannot be answered without asking numerous counter-questions: How large is the company? What is its current way of working? What goals does it want to reach? Why is it interested in product line engineering in the first place? What are its markets? etc.

Instead of giving a single answer, we will show *what* should be done, and *how* others have done it before. We have identified the ten steps[1] that are needed to successfully introduce product line engineering in an organisation. The steps are distributed over three phases:

- Decide
  1. Define a business strategy and vision.
  2. Learn about software product line engineering.
  3. Perform a risk analysis in the context of the organisation.
- Prepare
  4. Gain support for the new way of working.
  5. Set concrete goals for the transition.
  6. Scope the product line to determine its boundaries and contents.
  7. Evaluate the organisation for its current status and the ability to adopt the desired way of working.
  8. Plan the transition from the current development process to product line engineering.
- Transition
  9. Roll out and institutionalise the new way of working.

---

[1] We present them here as separate consecutive steps for readability. In practice, some of the steps will overlap, be taken in parallel, or their order changed. It is, however, important to address all of them in one way or another

10. Evolve the product line to continuously meet the goals of the organisation.[2]

We devote a separate section to each phase, with sub-sections per step. We explain what the steps mean and give examples of how the companies in our case studies have dealt with them. Armed with this knowledge, organisations can confidently start with software product line engineering.

19.1 Decide

The goal of this phase is to decide whether product line engineering is a suitable means to meet an organisation's goals. To make a well-informed decision, the goals and the potential solution must be well understood.

19.1.1 Define Business Strategy and Vision

Starting with software product line engineering is not something that an organisation does easily. It is not easy, and it certainly is not without risks. It means changing, sometimes radically, the way that software is developed, products are created and in some cases even how the company performs its business. Therefore, a deep understanding of the needs of the business is required before the decision on necessary changes can be made.

Software product line engineering is a long-term investment. It requires up-front investments in terms of effort, time and money. If the introduction is successful, the rewards are large and long lasting, but they will not come overnight. Therefore, it is important to have a good insight into the company's strategy. What can be expected for its future? How is the world changing? Are there customer needs that cannot be addressed in the future? What new systems will be developed and produced? Will new markets be addressed? Are there opportunities to enter adjacent markets by adapting products? It can be worthwhile to capture this information in a vision statement. Such a statement captures an (ambitious) goal in business terms. It sets a finish line towards which people work. DNV, for example, defined a long-term vision to express the company's ambitions to enter the market of vessel information services:

> To establish a common information repository containing or referring all information accumulated for an object, e.g. a vessel, throughout its life-cycle. This should enable the transfer of information on the object between all involved actors, including feedback of experiences accumulated during the object's life-cycle, for efficient delivery of high quality services and for continuous learning and improvement.

---

[2] Although evolving a product line extends from the starting phase to maturity, we address it here because evolution is something that starts as soon as a product line is started

Notice how DNV's vision does not mention product lines at all. This vision deals with *what* the company wants to achieve, not *how* it plans to achieve it. It describes a long-term goal in terms of products and services that DNV wants to bring to the market.

Often, current problems give rise to the introduction of product lines. At Bosch, for example, the platform could not handle the growing heap of functional requirements *and* preserve essential quality attributes like low resource consumption and keeping calibration procedures simple. The large range of variants (hundreds of programs versions per year) and the demand to share source code with customers indicated the need for a new way of working.

For Philips Consumer Electronics, it was a combination of problem, opportunity and future expectations that made the case for product lines. The company was faced with embedded software that grew exponentially in size and complexity. On the other hand, commonality in products had reached a level where televisions from different regions had less differences than that they had things in common. For the future, a new type of products was foreseen, namely hybrid systems such as television and video recorder combinations. These could not be dealt with efficiently with the current way of developing software.

19.1.2 Learn About Software Product Line Engineering

Software product line engineering is a powerful concept, but it is not a panacea. To make a founded decision, it is important to understand the pros and cons for the situation at hand.

Many of the companies described in this book have pioneered the concepts of software product line engineering. They had little or no information to guide them as they developed their processes and shaped their organisations. Still, in most cases knowledge was acquired beforehand. Some of the larger companies used their research and development capacities. Bosch set up small pilot projects within the research department to test their approach. Philips Consumer Electronics asked Philips Research for help on solving their problems. In some cases, external parties were contacted to help the companies find their way. Siemens used the testing expertise of the University of Duisberg-Essen to streamline their processes. Research institute Fraunhofer IESE helped market maker establish a product line using its PuLSE approach. Philips Medical Systems invited reuse expert Martin Griss to convince management and senior technical staff of the virtues of structured reuse.

19.1.3 Perform a Risk Analysis

Product line engineering can be a major leap forward for any software development organisation. However, it will almost certainly have a major impact on how the organisation is doing business. This leads to risks that any manager who is acting responsibly should assess prior to embarking on such a route. Just like in other projects, risk management should be an integral in transitioning to product line development [109].

The risks that are connected to product line engineering are manifold. The following list should only be seen as a short overview:

- The number of products that are developed as part of the product line may not be as high as initially expected.
- The developed assets (e.g. the components developed for reuse) may not be accepted by all developers, leading to wasted effort.
- It may be crucial to retain control and flexibility in every detail of the development to serve the customers appropriately.[3]
- The domain / product line thinking that is necessary may not be accepted in the development team.
- Existing systems that need to be maintained may hinder a transition to a different development approach.
- The overall business strategy may focus too strongly on "made to order", making it unrealistic to reuse a significant number of components.
- A customer may already exist for the products and may too strongly influence the direction of the product line.

Risk analysis should be a major aspect in software engineering management [87]; however, often it is not done or only to a limited extent. Also in transitioning to a product line approach, it is of immediate importance to perform risk management; however, if we analyse the various case studies in the Part II, we often see that risk management has often been done only superficially. Some positive examples of risk awareness are as follows:

- At DNV, a clear understanding existed that the differences in the culture of the various development centres may hinder any transitioning to a coordinated product line engineering approach. Thus, developing such an alignment, both on a technical and on a personal level was identified as a major issue.
- At Siemens, the risk analysis of management led to the decision to only perform a restricted form of product line engineering. The schedule was tight, management was unsure about success and a formal approach was seen as leading to too much organisational change. Thus, only testing was based on a product line approach.
- At Telvent, we actually see a case where the application of product line engineering was driven from the awareness of risks. Here, the risk was seen that strong volatility with customer requirements existed. Thus, product line engineering was seen as an approach to gain the necessary flexibility to adapt to these changing needs.

Despite these positive examples, especially risk analysis is a weak point in most attempts to transition to a product line approach. There are of course

---

[3] While in nine out of ten cases where this is claimed, it is actually not the case, there are still certain development contexts, where this is a serious issue

generic approaches to risk management that can be used like the RiskIT approach [81]. For our situation, there are certain approaches that specifically address the problem of benefit and risk analysis in a product line situation [120, 12, 58]. One of these approaches, which also addresses Scoping (cf. Sect. 19.2.1), is part of the PuLSE-Eco approach and shall be discussed here as a prototypical example. This approach works by analysing certain standard dimensions that should be assessed in order to determine (and compare) the costs, risks and benefits of a product line introduction situation [120]. The following dimensions cluster issues relevant to a product line benefit and risk analysis:

- *Maturity* – sufficient maturity of the domain in which the product line is situated is a pre-condition for stable concepts that are worth a significant investment. If the understanding of the domain has not yet sufficiently matured, it will not be possible to encode this basic knowledge into a product line infrastructure. On the other hand, the Telvent case study shows that product line development may also be introduced in relatively immature domains.
- *Stability* – even if the domain is mostly mature, this does per se not say much about the overall stability. However, a product line investment needs to take into account the impact of potentially rapid change. Once installed, the product line may be able to help the company act upon such changes as, for example, the market maker case shows.
- *Resource constraints* – as product line engineering will usually require a substantial investment, the impact of this has to be taken into account. But resources are not only money and time, they also cover the availability of experts. The Siemens example shows how a resource shortage led to initially cutting down on the extent of the product line initiative.
- *Organisational constraints* – this addresses any organisational restrictions as they become apparent in the example of DNV above.
- *Market potential (external and internal)* – this addresses any concerns regarding the market potential of the products. It is subdivided into an analysis of the external market (whether there are enough customers for the final products) and an analysis of the internal markets (whether the developed reusable components are actually used by the product organisations).
- *Commonality and variability* – this is of course the very basic question about product line engineering: Will we have sufficient commonality among the products, so that we will have enough reuse potential? In addition, is there sufficiently systematic variability, so that we can exploit it in terms of a product line approach?
- *Coupling and cohesion* – Can we identify features/ functionalities / components so that we can encapsulate reusable assets? The higher the coupling is, the more difficult (and costly) will it become to develop reusable assets.

- *Existing assets* – they can be both an advantage and a disadvantage. They can be an advantage as they may reduce the amount of effort required for developing reusable assets; they may be a disadvantage insofar as they may require the support of legacy systems and components.

Answering all these questions can be done in a manner very similar to other forms of assessments. The result is a benefit/ risk profile of the current situation. This may also be done on a fine-grained level, leading directly to a scope of the development as we will discuss below. However, the details of how risk analysis is performed are not so much in question. The issue is mostly that it is done at all.

19.2 Prepare

The preparation phase is all about preparing the organisation for the introduction of software product line engineering. This approach touches many facets of an organisation, and its introduction must be carefully prepared.

19.2.1 Gain Support

Right after the decision has been made to introduce software product line engineering to the organisation, the search for support begins and it never stops completely.[4] This ongoing activity needs to reach all the stakeholders of the change, most notably in (software) development, marketing and management. Companies that have successfully adopted software product lines have all taken this step seriously.

Bosch took a number of measures to make sure that the organisation would understand and, eventually, embrace the new way of working. Workshops were held with middle management to inform them of the process, learn from the feedback, and gain their trust and commitment. Enthusiastic and perseverant management were sought out to promote the new way of working. In order to communicate the idea behind the change, they used a vision statement.

> Software is built from a common architecture and a set of components using a product line approach, so that high quality individually tailored products can be built easily and predictably, using as few hardware resources as possible, thereby reducing overall development costs.[5]

---

[4] Actually, this step is *part of* the decision-making process. Although a select group may have taken the decision to go a certain way, a much larger group of people must make their own decision to give full support to the new way of working

[5] In contrast to the business vision, which focused on *what* a company wants to achieve, this vision focuses on *how* the company wants to achieve its goals, namely by introducing software product line engineering. This is a different perspective, for a different goal

DNV illustrated its vision for its second generation product line with a series of mock-ups. These illustrations of what types of products the new product line would establish were used to convince people in the development team, the customer organisations and top-level management.

Philips Medical Systems created a community of architects from all over the company to discuss their software, the common platform, ideas, problems, roadmaps and more. This community was kept alive and used to obtain agreements over the product line's technical course throughout its existence. In the beginning, e-mail was the primary communication tool for this community. Over time, more and more tools were put to use including an intranet website, teleconferencing facilities and regular face-to-face meetings.

Product groups have to be nurtured until long after they have decided to use common assets. Since this use requires an initial investment, the resistance in the group is growing up until the point that the payback becomes visible, after which it drops very fast. Those early periods of tension require the constant attention of the platform group's management. The most effective way of dealing with it is to help the adopting product groups to reach their break-even point sooner, for example by focusing platform development efforts on assets that are especially important to them.

The continuous nature of gaining support is also illustrated by the experiences of Philips Consumer Electronics. Having champions in the organisation that continuously promoted the way of working was an important success factor. Interestingly, with the approach being successful for a long period of time, it had started to be taken for granted. Newcomers, who did not personally experience the problems that the product line has solved, started to question the value of product line engineering in the organisation. Support is something that must be won continuously.

19.2.2 Set Concrete Goals

At this point, the organisation has a reasonable understanding of software product line engineering, the benefits and risks involved, and there is a business strategy that drives the effort. Now is a good time to set concrete and measurable goals for the change. These goals can then be used to guide the organisation through the transition phase and beyond. If chosen carefully, they help to avoid pitfalls like over-engineering or getting products out of the door without institutionalising the new process. Goals can also serve as finish lines that tell the organisation when it is done, or rather when the time has come to set new goals.

The following goals were mentioned most often in the case studies:

- *Reduce time to market*: both for new products and variants of existing ones.
- *Reduce costs*: the size and complexity of software is growing for many products, making the reduction of development and maintenance costs

an important goal for many companies. Siemens, for example, specifically aimed to reduce the costs of testing for their product line of highly reliable medical systems.

- *Raise the product quality level*: for individual products, or the portfolio as a whole. At Bosch, the software had grown to support a lot of functionality, but at the cost of some crucial quality attributes, like ease of use. Product line engineering was a way out of that situation.
- *Become more efficient*: to cut costs or reduce the time to market. DNV mentioned information sharing across disciplines as a driver for product line engineering. This increases the quality of their processes and therefore the efficiency and product quality.
- *Integrate the product portfolio*: establishing a common look-and-feel, and integrating products in other ways is often a goal for software product line engineering. For instance, AKVAsmart aimed for a common look-and-feel for different applications. Philips Medical Systems used its product line to integrate products of companies that it acquired.
- *Extend the product portfolio*: Telvent had a single customer for a single product, but it foresaw an opportunity to sell variants of it later and therefore chose product line engineering as their development process. Philips Consumer Electronics designed its product line to support the development of hybrid products that it foresaw would become important.

Most companies have several goals that they aim for. Bosch, for example, wanted to deal with the increasing complexity of their software while simultaneously lowering costs, shortening time to market, and increasing the product quality, along with more exotic goals like sharing source code with their customers.

One particular goal that can be helpful to define is the desired FEF-profile. In the previous step, the organisation evaluated its current position. Now, the desired situation can be described. The FEF-profile shows the organisation's ambition with respect to how it will use software product line engineering to achieve its goals. As explained in Chap. 6, the desired profile can help to identify where improvement is needed and thus effort should be focused on.

19.2.3 Scope the Product Line

Scoping the product line is a key step, which makes product line engineering a truly strategic approach. Determining the scope has many implications. In general three levels of scoping can be distinguished [119]:

1. *Product portfolio scoping:* this aims at identifying the products that shall be part of the product line.
2. *Domain scoping:* this aims at identifying major areas of functionalities that shall be supported by product line reuse.
3. *Asset scoping:* this aims at identifying the particular implementation components that shall be developed as product line assets.

The last two are in general closely related. Thus, we can regard the scoping problem as basically two-dimensional: which products shall be considered part of the product line and what functionality within these products shall be supported by reusable assets?

These two questions can not be answered clearly without relating to the previous steps. In particular, the strategy and vision will strongly impact the specific products that shall be developed. However, that a certain product shall be part of the overall strategy does not mean it also shall be part of the (technical) product line. Sometimes it is more meaningful to acquire certain products externally or develop it independently (e.g. if the products rely on a completely different platform like a mobile platform, or the product has only superficial resemblance).

Sometimes the specific products that shall be the basis for the product line are rather clear from the beginning. For example, in Chap. 16 on Siemens, it is mentioned that *"while planning to improve two existing (rather similar) applications and add a third, the decision was made to develop all three applications with the same assets"*; thus, the very decision that led to considering a product line approach also defined the specific products that should be taken into account. In contrast, Bosch and DNV define the scope very openly and broadly to rather general markets. The ambition there was to support all products relevant to the market. In particular, at DNV the concept was to create a plug-in architecture that supports the basic and common requirements, while extension of the product line can be done by the plug-in architecture. Based on the scoping results, Bosch decided to develop several product lines in parallel.

An intermediate strategy is demonstrated by the market maker case study. Here, a number of product types were defined; however, not all of them ultimately lead to instantiated products. Nevertheless, the effort of product definition was not considered wasted, but rather was regarded as a very helpful exercise that clarified much about the future products.

Scoping is directly based on the input from risk management. First of all, the risk management information is used to determine whether it is meaningful to define a scope at all. However, in a second step domain scoping is usually performed, i.e. individual functional areas are defined that are evaluated with respect to their reuse potential. Here, again risk analysis can be used as the benefit/risk situation of the various areas (sub-domains) may vary strongly. Some refined approaches make this decomposition of the overall product line functionality into sub-domains explicit and support the accompanying analysis [120].

The resulting analysis determines the product line potential in terms of the partial potentials of the various domains. This allows deriving a ranking of domains in terms of return-on-investment on reuse investments. Such a return-on-investment analysis can be performed in an even more fine-grained manner by making the utility of reuse relative to the various business goals explicit. (See Sect. 2 business goals for a list of goals). Some approaches support this kind of analysis [122]; however, in practice it is often not possible to apply these techniques for the simple reason that the necessary quantitative basis is not available in the organisation.

Sometimes scoping is misunderstood as an action that must be performed only when setting up a new product line; however, it is key that the scope of the product line is constantly managed throughout the lifetime of the product line. Managing the scope is a key part of change management in a product line situation [131]. Only when the scope is constantly managed, it can be ensured that the organisation adequately reacts to new developments and opportunities.

Product line development sometimes leads to unexpected opportunities for an organisation. Here, scoping is particularly relevant to recognise these opportunities [36]. Some examples of this are reported by Cummins [43] and Celsiustech [17]. In the case of Cummins, the product line was initially set up to support the development of engine software for diesel trucks. However, after developing the product line, the organisation realised that the product line could be easily extended to support any kind of industrial diesel engine as well. This led Cummins to move into this market. Similar, in the Celsiustech case study after the product line for navel battle ships was established, the company recognised that the surveillance software could also be used in land-based systems. This in turn led to an extension of the market.

This shows that product line engineering also creates options [53]. Adequate and continuous scoping can open ways to recognise and exploit these options.

19.2.4 Evaluate the Organisation

The evaluation of the organisation is needed to obtain knowledge of what are the best actions to take. It may be the case that certain elements of product line development already exist in the organisation. It may be wise to use them as a starting point. The Family Evaluation Framework (FEF, see Chap. 6) is developed for doing such an evaluation. The FEF allows preparing a goal profile that determines what the company prepares for.

The FEF as presented here is still at its initial stages. It is in use by several companies that were involved in its definition. In particular, it is used as an addition to CMM(I) evaluation, providing more details to certain aspects. However, there are no public reports on the use of FEF available yet. This is partially due to the fact that the involved companies consider the evaluation results as proprietary information that should not be shared with others.

An important aspect of the FEF is the explicit separation of the four BAPO concerns: Business, Architecture, Process and Organisation, all need attention to enable a healthy product line development.

The FEF is not the first model to evaluate or assess software development. In particular, in the area of software development processes, there are several capability evaluation models. The SEI published a Framework for Software

Product Line Practice [38] that distinguishes 29 practice areas, which are divided into three categories.

1. *Software engineering* practice areas are necessary to apply the appropriate technology to create and evolve both core assets and products.
2. *Technical management* practice areas are those management practices necessary to engineer the creation and evolution of the core assets and the products.
3. *Organisational management* practice areas are necessary for the synchronisation of the entire software product line activities.

The SEI's Product Line Technical Probe (PLTP) allows examining an organisation's capabilities to adopt a software product line engineering approach. The PLTP is based on the SEI's Framework for Software Product Line Practice as a reference model in collection and in analysis of data about an organisation. The results of applying the PLTP include a set of findings, which characterise an organisation's strengths and challenges relative to its product line effort, as well as a set of recommendations.

In addition, there exist several initial economic models to evaluate the business value of product lines; see e.g. [58, 125]. Jan Bosch proposed an initial model on evolution of software product line architectures in [28], and an initial investigation on organisational structures in [27].

19.2.5 Plan the Transition

The business goals are defined, the scope is clear and the organisation has an understanding of what software product lines are about. The next step is to plan the transition. That requires designing the right architecture, process and organisation that support the business goals for the software product line, and making plans for getting from the current situation to the new one.

The current architectures, processes and organisation structures are crucial in deciding upon the new ones. The Philips Medical Systems case study is a good illustration. Its decentralised organisation heavily influenced the way in which it established a common platform. Product development groups were responsible for their own product portfolio, and many had a product line of their own. Establishing a new product line that spanned the product groups meant dealing with the needs and desires of each individual group. This led to a process where the platform definition was a joint effort, whereas its implementation was more centralised. One product group was selected to implement the platform. Change-control boards, with representatives of all product groups, oversaw the platform's evolution.

With the architecture, process and organisation in place, two groups were selected to be the first customers of the new platform. After that, it was left up to the product groups to plan their own transition to using the common platform. The functional scope of the platform was gradually extended using a component-based architecture. Existing software was transformed into platform components on a piece-by-piece basis.

Different companies require different approaches. Being a small company, market maker did not feel the need for heavy processes and organisation structures. A single team of five developers was enough to set up their product line. Although this team was process aware, it did not have a fully defined and documented development process. That was considered too much overhead for a small company. Instead, people were assigned roles that made clear what their responsibilities were. Examples of such roles are scoping team, architecture manager and component developer. People were left free to fulfil their responsibilities as they saw fit, although their results were carefully controlled. Within twelve months, the team set up a product line and released their first products.

As a final example we consider AKVAsmart. The company wanted to minimise the risks involved by gradually growing their software product line. Their plan was to reimplement each of their existing products using the common assets. For each product added to the line, the software platform grew to support that product's needs, but not more. At no point the software platform should contain more functionality than was needed to support the products that used it at the time. The architecture that was designed to support this gradual transition was based on a plug-in framework. The framework itself was the responsibility of domain engineering, while the plug-ins were developed and maintained by application engineers. At the time of writing their case study, the first two products had been successfully ported to the platform and the next one was in line.

19.3 Transition

The last phase is where the plans are created before they are actually implemented. In practice, the last two phases are often intertwined, unless a big-bang introduction strategy was chosen.

19.3.1 Roll Out and Institutionalise

Product line engineering can be introduced in a company in many different ways. Ultimately, the approach used should fit the organisation and its goals.

One of the goals that every organisation that starts with software product lines should have is to institutionalise the new way of working. Without product line engineering, a product line quickly looses its advantages, diminishing to a set of more and more independent products. Product line engineering must become the standard way of working with the product line. Changing the way things are being done can be a slow and painful process. Special attention must be paid to managing this process and making sure it goes all the way. Education and gaining support go hand in hand.

market maker identified an opportunity for a range of products that could be based on a new technology. The company decided to attract new people and let them build the product line up from the ground. This enabled them to quickly grow this new line of products without cannibalising on the resources of its existing portfolio. Close integration with the rest of the company let the team benefit from the knowledge of their colleagues. Existing software assets were used to give the new team a running start, and the team was given a firm deadline to serve as a focus point. As a result, the first product was ready within twelve months. By then, software product line engineering was institutionalised as the team's way of working.

Being in a totally different situation, Philips Consumer Electronics took a more cautious approach. It spent the first three years to set up an architecture and build two lead products with it. These products were carefully selected: they were highly visible but represented a low risk. When the second lead product was successful, the product line engineering approach was rolled out across the full range of products in two years. The organisation changed from one with large, product-oriented teams to one with small product teams and medium-sized asset teams. The way of working was changed from waterfall to iterative development. During the transition, developers gradually moved from the old way of working to the new one, while Philips Research remained involved to make sure that the processes were carried out consistently.

At Bosch, analysis of market segments lead to the conclusion that there was a need for not one but two product lines, besides single system development projects. Rolling out product line engineering was done using a stepwise approach. Small pilot projects carried out in corporate research established the much needed experience inside the company. Next, a single business unit project was put in place. This project was carefully set up to maximise its impact on the whole organisation. Its project manager, for example, was well respected in the business unit. Furthermore, the team was filled with representatives from several development departments, complemented with consultants from corporate research. The project had a champion in middle management, who could ensure that funding was not an issue. Most importantly, of course, was that the project actually delivered what was promised, paving the way for similar projects in other parts of the organisation.

Bosch acknowledged that there was a risk that developers and management would focus on the technical aspects of the implementation at the cost of embedding the new processes in the organisation. They used product line engineering coaches to support the developers and make sure that the new processes were executed in the right way. A training program for the processes and the common architecture was set up to help developers become productive quickly. The new processes were also documented in the development handbook on the company's intranet.

One particular pitfall that needs to be avoided is overdoing it: domain engineering continues to make ever better and more generic assets, but no-one bothers to make products out of them. A common asset does not bring any value to the company until it is used in a product. Even worse, the costs for maintaining the asset begin to pile up as soon as its development begins.

DNV attacks this problem by accepting only those ideas for common assets that come with a product development project willing to use it. market maker started discussions with potential customers soon after the development of its new product line began. It also set a deadline for the first product to be delivered within twelve months. Philips Consumer Electronics used various ways to make sure their common assets were useful and used in products, including asset developers joining product teams for periods of time and product-specific branches of asset archives. But it also acknowledges that for every force a counter-force is needed to keep the balance. Therefore, they made it the personal responsibility of asset teams that their assets are product-independent and have long-term value.

19.3.2 Evolving the Product Line

Things change, and product lines are no exception. One particular advantage of product line engineering is that it increases the freedom of choice that a company has. Reducing the time and effort it takes to bring new products to the market means that there is a lot more that can be done. But to keep this advantage, the product line should evolve to continue to support the needs and wishes of its owners. Is the architecture still in top condition? Are the processes surrounding the product line still effective and efficient enough? Do the organisational structures fit with the current business goals? What opportunities and threats do we see approaching in the future? These kinds of questions need to be asked and answered regularly to make sure that the product line engineering effort continues to bring value to the company.

One way to keep these items on the agenda is to use roadmapping. A roadmap is like a plan for the long-term future, but with this respect that nobody believes it. The further a plan looks ahead, the less precise it can be, as the uncertainty increases the further one looks into the future. A roadmap can start in the near future with well-defined and planned items, continue with resolutions in the mid-term, and change to vague expectations and predictions in the longer-term. The idea is not to predict the future but to be aware of the fact that things change and to continuously steer the product line in the right direction. In a situation where multiple groups depend on each other, as is often the case with software product lines, sharing roadmaps for the applications and the platform can be a good way of ensuring that all groups agree on the direction in which the product line evolves.

At Philips Medical Systems, the scope of the product line grew in both foreseen and unforeseen ways. Although it was part of the institutionalisation plan to start with a limited scope in both functionality and number of applications, the latter grew larger than was expected beforehand. Along the years, Philips acquired several medical companies. Each of them became involved in the product line engineering effort, with key people of the acquired companies joining this product line's community.

The organisation changed in another way as well. The domain engineering effort started as a task of an established product group. Over time, this platform team was separated more and more from the application teams, became a separate department within the product group and finally a sub-organisation of its own. These changes reflected the needs of the domain engineers at the different times in the life of the product line. At first, the experience and domain knowledge of the people in the product group were much needed to get things going. Later, conflicts of interest started to arise because the resources of a single department needed to be shared between domain and application engineering. Currently, the size of the domain engineering group justifies it being a sub-organisation within the company.

Roadmapping is a continuous activity at both the domain and the application levels in Philips Medical Systems. The planned use of the platform is on the roadmaps of the product groups, and the platform's roadmap reflects that.

19.4 Conclusion

In short, these are the steps to be taken when starting with software product line engineering:

- *Define a business strategy and vision*: if the company's strategy does not support the investments that are needed to make product line engineering work, the introduction makes no sense and will most likely fail.
- *Learn about software product line engineering*: without a solid understanding of the pros and cons of this approach, a sensible decision cannot be made.
- *Perform a risk analysis* in the context of the organisation: the companies in our case studies barely mention risk analysis as a part of their approach. This is not so surprising, given that these companies were pioneering a new approach to software development. Had these companies done a thorough risk analysis, they probably would have backed off, and thus never made it as a case study for this book. The Siemens case, where a risk analysis led to a very partial adoption of product line engineering, illustrates this. Today, the situation is different. Much more is known about software product lines, and many companies have successfully deployed them. Therefore, it makes sense to do a good risk analysis now, before making a decision.
- *Gain support for the new way of working*: a broad range of stakeholders must understand and ultimately embrace the concepts of software product line engineering to make it work.

- *Set concrete goals for the transition*: well-chosen goals help an organisation to stay focused on what is important, and to avoid pitfalls like over-engineering or forgetting to institutionalise the new way of working.
- *Scope the product line* to determine its boundaries and contents: with the strategy, risks and goals set, the scope of the product line actually describes what it is that will be created.
- *Evaluate the organisation* for its current status and the ability to adopt the desired way of working: without knowing where you are now, it is very hard to determine the best route to your destination. Here, all BAPO aspects are relevant.
- *Plan the transition* from the current development process to product line engineering: the transition plan depends heavily on the business strategy, risk profile, and current situation of the company among others. A good plan helps a company to stick to its course and successfully deploy product line engineering in the organisation.
- *Roll out and institutionalise* the new way of working: the main goal is to get a product line up and running. But just as important is to embed this way of working into the organisation.
- *Evolve the product line* to continuously meet the goals of the organisation: a product line that fits the organisation's needs is a valuable asset. To keep this value, the product line should evolve with these needs. To keep up with all the changes that a company deals with, roadmapping should be an ongoing activity.

20

Outlook

Product line engineering has come a long way since the initial work by Parnas in the 1970s [101]. For quite some years, it seemed that product line engineering would not make the transition into industrial practice, but finally it became a reality. In hindsight, it becomes clear why such a long time was needed in order to transition the concepts into practice: software business needed to become a more "normal" kind of business, one in which companies do not develop one kind of software on one day and a completely different kind on another. Today, we are in a situation where companies are in fierce competition based on similar products and thus need to provide a wide range of well-adapted solutions for their customers. Further, software systems have grown considerably in size, making development effort for software a key part of total costs for most organisations.

This also sheds some light on what kind of companies should *not* look at product line engineering if it is sufficient for you to provide a single product version for your customer, if you make completely different projects today from the ones you made yesterday, if being at the forefront of innovation means to you that each new product has to be developed from scratch, than product line engineering is not made for you.

For all other kinds of cases, companies can expect substantial return on investment from their decision to start a product line effort. Our case studies have shown this across a large range of businesses, organisation sizes, industries and even approaches taken towards product line engineering. Now, the questions are Where to go from here? What needs further research? Where do companies venture into new grounds where no well-established routes are available, yet?

20.1 Where We Are

A lot of companies have started product line initiatives over recent years. These companies range from very small to very large. The approach has gained significant attention and proves to be a basis for significant cost reductions in software development. However, product line engineering has not yet received the strong attention that should be connected to the level of improvements that can be derived from it. It is important to note that there is currently a strong focus on embedded systems, but only comparatively little work from the information systems world. However, it can be applied there as well as the market maker case study in this book (Chap. 11) and other reports show (e.g. [34, 126]). It is difficult to precisely pin down the reasons for this embedded focus, but certainly significant effort is required to make the approach for information systems as well-known as it is in the embedded systems context.

Another commonality among the different case studies we discussed in Part II of this book is that most of them applied an approach to product line engineering that was invented as the companies undertook the effort of applying product line engineering. While at this point a significant body of knowledge on product line engineering has been established and also certain guidelines are known, there is not yet a sound portfolio of approaches from which techniques can be selected on a rational basis. Although good general guidelines can be given now, systematic and precise customisation guidelines are not yet available.

Most of the companies of our case studies are large organisations. While this might be due to some bias in our selection, it currently seems that especially large organisations address the challenge of product line engineering systematically. However, experience shows that also small organisations can profit considerably from product line engineering. This has been shown among other cases in the market maker case study (cf. Chap. 11). Again, it seems there is the major issue that awareness must be created among smaller companies about the opportunities of product line development.

So far, product line engineering can still be regarded as a rather new technology in software engineering with about half a dozen years since it is really heading into mainstream and about ten years since it was accepted as a vision in many companies. Thus, while product line engineering is already somewhat established it still has some shortcomings. We will discuss those and potential remedies in the following section.

20.2 Current Shortcomings of Product Line Engineering

If we look at ways to improve product line engineering, we can distinguish two major perspectives:

1. True shortcomings may actually provide obstacles in the wide-spread adoption of product line engineering.
2. Ways in which we could go beyond the state of the art in product line engineering, focusing mostly on more efficient and potent approaches.

In this section, we will focus on shortcomings that may hinder product line adoption. In the next section, we will focus on making product line engineering an even more potent approach.

Unfortunately, there are quite a number of shortcomings that may hinder effective product line adoption. Although it is possible to effectively deal with each of them, we believe that product line engineering will need to provide better solutions in order to further improve its acceptance. We can distinguish two major areas of improvement:

1. Improvement of methods.
2. Improvement in technology and tools.

20.2.1 Methodological Shortcomings

The first and perhaps most profound shortcoming is still the *lack of experimental analysis and detailed comparisons* of product line engineering techniques. Luckily over the last ten years a lot of research has been devoted to the question whether product line engineering is a viable and successful approach for organisations in comparison with standard (single-system) software engineering methods. Last but not least, the wealth of case studies we report on in this book and our cross-sectional analysis improves this situation. The general outcome can simply be summarised as follows: product line engineering enables organisations to achieve significant reductions in development effort while simultaneously improving overall software quality.

However, while many different approaches to product line engineering were established, only little analysis was devoted to the comparison of their respective advantages and disadvantages. Thus, we can currently only observe the multitude of approaches (e.g. for variability modelling), but cannot thoroughly define their respective advantages and disadvantages. This is less problematic from a practical point of view, as so far all approaches to product line engineering seem to be at least better than single system engineering. Nevertheless, it is still a rather unsatisfactory situation. Here, we need a step towards the comparative analysis of different product line engineering techniques in order to provide the practitioner with a qualified portfolio of techniques.

The second shortcoming is particularly important for practitioners that ponder the question of whether they should move towards a product line engineering approach. This is the *lack of detailed and sound business and economical models* of product line engineering. This makes it currently very difficult to perform product line engineering in a manner explicitly driven by business goals. While all our case study contributors experienced significant benefits from product line engineering, they were not able beforehand to quantitatively estimate the benefits they would gain from product line engineering. While economical models of product line engineering and software reuse in general exist [52, 86, 22, 125], they do not provide sufficiently detailed guidance and there is a lack of adequate and well-supported parameter estimates for determining the benefits beforehand with an acceptable margin of error. Again, while unsatisfactorily, this situation need not haunt the practitioner as still the general agreement is that significant benefits can be derived from product line engineering that cannot be achieved with traditional software engineering approaches.

Variability management is a key aspect of product line engineering. Nevertheless, we must currently accept the *lack of a generally accepted theory of variability*. While a vast range of variability management techniques were proposed so far, there is agreement only on the general aspects of variability and not on the details of the required expressiveness. The availability of these techniques is currently a major bonus of product line engineering, as they constitute a core element of product line engineering. However, there is no systematic guidance for selecting (or constructing) a variability management approach for specific development situations and contexts. A brief overview of variability management approaches already shows that the various approaches share a significant amount of commonality. Nevertheless, a generalisation model encompassing the large number of different approaches is still lacking, although currently work along these lines is under way [42, 1]. Also, the traceability of variability (identifying and understanding parts of documents and products related to a specific variability) is an important issue.

At this point, even in organisations that systematically perform product line development, *quality assurance* is often done very similar to a single systems approach. Here, further work is required. This includes both review techniques and testing. In particular, the question how to benefit from commonalities in the system functionality in order to reduce overall testing effort (not only test case derivation) will require substantial effort for some time to come. Certain effort reductions are already today part of industrial practice as the Siemens case study (cf. Chap. 16) shows.

Current *frameworks for software process assessment* like the CMMI do not address product line engineering at all. As a result, they are not capable of assessing the product line maturity of an organisation; they are not even able to assist in this undertaking. Especially for the CMMI, extensions for product line engineering have been developed [145], but these are not yet generally known and accepted. In this book we presented the Families Evaluation Framework (cf. Chap. 6). This does not only include extensions to the CMMI for addressing the concerns mentioned above, it also addresses a wider range of aspects: business, architecture and organisation.

As product line engineering will become an increasingly accepted and widespread approach, problems which have so far hardly surfaced will become major issues. A prime example of this is *evolution support*. While so far the focus in the product line engineering community was on the successful adoption of product lines, it will shift to the evolution and sustained development of product line engineering. This becomes a more complex concern, compared to single system development, as successful product lines are inherently long-lived and need to support a rapidly growing number of products over time.

Software product line engineering will increasingly be used in a very complex situation, see e.g. Chap. 13. Several product lines are connected and built upon each other. Moreover, development is distributed in the organisation and it even crosses organisational boundaries. In most cases, such a complex situation is mastered by the introduction of a hierarchy. Products developed by one product line are used as basic building blocks in another. This introduces a series of dependencies among the product lines that must be managed correctly through traceability for maintenance. This is still not solved appropriately today and the involved business models are much more complicated than those for a single product line.

20.2.2 Technology and Tools

From a technology perspective, product line engineering has been combined and applied in connection with a large number of different implementation technologies. Some collections do also provide catalogues of implementation techniques.

A particularly interesting area is *Domain-Specific Languages (DSLs)*. In some sense, they can be regarded as an extreme form of product lines. The core idea of a domain-specific languages approach is to describe the variability of a product line based on a specifically developed high-level language. Commonalities are not made explicit in the language. They are treated as part of the domain. This is certainly not an approach for all cases; however, it has clear advantages under certain circumstances [127].

So far work on product lines typically focuses on using a single approach to product line engineering throughout the development. This certainly results in certain simplifications in the development process, but it fails to achieve certain benefits that could result from a systematic integration of domain-specific languages and traditional variability management approaches like feature modelling. So far this integration is only weakly explored. Being strongly related to domain-specific languages the software factory approach is currently advocated by Microsoft [63].

A generative approach that is currently explored is the area of model-based development. Here, in particular, the *Model-Driven Architecture Approach (MDA)* attracts a lot of attention. While some work has been done so far to integrate model-driven approaches and product line engineering, the field is so far explored only very little. It seems that both MDA and product line engineering are complementary to some extend. MDA focuses on implementing technical variability, e.g. the alternative platforms .NET or J2EE, while product line engineering focuses mostly on the customer-oriented flexibility, i.e. in particular the variability in functional and non-functional requirements that results from different customer requirements. As generative techniques are increasingly accepted in industrial practice, we expect a stronger integration of product line engineering with MDA also for the near future. The potential for further cost reduction can be expected to be significant.

From a practical perspective the current *lack of tool integration* of product line approaches is very important. None of the mainstream software engineering environments currently explicitly support the notion of variability or of a product line. So far only few specialised companies offer product line tool support. This is typically handled by extending existing tools in the form of a plug-in. Examples for such tool extensions are the GEARS-tool [60], which provides a layer on top of configuration management, or Pure::Variants [110], which provides an extension to such tools as requirements engineering tools. Besides those commercialised tools, there also exists a large number of product line tools, which have mostly been developed from a research context and thus typically do not provide a stable production environment [7, 33, 130].

20.3 Going Beyond Product Lines

If there is a general trend that can be seen in software engineering, then it is certainly the trend to *higher flexibility and adaptation* to customer needs. Product line engineering as we see it today is a result of this development. At its core we see a strong demand of organisations to provide tailored solutions to their customers. However, the demand for customisation is constantly increasing; plug-in architectures that enable run-time addition of functionality are a result of this trend. Thus, it does not require much guess-work to expect run-time dynamism, end-user customisation and context-awareness to be key topics of future product lines. First attempts at expanding product line engineering to address these problems have already been made [85, 65].

A key issue in these areas is the notion of binding time: When will the decision be made? What functionality shall be provided as part of the systems? Generally, this is constantly moving to later and later points in time. Traditionally, this has been done mostly statically. Often the last point was compile time or link time. To some extend also startup of the system played a role as some systems performed self-configuration during initialisation.

Systematic approaches to end-user customisation require open architectures that can integrate a wide range of external functionality which is not yet known at development time. At the same time quality guarantees for the resulting systems must be given. This requires new ways of integrating these components as well as new ways of assuring the component quality at run-time.

A different dimension of end-user customisation that goes also in terms of expressiveness beyond the traditional forms of product line engineering is the customisation to user-specific business processes. This form of customisation is very well known in information systems, but has hardly been addressed from a product line perspective so far. Traditionally, variability management is strongly focused on feature-based approaches; however, business processes go beyond this in terms of their expressiveness. Here, new approaches for describing the customisation like the business process execution language (BPEL) have emerged [76]. This is typically combined with a service-oriented architecture (SOA). BPEL can be regarded as a domain-specific language particularly adapted to business process customisation.

Context-aware and autonomous systems have recently become rather popular, especially in combination with ambient intelligence and pervasive computing [152, 64]. This concept goes even a step further, as here the decision about the potential form of adaptation is made by the system itself. Current variability management approaches are not yet able to capture these decisions and the conditions under which they should be triggered. However, as these forms of end-user customisation and self-adaptivity will become increasingly relevant, their integration with product line engineering must be addressed. Especially, as some products in a single product line might be producer-customised, some products may support end-user customisation, while some products may even support context-awareness – all for the same variation.

20.4 Product Line Engineering for Practitioners

A few years ago product line engineering was only an approach that was used by a few companies. Of course many organisations had already developed product lines for a market, but only few were able to fully exploit the large potential that such a situation entails. Currently, we see the number of companies that aim to transition to a product line engineering significantly increasing. Like other technologies before, product line engineering goes mainstream. The case studies we were able to collect and analyse in this chapter emphasised this lesson. We are certain that while currently companies that transition to a product line approach are able to gain significant advantages over their competitors, in a few years, time organisations will *have to adopt* product line engineering in order not to suffer from a significant disadvantage over their competitors.

As a result of the analysis of the various case studies in this book, we were able to provide some general guidelines for practitioners who are interested in product line engineering as a way forward for their development organisation. We will now briefly summarise some of these guidelines:

- Product line engineering adoption becomes much more systematic if an appropriate evaluation of the current situation and the particular benefits that are planned to achieve are made. An approach for performing such an assessment has been introduced with the Families Evaluation Framework (FEF). By using such an approach, an organisation can determine where it is currently situated and determine a potential future development approach.
- A commonality across all observed case studies was that architecture played a significant role. A clear technical vision needs to be established that allows to support the specific variabilities required by future products in the product line. Thus, any organisation which is currently weak

on architecting will need to improve this capability in order to succeed at product line engineering.

- On the other hand, process competence does not seem to be as important as it is sometimes taken. You do not need to be at CMMI level 5 in order to be successful at product line engineering. Level 2 is enough (at least you should follow your process). While improvements in process competence will enable to more reliably achieve product line benefits, sufficient case studies establish that CMMI levels alone will not significantly impact your product line performance.
- Organisation is an issue. Clear roles for developing the reuse infrastructure (domain engineering) and for developing the individual products must be established. Even if the same person may fill the same role, it is important that the focus of the current work at each moment in time is clear. As a consequence, while such an organisational structure needs to be established, this does not mean that a formal reorganisation needs to take place. Such a scheme can actually be superimposed on rather traditional role schemata.

There are many ways of performing product line engineering. Despite these differences, there are some commonalities, which we tried to highlight in this book. The above list shows only some of the key aspects one should have in mind when starting product line engineering.

Product line engineering is finally here – and it is here to stay. If you are in a software business where development costs, time to market and quality matter – and who is not – then the question is how long can you afford to work without product line engineering or with a sub-optimal approach? We hope this book helps you to systematically go forward in terms of the cost-effectiveness of your software development.

Glossary

Application Assets are the *development assets* of specific product line applications.

Application Design is the sub-process of *application engineering* where the *reference architecture* is specialised into the application architecture.

Application Engineering is the process of software product line engineering in which the applications of the product line are built by reusing *domain assets* and exploiting the variability of the product line.

Application Realisation is the sub-process of *application engineering* where a single application is realised according to the application architecture by reusing domain realisation assets.

Application Requirements Engineering is the sub-process of *application engineering* dealing with the elicitation of stakeholder requirements, the creation of the application requirements specification, and the management of application requirements.

Application Testing is the sub-process of *application engineering* where domain test assets are reused to uncover the evidence of defects in the application.

Architecture, *see software architecture.*

Architectural Structure is the decomposition of a software system into parts and relationships.

Architectural Texture is the collection of common development rules for realising the applications of a software product line.

BAPO is an acronym that refers to Business, Architecture, Process, and Organisation. Based on these four dimensions a specific product line engineering approach can be characterised.

Binding Time defines points in time when the decision must be made whether a feature that is available in the product line infrastructure will be part of a specific product.

Component is a unit of composition with contractually specified component interfaces and explicit context dependencies only; it can be deployed independently and is subject to composition by third parties.

CMMI is an abbreviation for Capability Maturity Model Integration. This is a widely used approach for process improvement approach to succeed the CMM approach.

Configuration describes the specific assets that together constitute a final product. The assets can be domain and application assets.

Development Asset is the output of a sub-process of *domain* or *application engineering*. Development assets encompass requirements, architecture, components and tests.

Development for Reuse refers to any development activity that does not directly aim at developing a product, but rather aims at developing assets which will be reused by other activities.

Development with Reuse refers to any development activity which takes advantage of existing, reusable assets.

Domain is an area of process or knowledge driven by business requirements and characterised by a set of concepts and terminology understood by stakeholders in that area. The problem domain and the solution domain are two kinds of domains.

Domain Assets are reusable *development assets* created in the sub-processes of *domain engineering*. Synonyms are platform assets and *product line assets*.

Domain Design is the sub-process of domain engineering where a reference architecture for the entire software product line is developed.

Domain Engineering is the process of *software product line engineering* in which the commonality and the variability of the product line are defined and realised.

Domain Realisation is the sub-process of *domain engineering* where the set of reusable *components* and interfaces of the product line is developed.

Domain Requirements Engineering is the sub-process of *domain engineering* where the common and variable *requirements* of the product line are defined, documented in reusable *requirements assets* and continuously managed.

Domain Testing is the sub-process of *domain engineering* where the evidence of defects in domain assets is uncovered and where reusable *test assets* for *application testing* are created.

Families Evaluation Framework (FEF) is a reference framework for characterizing certain properties of a product line engineering approach. The framework can be used by a comparison of a desired state with the actual state to improve the product line engineering approach of an organisation. The framework was developed within the Families project, hence the name.

Opportunistic Reuse refers to a development model where appropriate assets are reused from other projects if they can be identified and adapted during product development. In this case, no specific process exists for developing explicit assets for reuse.

Platform, see *software platform*.

Platform Assets, see *domain assets.*

Process defines how software development is – or should be — performed, i.e. the specific activities that need to be conducted. In order to perform product line engineering, a single system development process needs to be adequately adapted.

Product Line Assets, see *domain assets.*

Product Line Adoption describes the process of changing to a product line engineering approach.

Product Line Engineering, see *software product line engineering.*

Product Management is the process of controlling the development, production and marketing of the software product line and its applications.

Product-Specific is a functionality or a characteristic of a final system that is not shared with other products in the software product line.

Product Portfolio defines the particular products that shall be developed. In general, a product portfolio defines all the products relevant to a company (marketed product line). In the context of a product line, it usually refers to the products that are developed based on the product line assets (engineered product line).

Reference Architecture is a core *software architecture* that captures the high-level design of a software product line.

Requirement is (1) A condition or capability needed by a user to solve a problem or achieve an objective. (2) A condition or capability that must be met or possessed by a system or system component to satisfy a contract, standard, specification or other formally imposed document. (3) A documented representation of a condition or capability as in (1) or (2) [IEEE Std 610.12-1990].

Requirements Assets are products of the requirements engineering process specified using natural language and/or requirements models.

Scoping is the process of determining the boundaries of the product line engineering activity. This can be performed on three levels: product portfolio, domain and assets.

Software Architecture is the set of the main guiding development principles for one or more software applications. The principles are the solution for one or more architectural concerns dealing with quality. There are other, more instrumental, definitions in the literature.

Software Platform is a set of software sub-systems and interfaces that form a common structure from which a set of derivative products can be efficiently developed and produced.

Software Product Line Infrastructure is the collection of all assets that support the development of products in the product line. This does encompass the software platform and does also include all forms of documentation that is generated as part of the development. Common tooling is also part of the infrastructure.

Software Product Line Engineering is a paradigm to develop software applications (software intensive systems and software products) using *software platforms* and *mass customisation.*

Systematic Reuse refers to a development model where appropriate assets are developed specifically in a planned way for reuse. More generally it can be said that systematic reuse is characterised by an explicit domain engineering activity.

Two-Life-Cycle Approach this refers to the fact that domain engineering and application engineering can be seen as two loosely coupled life cycles that together define product line engineering.

Variability is any aspect where characteristics in the product line (respectively in the assets) differ for different products.

Variability in Space is the existence of an asset in different shapes at the same time.

Variability in Time is the existence of different versions of an asset that are valid at different times.

Variation Point is a point where variation occurs in a domain asset, i.e. at this point in the fact a selection needs to be made to arrive at an instantiated asset.

References

1. T. Aikainen, T. Männistö, and T. Soininen. A unified conceptual foundation for feature modelling. In *Proceedings of the Tenth International Software Product Line Conference, SPLC 10*, pages 31–40, 2006.
2. J. Airaksinen, K. Koskimies, J. Koskinen, J. Peltonen, P. Selonen, M. Siikarla, and T. Systä. xUMLi: Towards a tool-independent UML processing platform. In K. Osterbye, editor, *Proceedings of the Nordic Workshop on Software Development Tools and Techniques, 10th NWPER Workshop*. IT University of Copenhagen, 2002.
3. P. America, H. Obbink, R. van Ommering, and F. van der Linden. CoPaM: A component-oriented platform architecting method family for product family engineering. In *Proceedings of the First Software Product Line Conference (SPLC-1)*, pages 167–180. Kluwer, 2000.
4. E. Andersen. Information models for component design and implementation. In *ICSSEA'99, 12th International Conference on Software Systems Engineering and Applications*, 1999. ftp://ftp.nr.no/pub/egil/icssea99-slides-im-comp.ppt.
5. E. Andersen. SINAI - a UML-based architectural framework for evolutionary information systems. Technical report, Norwegian Computer Center, June 2001.
6. E. Andersen and B. Hansen. Providing persistent objects to globally distributed sites. In *NOSA'99, second Nordic Workshop on Software Architecture*. University of Karlskrona/Ronneby, 1999. ftp://ftp.nr.no/pub/egil/brix-ws.pdf.
7. M. Antkiewicz and K. Czarnecki. Featureplugin: Feature modeling plug-in for eclipse. In *OOPSLA'04 Eclipse Technology eXchange (ETX) Workshop*, 2004.
8. Automotive open system architecture website. http://www.autosar.org/.
9. F. Bachmann and L. Bass. Managing variability in software architectures. In *ACM SIGSOFT Symposium on Software Reusability*, pages 126–132, 2001.
10. F. Bachmann, M. Goedicke, J. Leite, R. Nord, K. Pohl, B. Ramesh, and A. Vilbig. A meta-model for representing variability in product family development. In *Proceedings in the 5th International Workshop on Product Family Engineering (PFE'5)*, pages 66–80, 2003.
11. R. Balzer. An architectural infrastructure for product families. In *Proceedings of the Second International ESPRIT ARES Workshop*, volume 1429 of *Lecture Notes in Computer Science*, pages 158–160. Springer, 1998.

12. S. Bandinelli and G. Mendieta. Domain potential analysis: Getting serious about product-lines. In *Third International Workshop on Software Architectures for Product Families (IW-SAPF'3), Las Palmas de Gran Canaria, Spain, March 15–17*, pages 75–81, 2000. Also as LNCS 1951.

13. V. Basili. The experimental paradigm in software engineering. In H. Rombach, V. Basili, and R. Selby, editors, *Experimental Software Engineering Issues: A critical assessment and future directions*, pages 3–12. Lecture Notes in Computer Science Nr. 706, Springer, September 1992.

14. V. Basili, F. McGarry, R. Pajerski, and M. Zelkowitz. Lessons learned from 25 years of process improvement: The rise and fall of the NASA software engineering laboratory. In *Proceedings of International Conference on Software Engineering (ICSE 2002)*, 2002.

15. V. Basili and H. Rombach. Support for comprehensive reuse. *IEEE Software Engineering Journal*, 6(5):303–316, September 1991.

16. V. Basili, R. Selby, and D. Hutchens. Experimentation in software engineering. *IEEE Transactions on Software Engineering*, SE-12(7):733–743, July 1986.

17. L. Bass, P. Clements, R. Kazman, and L. Brownsword. Celsiustech: A case study in product line development. In *Software Architecture in Practice*, chapter 16. Addison–Wesley, 1998.

18. L. Bass, M. Klein, and F. Bachmann. Quality attribute design primitives and the attribute driven design method. In *Proceedings of the 4th International Workshop on Product Family Engineering (PFE'4)*, 2004.

19. J. Bayer, O. Flege, P. Knauber, R. L., D. Muthig, K. Schmid, T. Widen, and J.-M. DeBaud. PuLSE: A methodology to develop software product lines. In *Proceedings of the ACM SIGSOFT Symposium on Software Reusability*, pages 122–131, 1999.

20. A. Birk, G. Heller, I. John, T. von der Maßen, K. Müller, and K. Schmid. Product line engineering: The state of the practice. *IEEE Software*, 20(6):52–60, 2003.

21. Joshua Bloch. *Effective Java Programming Language Guide*. Sun Microsystems Inc., 2001.

22. G. Böckle, P. Clements, J. McGregor, D. Muthig, and K. Schmid. A cost model for software product lines. In *Proceedings in the 5th International Workshop on Product Family Engineering (PFE'5)*, pages 310–316, 2003.

23. G. Böckle, P. Clements, J. McGregor, D. Muthig, and K. Schmid. Calculating ROI for software product lines. *IEEE Software*, 21(3):23–31, 2004.

24. B. Boehm, C. Abts, W. Brown, S. Chulani, B. Clark, E. Horowitz, R. Madachy, D. Reifer, and B. Steece. *Software Cost Estimation with COCOMO II*. Prentice Hall PTR, 2000.

25. J. Bosch. *Design and Use of Software Architectures*. Addison–Wesley, 2000.

26. J. Bosch. Organizing for software product lines. In *Third International Workshop on Software Architectures for Product Families (IW-SAPF'3), Las Palmas de Gran Canaria, Spain, March 15–17*, pages 126–143, 2000. Also as LNCS 1951.

27. J. Bosch. Software product lines: Organizational alternatives. In *Proceedings of the 23rd International Conference on Software Engineering*, pages 91–100. IEEE Computer Society Press, 2001.

28. J. Bosch. Maturity and evolution in software product lines: Approaches, artefacts and organisation. In *Software Product Lines – Proceedings of the Second*

International Conference, SPLC 2, volume 2379 of *Lecture Notes in Computer Science*, pages 257–271. Springer, 2002.

29. R. Bourgonjon. The evolution of embedded software in consumer products. In *International Conference on Engineering of Complex Computer Systems*, 1995. unpublished keynote address.

30. D. Bredemeyer. Software architecture workshop, course handouts. http://www.bredemeyer.com/, 2002.

31. BRIX workflow. http://www.dnv.com/software/workflow.

32. K. Brockschmidt. *Inside OLE, second edition*. Microsoft Press, 1995.

33. S. Bühne, K. Lauenroth, and K. Pohl. Modelling requirements variability across product lines. In *Proceedings of the Requirements Engineering Conference (RE'05)*, pages 41–50, 2005.

34. R. Buhrdorf, D. Churchett, and C. Krueger. Salion's experience with a reactive software product line approach. In *Proceedings of the 5th International Workshop on Product Family Engineering (PFE'5)*, pages 317–322, 2003.

35. CAFÉ project website. http://www.esi.es/Projects/Cafe, 2003.

36. P. Clements. On the importance of product line scoping, 2001.

37. P. Clements, R. Kazman, and M. Klein. *Evaluating Software Architectures: Methods and Case Studies*. Addison–Wesley, 2002.

38. P. Clements and L. Northrop. *Software Product Lines: Practices and Patterns*. Addison–Wesley, 2001.

39. Software engineering institute: CMMI web site. http://www.sei.cmu.edu/cmmi/cmmi.html.

40. M. Conway. How do committees invent. *Datamation*, 14(4):28–31, April 1968.

41. Cruise control. http://cruisecontrol.sourceforge.net.

42. K. Czarnecki, C. Kim, and K. Kalleberg. Feature models are views on ontologies. In *Proceedings of the 10th International Software Product Line Conference (SPLC 2006)*, pages 41–51, 2006.

43. J. Dager. Cummin's experience in developing a software product line architecture for real-time embedded diesel engine controls. In P. Donohoe, editor, *Software Product Lines: Experience and Research Directions, Proceedings of the First Software Product Line Conference, SPLC1*, pages 23–46. Kluwer Academic Publishers, 2000.

44. S. Deelstra, M. Sinnema, and J. Bosch. Experiences in software product families: Problems and issues during product derivation. In *Proceedings of the Software Product Line Conference, SPLC'04*, pages 165–182, 2004.

45. Department of Defense — Software Reuse Initiative, Version 3.1. *Domain Scoping Framework, Volume 2: Technical Description*, 1995.

46. DICOM. http://medical.nema.org/.

47. D. Dikel, D. Kane, S. Ornburn, W. Loftus, and J. Wilson. Applying software product-line architecture. *IEEE Computer*, 30(8):49–55, August 1997.

48. DNV software: Best engineering practice. http://www.dnv.com/software/workflow/bestEngineeringPractise.asp.

49. ESAPS project website. http://www.esi.es/Projects/Esaps, 2001.

50. M. Paulk et al. Capability maturity model of software, version 1.1. Technical report, Software Engineering Institute, Carnegie Mellon University, 1993.

51. FAMILIES project website. http://www.esi.es/Projects/Families, 2005.

52. J. Favaro. A comparison of approaches to reuse investment analysis. In *Proceedings of the Fourth International Conference on Software Reuse*, pages 136–145, 1996.

53. J. Favaro, K. Favaro, and P. Favaro. Value based software reuse investment. *Annals of Software Engineering*, 5:5–52, 1998.
54. S. Ferber, J. Haag, and J. Savolainen. Feature interaction and dependencies: Modeling features for reengineering a legacy product line. In *Software Product Lines – Proceedings of the Second International Conference, SPLC 2*, pages 235–256. Springer, 2002.
55. M. Fowler. *Analysis Patterns: Reusable Object Models*. Addison–Wesley, 1997.
56. M. Fowler. Dealing with roles. In *Proceedings of the 4th Annual Conference on Pattern Languages of Programs*, 1997.
57. M. Fowler, K. Beck, J. Brant, W. Opdyke, and D. Roberts. *Refactoring: Improving the Design of Existing Code*. Addison–Wesley, 2000.
58. C. Fritsch and R. Hahn. Product line potential analysis. In *Proceedings of the Software Product Line Conference, SPLC'04*, pages 228–237, 2004.
59. E. Gamma, R. Helm, R. Johnson, and J. Vlissides. *Design Patterns: Elements of Reusable Object-Oriented Software*. Addison–Wesley, 1995.
60. Product demo Gears. http://www.biglever.com/demo/GearsSelfGuided Tour.html, September 2006.
61. J. Girard, M. Verlage, and D. Ganesan. Monitoring the evolution of an OO system with metrics: an experience from the stock market software domain. In *Proceedings of the 20th International Conference on Software Maintenance*, September 2004.
62. M. Glaser, W. Grimm, A. Schneider, W.Stolz, H. Hönninger, H.-J. Kugler, and P. Kirwan. Success factors for software processes at Bosch Gasoline Systems GS. In *11. Internationaler Kongress Elektronik im Kraftfahrzeug (VDI)*, 2003.
63. J. Greenfield. *Software Factories*. Hungry Minds, 2004.
64. IST Advisory Group. Ambient intelligence: from vision to reality. ftp://ftp. cordis.europa.eu/pub/ist/docs/istag-ist2003_consolidated_report.pdf, September 2006.
65. S. Hallsteinsen, E. Stav, A. Solberg, and J. Floch. Using product line techniques to build adaptive systems. In *Proceedings of the 10th International Software Product Line Conference (SPLC 2006)*, pages 141–150, 2006.
66. C. Hammel, H. Jessen, B. Boss, A. Traub, C. Tischer, and H. Hönninger. A common software architecture for diesel and gasoline engine control systems of the new generation EDC/ME(D)17. In *2003 SAE World Congress*, 2003.
67. A. Helferich, K. Schmid, and G. Herzwurm. Reconciling marketed and engineered software product lines. In *Proceedings of the 10th International Software Product Line Conference (SPLC'06)*, pages 23–27, 2006.
68. A. Helferich, K. Schmid, and G. Herzwurm. Softwareproduktlinien für Anwendungssysteme: eine Analyse aus Techniksicht und Marktsicht. In *Multikonferenz Wirtschaftsinformatik 2006; Band 2: Software-Produktmanagement*, pages 237–248, 2006. In German.
69. Integrating the healthcare enterprise — radiology technical frameworks. http://www.rsna.org/IHE/tf/ihe_tf_index.shtml, 2003.
70. *ISO/IEC FCD 9126 "Information Technology — Software Product Quality-Part 1: Quality Model"*, 1998.
71. I. Jacobson, M. Griss, and P. Jonsson. *Software Reuse — Architecture, Process, and Organization for Business Success*. Addison–Wesley, 1997.
72. M. Jaring, R. Krikhaar, and J. Bosch. Representing variability in a product line of MRI scanners. *Software, Practice and Experience*, 34:69–100, 2004.

73. M. Jazayeri, A. Ran, and F. van der Linden. *Software Architecture for Product Families.* Addison–Wesley, 2000.

74. L. Jones and L. Northrop. Product line adoption in a CMMI environment. Technical Report CMU/SEI-2005-TN-028, Software Engineering Institute, Carnegie Mellon University, 2005. http://www.sei.cmu.edu/publications/documents/05.reports/05tn028/05tn028.html.

75. H. Jonkers. Interface-centric architecture descriptions. In *Working IEEE/IFIP Conference on Software Architecture (WICSA'01)*, 2001.

76. D. Jordan and J. Evdemon. Oasis web services business process execution language (WSBPEL) TC. http://www.oasis-open.org/committees/tc_home.php?wg_abbrev=wsbpel, September 2006.

77. junit testing framework. http://www.junit.org.

78. E. Kamsties, K. Pohl, S. Reis, and A. Reuys. Testing variabilities in use case models. In *Proceedings of 5th International Workshop on Product Family Engineering (PFE-5)*, volume 3014 of *Lecture Notes in Computer Science*, pages 5–18. Springer, November 2003.

79. E. Kamsties, K. Pohl, and A. Reuys. Supporting test case derivation in domain engineering. In *7th World Conference on Integrated Design and Process Technology (IDPT-2003)*, December 2003.

80. K. Kang, S. Cohen, J. Hess, W. Novak, and S. Peterson. Feature-oriented domain analysis (FODA) feasibility study. Technical Report CMU/SEI-90-TR-21, Software Engineering Institute, Carnegie Mellon University, November 1990.

81. J. Kontio. The riskit method for software risk management, version 1.00. Technical Report CS-TR-3782, University of Maryland, 1997.

82. P. Kotler and F. Bliemel. *Marketing Management.* Schäffer-Poeschel, 2001.

83. B. Kristensen. Object-oriented modeling with roles. In *Proceedings of the 2nd International Conference on Object-Oriented Information Systems, OOIS'95*, 1995.

84. D. Lea. Draft java coding standard. http://gee.cs.oswego.edu/dl/html/javaCodingStd.html.

85. J. Lee and K. Kang. A feature-oriented approach to developing dynamically reconfigurable products in product line engineering. In *Proceedings of the 10th International Software Product Line Conference (SPLC 2006)*, pages 131–140, 2006.

86. W. Lim. Reuse economics: A comparison of seventeen models and directions for future research. In *Proceedings of the Fourth International Conference on Software Reuse*, pages 41–50, 1996.

87. T. Lister. Point: Risk management is project management for adults. *IEEE Software*, 14(3):20–22, 1997.

88. R. Macala, L. Stuckey, and D. Gross. Managing domain-specific, product-line development. *IEEE Software*, 13(3):57–67, 1996.

89. J. Magee, N. Dulay, S. Eisenbach, and J. Kramer. Specifying distributed software architectures. In Wilhelm Schäfer and Pere Botella, editors, *Proceedings of the European Software Engineering Conference (ESEC'95)*, volume 989 of *Lecture Notes in Computer Science*, pages 137–153. Springer, 1995.

90. C. Mason and G. Milne. An approach for identifying cannibalization within product line extensions and multi-brand strategies. *Journal of Business Research*, 31:163–170, 1994.

91. M. Matinlassi. Comparison of software product line architecture design methods: COPA, FAST, FORM, KobrA and QADA. In *ICSE '04: Proceedings of the 26th International Conference on Software Engineering*, pages 127–136, Washington, DC, USA, 2004. IEEE Computer Society.

92. J. McGregor. Testing a software product line. Technical Report CMU/SEI- 2001-TR-022, Software Engineering Institute, Carnegie Mellon University, 2001. http://www.sei.cmu.edu/publications/documents/01.reports/01tr022.html.

93. J. McGregor and D. Sykes. *A Practical Guide to Testing Object-Oriented Software*. Addison–Wesley, 2001.

94. W. Mellis. Process and product orientation in software development and their effect on software quality management. In M. Wieczorek and D. Meyerhoff, editors, *Software Quality — State of the Art in Management, Testing, and Tools*. Springer, 2000.

95. Microsoft .NET technology. http://msdn.microsoft.com/netframework.

96. D. Muthig. *A Light-Weight Approach Facilitating an Evolutionary Transition Towards Software Product Lines*. PhD thesis, University of Kaiserslautern, IRB Verlag, 2002.

97. J. Neighbors. The draco approach to constructing software from reusable components. *IEEE Transactions on Software Engineering*, 10(5):564–573, September 1984.

98. E. Niemela. Strategies of product family architecture development. In *Proceedings of the Ninth International Conference on Software Product Lines (SPLC 2005)*, pages 186–197, 2005.

99. H. Obbink, J. Müller, P. America, and R. van Ommering. COPA — a component-oriented platform architecting method for families of software-intensive electronic products. Available at: http://www.extra.research.philips.com/SAE/COPA/COPA_Tutorial.pdf, 2000. Presented as Tutorial at SPLC'01.

100. Object Management Group (OMG). Model driven architecture. http://www.omg.org/mda/.

101. D. Parnas. On the design and development of program families. *IEEE Transactions on Software Engineering*, 2(1):1–9, March 1976.

102. J. Peltonen. Visual scripting for UML-based tools. In *Proceedings of the International Conference on Software and Systems Engineering and their Applications(ICSSEA 2000)*, volume 3, 2001.

103. Royal philips. http://www.philips.com/.

104. Product line hall of fame. Available on the Internet at: http://www.sei.cmu.edu/plp/plp_hof.html.

105. K. Pohl. *Process-Centered Requirements Engineering*. John Wiley & Sons, 1996.

106. K. Pohl, G. Böckle, and F. van der Linden. *Software Product Line Engineering: Foundations, Principles, and Techniques*. Springer, 2005.

107. M. Porter. *Wettbewerbsstrategie*. Campus, 1999.

108. J. Poulin. *Measuring Software Reuse — Principles, Practices, and Economic Models*. Addison-Wesley, 1997.

109. Project Management Institute, Four Campus Boulevard, Newtown Square, PA 19073-3299. *A Guide to the Project Management Body of Knowledge (PM-BOK) GUIDE*, 2000.

110. Product pure::variants. http://www.pure-systems.com/Variant_Management. 49.0.html, September 2006.

111. M. Raatikainen, T. Soinine, T. Männistö, and A. Mattila. A case study of two configurable software product families. In *Proceedings of Product Family Engineering, 5th International Workshop, PFE 2003*, pages 403–421, 2003.

112. A. Reuys, E. Kamsties, K. Pohl, H. Goetz, J. Neumann, and J. Weingaertner. Testen von Software-Produktvarianten — Ein Erfahrungsbericht. In *Proceedings der Teilkonferenz zu Software-Produktlinien im Rahmen der Multi-Konferenz Wirtschaftsinformatik (MKWI 2004)*, March 2004.

113. A. Reuys, S. Reis, E. Kamsties, and K. Pohl. Derivation of domain test scenarios from activity diagrams. In *Proceedings of the International Workshop on Product Line Engineering The Early Steps: Planning, Modeling, and Managing (PLEES'03)*, September 2003.

114. A. Reuys, S. Reis, E. Kamsties, and K. Pohl. *The ScenTED Method for Testing Software Product Lines*, chapter 13, pages 479–518. Springer, 2006.

115. C. Riva, P. Selonen, T. Systä, A.-P. Tuovinen, J. Xu, and Y. Yang. Establishing a software architecting environment. In *Proceedings of the Working IFIP/IEEE Conference on Software Architecture (WICSA 2004*, 2004.

116. C. Riva, P. Selonen, T. Systä, and J. Xu. UML-based reverse engineering and model analysis approaches for software architecture maintenance. In *Proceedings of the International Conference on System Maintenance (ICSM'04)*, 2004.

117. S. Sanderson and M. Uzumeri. *The Innovation Imperative — Strategies for Managing Product Models and Families*. Irwin Professional Publishing, 1997.

118. K. Schmid. The product line mapping method. Technical Report 028.00/E, Fraunhofer IESE, 2000.

119. K. Schmid. Scoping software product lines — an analysis of an emerging technology. In Patrick Donohoe, editor, *Software Product Lines: Experience and Research Directions; Proceedings of the First Software Product Line Conference (SPLC1)*, pages 513–532. Kluwer Academic Publishers, 2000.

120. K. Schmid. An assessment approach to analyzing benefits and risks of product lines. In *The Twenty-Fifth Annual International Computer Software and Applications Conference (Compsac'01)*, pages 525–530, 2001.

121. K. Schmid. An initial model of product line economics. In F. van der Linden, editor, *Proceedings of the Fourth International Workshop on Product Family Engineering (PFE-4), 2001*, volume 2290 of *Lecture Notes in Computer Science*, pages 38–50. Springer, 2001.

122. K. Schmid. A comprehensive product line scoping approach and its validation. In *Proceedings of the 24th International Conference on Software Engineering*, pages 593–603, 2002.

123. K. Schmid. *Planning Software Reuse — A Disciplined Scoping Approach for Software Product Lines*. PhD thesis, University of Kaiserslautern, IRB Verlag, 2002.

124. K. Schmid. People management in institutionalizing product lines. Technical Report 102.03/E, Fraunhofer Institute for Experimental Software Engineering (IESE), 2003.

125. K. Schmid. A quantitative model of the value of architecture in product line adoption. In *Proceedings in the 5th International Workshop on Product Family Engineering (PFE'5)*, 2003.

126. K. Schmid, U. Becker-Kornstaedt, P. Knauber, and F. Bernauer. Introducing a software modeling concept in a medium-sized company. In *Proceedings of the 22nd International Conference on Software Engineering*, pages 558–567, 2000.

127. K. Schmid and C. Gacek. Implementation issues in product line scoping. In William B. Frakes, editor, *Software Reuse: Advances in Software Reusability — Proceedings of the 6th International Conference, ICSR'6, Vienna, Austria, June 2000*, number 1844 in Lecture Notes in Computer Science, pages 170–189. Springer, 2000.

128. K. Schmid and I. John. A customizable approach to full lifecycle variability management. *Science of computer programming*, 53(3):259–284, 2004.

129. K. Schmid, I. John, R. Kolb, and G. Meier. Introducing the PuLSE approach to an embedded system population at Testo AG. In *Proceedings of the 27th International Conference on Software Engineering(ICSE'27)*, pages 544–552, 2005.

130. K. Schmid, K. Krennrich, and M. Eisenbarth. Requirements management for product lines: Extending professional tools. In *Proceedings of the 10th International Software Product Line Conference (SPLC 2006)*, pages 113–122, 2006.

131. K. Schmid and M. Verlage. The economic impact of product line adoption and evolution. *IEEE Software*, 19(6):50–57, July/August 2002.

132. Staged event-driven architecture. http://www.eecs.harvard.edu/ mdw/proj/ seda/.

133. M. Shaw and D. Garlan. *Software Architecture: Perspectives on an Emerging Discipline*. Prentice Hall, 1996.

134. Software Productivity Consortium Services Corporation. *Reuse Adoption Guidebook, Version 02.00.05*, November 1993.

135. Software Productivity Consortium Services Corporation, Technical Report SPC-92019-CMC. *Reuse-Driven Software Processes Guidebook, Version 02.00.03*, November 1993.

136. M. Steger, C. Tischer, B. Boss, A. Müller, O. Pertler, W. Stolz, and S. Ferber. Introducing PLA at Bosch Gasoline Systems: Experiences and practices. In *Proceedings of the Software Product Line Conference, SPLC'04*, pages 34–50, 2004.

137. M. Svahnberg and J. Bosch. Evolution in software product lines: Two cases. *Journal of Software Maintenance: Research and Practice*, 11:399–422, 1999.

138. L. Taborda. Generalized release planning for product line architectures. In R. Nord, editor, *Software Product Lines, Third International Conference*, volume 3154 of *Lecture Notes in Computer Science*, pages 238–254. Springer, 2004.

139. CMMI Product Team. Capability maturity model integration (CMMI), version 1.1 - CMMI for systems engineering and software engineering (CMMI-SE/SW, v1.1) -staged representation. Technical Report CMU/SEI-2002-TR-002, Software Engineering Institute, Carnegie Mellon University, 2002. http://www.sei.cmu.edu/cmmi/adoption/pdf/cmmi-overview05.pdf.

140. CMMI Product Team. Capability maturity model integration (CMMI) overview. Technical report, Software Engineering Institute, Carnegie Mellon University, 2005. http://www.sei.cmu.edu/cmmi/adoption/pdf/cmmi-overview05.pdf.

141. P. Toft, D. Coleman, and J. Ohta. A cooperative model for cross-divisional product development for a software product line. In P. Donohoe, editor, *Software Product Lines: Experience and Research Directions; Proceedings of the*

First Software Product Line Conference (SPLC1), pages 111–132. Kluwer Academic Publishers, 2000.

142. J.-P. Tolvanen and S. Kelly. Defining domain-specific modelling languages to automate product derviation: Collected experiences. In *Proceedings of the Ninth International Conference on Software Product Lines (SPLC 2005)*, pages 198–209, 2005.

143. F. van der Linden. Engineering software architectures, processes and platforms for software product families. In *Software Product Lines – Proceedings of the Second International Conference, SPLC 2*, volume 2379 of *Lecture Notes in Computer Science*, pages 383–397. Springer, August 2002.

144. F. van der Linden. Software product families in europe: The ESAPS and CAFÉ projects. *IEEE Software*, 19(4):41–49, July/August 2002.

145. F. van der Linden, J. Bosch, E. Kamsties, K. Kansala, L. Krzanik, and H. Obbink. Software product family evaluation. In *Proceedings of Product Family Engineering, 5th International Workshop, PFE 2003*, pages 352–369, 2003.

146. F. van der Linden and J. Müller. Creating architectures with building blocks. *IEEE Software*, 12(6):51–60, 1995.

147. F. van der Linden and J. Wijnstra. Platform engineering for the medical domain. In *Proceedings of the fourth Workshop on Product Family Engineering (PFE-4)*, volume 2290 of *Lecture Notes in Computer Science*, pages 224–237. Springer, 2001.

148. R. van Ommering. *Building Product Populations with Software Components*. PhD thesis, Rijksuniversiteits Groningen, 2004.

149. R. van Ommering. Software reuse in product populations. *IEEE Transactions on Software Engineering*, 31(7):537–550, July 2005.

150. Velocity website. http://jakarta.apache.org/velocity/.

151. B. Weichel. A backbone in automotive software development based on XML and ASAM/MSR. In *2004 SAE World Congress*, 2004.

152. M. Weiser. The computer of the 21st century. *Scientific American*, 265(3): 94–104, 1991.

153. D. Weiss. Product-line engineering as the basis for reuse. In *The 8th International Conference on Software Reuse*, 2004. keynote speech.

154. J. Wijnstra. Critical factors for a successful platform-based product software product family approach. In *Software Product Lines – Proceedings of the Second International Conference, SPLC 2*, pages 68–89, 2002.

155. J. Withey. Investment analysis of software assets for product lines. Technical Report CMU/SEI-96-TR-010, Software Engineering Institute, Carnegie Mellon University, 1996.

156. B. Witt, F. Baker, and E. Merritt. *Software Architecture and Design: Principles, Models, and Methods*. J. Wiley & Sons, Inc., New York, NY, USA, 1993.

157. W. Zhang and S. Jarzabek. Reuse without compromising performance: Industrial experience from RPG software product line for mobile devices. In *Proceedings of the Ninth International Conference on Software Product Lines (SPLC 2005)*, pages 45–56, 2005.

About the Authors

Frank van der Linden has worked at Philips Medical Systems in the Netherlands since 1999 and has been involved with software product lines since then. He was programme chair of a series of five workshops on product line engineering, is a member of the steering committee of the SPLC conferences, and has co-authored *Software Product Line Engineering* published by Springer in 2005.

Klaus Schmid is Professor for software engineering at the University of Hildesheim, Germany. Previously, he was department head for requirements engineering and usability engineering at the Fraunhofer Institute for Experimental Software Engineering (IESE) in Kaiserslautern, Germany. He has been involved in numerous research and industrial projects in product line engineering.

Eelco Rommes worked at Philips Research in the area of software architecture for medical systems from 2001 to 2006. During that time he was involved in several research projects and he has published on software product lines and related topics.

Index